Practical Bakery

Paul Connelly

LCGI, Cert.Ed

Malcolm Pittam

LCGI, Cert.Ed

Hodder & Stoughton

A MEMBER OF THE HODDER HEADLINE GROUP

A catalogue record for this title is available from the British Library

ISBN 0 340 669934

First published 1997

Impression number	10	9	8	7	6	5	4	3	2	1
Year	2001		2000		1999		1998		1997	

Typeset by Wearset, Boldon, Tyne and Wear.
Printed in Great Britain for Hodder & Stoughton Educational, a division of Hodder Headline Plc, 338 Euston Road, London NW1 3BH by Bath Press

contents

acknowledgements

We wish to extend our grateful thanks to all those who helped us to produce this book:

- Dawn Gregan for typing the original manuscript
- The Principal, Michael Rowarth, OBE and Governors of Newcastle College
- Keith Jobson, Bakery Manager of the working bakery at Newcastle College; and the baking students
- The management and staff of the Faculty of Humanities, Hospitality and Science, Newcastle College
- Bob Shiels, Production Director of Greggs Bakery, Gosforth
- Harry Holland, former bakery lecturer of Newcastle College
- Thomas Davison, pastry chef, the Victoria, P&O Cruises
- Simon Tennet, executive chef, the Fisherman's Wharf, Newcastle-upon-Tyne
- Jim McAddam for the commissioned photography

We would also like to thank Ian Gregg, Chairman of Greggs plc for kindly providing the foreword; our publisher Elisabeth Tribe for her confidence in our book, and our desk editor Llinos Davies for her professional help and guidance.

Finally, thanks are due to our families for their understanding and support.

We would like to dedicate this book to our wives and daughters, Jacqueline and Rachael Pittam, and Dawn and Sophie Connelly.

foreword

Paul Connelly and Malcolm Pittam share over 40 years of experience in the baking industry. They have both worked at our Gosforth bakery, where they worked their way up to management positions before changing to academic careers at Newcastle College.

During this period the authors accumulated a vast store of knowledge and experience of bakery products and recipe formulation. They are to be warmly congratulated, firstly for identifying the need for a modern practical bakery text book which sets out the most popular bakery products and how to make them; and secondly, for producing a reference book with such clear and well organised text.

The greatest challenge facing the bakery student and the working baker today is the very wide range of products, raw materials and processes which must be understood and correctly applied, in order to create products which are consistently good to eat.

Practical Bakery makes it all much simpler, and will undoubtedly help students and bakers to meet this challenge. The detailed recipes, the description of raw materials and how they should be handled, the carefully laid out processes together with the helpful illustrations and photographs, will ensure that this book becomes a companion and reference point for everyone involved in the baking industry.

Ian Gregg
Greggs plc

introduction

Practical Bakery is written for people with an interest in baking, whether it be in a professional or non-professional capacity. It will provide a source of reference for the bakery student, catering student, baker and confectioner, caterer and non-vocational person.

The most popular products and processes are included to assist anyone following an NVQ programme of learning within bakery and catering. A study of the main raw materials used in the production of bakery products provides the reader with an understanding of each ingredient. Each chapter of recipes is headed by an oven chart which provides the reader with a helpful reference at a glance, for baking temperatures, times and techniques. Many aspects within the production of bakery products require careful control to ensure a successful product is obtained. With this in mind, it was our aim to produce recipes, mixing methods, processing methods and theoretical content in a detailed yet easy to understand format.

FORMAT OF THIS BOOK

These features have been included to help the reader.

1 *Recipes*
- All weights are given in Metric and Imperial and the conversions are as accurate as possible to maintain a balanced recipe.
- Each ingredient within a recipe is expressed as a percentage to help the reader become familiar with the usage levels that achieve a balanced recipe.
- The ingredients are listed in an efficient order for weighing.
- The gross weight and net weight of ingredients are stated to indicate the amount of mixture required to obtain the yield. The accepted production losses are:
  Bread and Fermented Products – 2.5% subtracted from the gross weight equals the net weight.

Confectionery Products – 4% subtracted from the gross weight equals the net weight.
Note: The yields stated are as accurate as possible. They may vary depending upon the care taken by the individual during production.

2 *Production points*
Essential information is available at a glance and is located next to each recipe.

3 *Mixing method*
The mixing method for each product is stated in a clear and detailed step by step approach.

4 *Processing method*
- The processing method for each product is also stated in a clear and detailed step by step approach.
- Illustrations and photographs are included to help convey processing methods that are difficult to explain.

5 *Cross references*
- Cross referencing has been kept to a minimum to avoid confusion and repetition.
- The quantity of additions and filling are calculated to correspond with the yield of the relevant base.
- From the options provided the reader has an opportunity to select the recipe and mixing process appropriate to their practical resources.

Finally, an explanation of terminology used in bakery is provided.

Paul Connelly

Malcolm Pittam

Conversion charts

METRIC–IMPERIAL

Metric working equivalent grams	Imperial oz
14	0.5
28	1
42	1.5
56	2
71	2.5
85	3
99	3.5
113	4
127	4.5
142	5
156	5.5
170	6
184	6.5
198	7
212	7.5
226	8
241	8.5
255	9
269	9.5
283	10
297	10.5
311	11
326	11.5
340	12
354	12.5
368	13
382	13.5
396	14
410	14.5
425	15
439	15.5
454	1 lb
907	2 lb
1361	3 lb
1814	4 lb
2268	5 lb
2722	6 lb
3175	7 lb
3629	8 lb
4082	9 lb
4536	10 lb

CENTIGRADE–FAHRENHEIT

Centigrade	Fahrenheit working equivalent
−22	−8
−18	0
−12	10
−6	21
0	32
4	39
8	46
12	54
16	61
20	68
24	75
28	82
32	90
36	97
40	104
44	111
48	118
52	126
56	133
60	140
64	147
68	154
72	162
76	169
80	176
84	183
88	190
92	198
96	205
100	212
110	230
120	248
130	266
140	284
150	302
160	320
170	338
180	356
190	374
200	392
210	410
220	428
230	446
240	464
250	482

C H A P T E R

one

Health and safety during the manufacture of bakery products

Food hygiene is the manufacture of safe bakery products in a clean work environment, using hygienic practices during each stage of the production process. The responsibility for the safe production of food includes everyone involved in the production process. The aim of good hygiene is to prevent food from becoming contaminated by bacteria which can lead to cases of food poisoning.

Contamination of food is prevented by the manufacturers of bakery products following these basic principles:

1 Good personal hygiene practices.
2 Maintain a clean work environment.
3 Keep utensils and equipment clean.

Finally, food hygiene is controlled by legislation, and any offence may incur a penalty ranging from a fine to imprisonment. The Food Safety (General Food Hygiene) Regulations 1995 state the standards for safe and hygienic practice that must be met by every food production establishment.

PERSONAL HYGIENE

It is the responsibility of every food worker to adopt and maintain the high standard of personal hygiene as outlined below:

Hands

Hands must be washed regularly, especially:

- before starting work
- after visiting the toilet
- after handling raw food
- after handling rubbish
- after meal breaks
- after blowing your nose
- after smoking
- after cleaning processes.

Fingernails:

- must be kept short
- must not be bitten
- should not be varnished.

Avoid:

- licking fingers
- touching food with your hands.

Skin

Food workers must keep the skin clean by showering and bathing every day to remove bacteria and odour. Cuts and wounds contain bacteria, so they must be covered up with a coloured, waterproof dressing.

Mouth, nose and ears

The mouth, nose and ears can contain harmful bacteria. The food worker can reduce the risk of transferring bacteria from these areas to food, by observing these guidelines:

1 Do not pick your nose.
2 Do not eat.
3 Do not spit.

4 Do not cough over food.
5 Do not sneeze over food.
6 Do not touch your ears.

Hair

In addition to the risk of hair falling out onto food, bacteria is present in the hair. To ensure it is not able to contaminate food during production, you must:

- keep hair clean
- tie hair back
- keep hair covered
- avoid touching your hair.

Jewellery

All jewellery is capable of harbouring bacteria which can be transferred to food through handling, or it may fall off into food. Therefore, before production begins, remove rings, watches, bracelets, earrings, necklaces, nose rings etc.

Make-up, perfume and aftershave

Strong odours can be transferred to food, so make-up, perfume and aftershave that has a powerful fragrance should be avoided.

Protective clothing

Outdoor clothing may carry bacteria and should not be worn during the production process. Clean, light-coloured clothing that will protect food from contamination must be worn:

- a suitable white head covering
- a white tunic, coat or overall
- white trousers
- fastenings such as press studs, velcro and tapes
- non-absorbent, clean footwear.

Illness

The symptoms of certain illnesses can place food at risk from contamination by bacteria. You should report to your supervisor immediately if you are suffering from any of the following:

- diarrhoea
- vomiting
- a septic wound
- a cold or flu
- a sore throat
- boils.

A CLEAN WORK ENVIRONMENT

A clean work environment is essential in which to produce bakery products that are free from contamination and safe to eat. A work environment that is kept clean and tidy is a much more efficient and comfortable workplace. Some of the important areas of the work environment to concentrate on are:

- floors and walls
- work surfaces
- sinks
- storage areas
- hand contact surfaces, for example, fridge door handles
- refuse areas
- cupboards and storage areas
- refrigerators and freezers
- tin and tray preparation areas.

The cleaning process

To clean each area of the work environment effectively, follow this procedure:

1 Remove debris.
2 Clean with hot water and detergent.
3 Rinse.
4 Disinfect.
5 Rinse.
6 Dry.

Note: When using cleaning materials, always follow the manufacturer's recommendations.

Clean as you go

The work environment must be kept clean throughout the production period to:

- reduce the risk of food becoming contaminated
- maintain an efficient and comfortable workplace
- prevent a build-up of cleaning processes occurring.

Utensils and equipment

Utensils and equipment are designed and made from materials that make the cleaning process easy and efficient. It is the responsibility of the food worker to inspect the cleanliness of utensils and equipment before the production process begins. During production, utensils and equipment should be cleaned as and when necessary, to prevent a build-up occurring. At the end of the production process, the utensils and equipment should be cleaned and stored in hygienic conditions. Important utensils and equipment that must be given attention include:

- knives
- scrapers
- hand whisks
- hand brushes
- savoy bags and piping tubes
- chopping boards
- rolling pins
- cloths
- bowls and food containers
- moulding machines
- mixing machines and bowls
- depositing machines
- racks, tins and trays.

Many of these examples can be cleaned using the six-stage cleaning process described on p. 4. However, other examples from the list require a more thorough cleaning process, involving steeping, sterilising and disassembly prior to cleaning.

SAFE WORKING PRACTICES

Safe working practice during the manufacture of bakery products is the responsibility of everyone involved in the

production process. Your own personal well-being and the welfare of others must be a constant priority to prevent the occurrence of accidents and injury.
As with food hygiene, safety at work is controlled by legislation, and any offence may incur a penalty ranging from a fine to imprisonment. The Health and Safety at Work Act 1974 states the standards for safe working practices that must be followed in every food production establishment.

Personal safety

To safeguard yourself from the risk of injury during the production process, you should follow these guidelines:

1 To avoid entanglement with machinery,
   - ensure work clothes are properly fastened
   - contain long hair in suitable head wear
   - remove all jewellery
   - never attempt to touch mixture whilst a machine is in motion.
2 Do not be easily distracted or inattentive, as your behaviour could result in serious injury or death.
3 Treat all equipment and utensils with respect.
4 Never attempt to lift materials or equipment that are too heavy for you and which may cause injury.
5 Wear protective clothing, eg masks, safety shoes etc.

The safe use of equipment and machinery

All equipment and machinery is potentially dangerous if misused. The food worker must recognise and appreciate the potential dangers present in a food establishment. While using equipment and machinery during the production of bakery products, follow these guidelines:

1 Do not use equipment and machinery without having received adequate training and supervision.
2 Before using any equipment and machinery, always ensure that safety guards and attachments are securely in place.
3 In case of an emergency, make sure you know where the stop button is located.
4 Never attempt to interfere during the production process while the machine is in motion.

5 Equipment and machinery should be left in neutral or on slow speed whenever possible.
6 Always isolate equipment and machinery from the mains electricity before cleaning.
7 Any uncertainties or defects should be reported to your supervisor.

General safety measures

There are many hazards within the work environment. Stated below are some of the general safety measures that must be observed by the food worker.

1 In the production area you should *walk* at all times – never run.
2 Horseplay is unacceptable behaviour in the production area.
3 Exercise great care when handling hot equipment and products, and bring any possible dangers to the attention of others.
4 Beware of possible dangers when handling corrosive and toxic substances.
5 Keep all work areas and floors free from obstructions and spillages at all times.
6 Adopt the accepted stacking procedures for bags and boxes.
7 In case of an emergency evacuation, ensure that you know the quickest exit routes from the production area and assembly points.
8 Finally, do not take any unnecessary risks to yourself or others, because prevention is always the better option.

C H A P T E R

two

Selecting raw materials for bakery

It is necessary to select raw materials suitable for the product and of the appropriate quality to enable good bakery products to be produced. Therefore, it is essential for the baker to have a working knowledge of raw materials – how they perform and the effect on the final product. Where it is applicable, knowledge and understanding is required of the following topics related to each raw material:

- the source of the raw material
- the types available
- properties of the raw materials
- suitability for the characteristics of the product
- features of materials in good condition
- accurate weighing
- preparation for use
- suitable storage conditions
- relevant legislation.

DRY INGREDIENTS

Flours and meals

SOURCE

Flour is obtained from the cereal *wheat*. A grain of wheat consists of three main parts, the endosperm, bran and germ:

1 Endosperm is the white part of the wheat grain from which white flour is obtained.
2 Bran is the outside skin of the wheat grain and is blended with the endosperm to produce brown flours.
3 Germ is located inside the wheat grain and is the embryo from which wheat can reproduce itself. The germ is used in germ meal and wholemeal flour.

The main wheat growing countries are Canada, USA, Argentina, England, France, Russia and Australia.

FLOUR MILLING

Flour millers clean the grains of wheat and bring them to the appropriate condition for the milling process. The grains are arranged into appropriate blends, and are separated and reduced during the milling process into very fine particles. The *extraction rate* is the quantity of flour that is obtained from a given amount of wheat; for example:

- If a flour miller obtains 70 kg of white flour from 100 kg of wheat, the extraction rate equals 70%.
- If the flour miller obtains 100 kg of wholemeal flour from 100 kg of wheat, the extraction rate equals 100%.

CONSTITUENTS OF FLOUR

1 White flour – see Table 1.

Table 1 Constituents of white flour

Strong flour %	Constituents	Soft flour %
69.00	starch	71.50
13.00	insoluble gluten forming proteins	8.30
13.00	moisture	14.50
2.50	sugar	2.20
1.00	fat	1.50
1.00	soluble proteins	1.00
0.50	mineral salts	1.00

2 Brown flour and meals – the Bread and Flour (Amended) Regulations 1972 state that:
   - Brown flour contains a minimum of 0.6% fibre.
   - Wholemeal flour contains 100% of the wheat grain.
   - Germ meal contains a minimum of 10% wheat germ.

INSOLUBLE GLUTEN FORMING PROTEINS

The insoluble proteins are known as gluten which is produced in a bread dough for example, when water has been added and the dough has been mixed sufficiently to develop the gluten. The suitability of a flour for bakery products is determined by the quality of gluten and in some cases the quantity it contains. Flour that contains good quality gluten is known as *strong* flour; flour that contains low quality gluten is known as *soft* flour.

TYPES

The type of flours used to make bakery products can be classified into five categories:

1 Strong flours.
2 Medium flours.
3 Soft flours.
4 Special white flours.
5 Brown flours and meals.

PROPERTIES

Flour is a major structural agent and has an important effect upon the formation of these characteristics of a product:

- volume
- colour
- eating qualities
- texture
- flavour
- nutritional value.

SUITABILITY FOR THE PRODUCT

1 *Strong* flours are used to make bread and fermented products and puff pastry.
2 *Medium* flours are used to make short pastries, powder aerated products and some fruit cakes.
3 *Soft* flours are used to make cake and sponge products.
4 *Special white* flours are known as *high ratio cake flour* and *high protein cake flour.* High ratio flour is used to make

cakes that contain a high level of sugar and liquid to the quantity of flour. High protein flour is used to make cakes that contain a high level of fruit to the quantity of flour.

5 *Brown* flours and meals are used to make bread and fermented products, short pastry, powder aerated products, and cake and sponge products. These flours and meals contain larger particles than white flour because of the presence of bran and germ. They confer a pronounced flavour to a product and are particularly popular with consumers who follow a healthy diet.

Note: Flour is an important dusting material which prevents sticking during processing methods, and can be used as a finish for products prior to baking.

FEATURES OF GOOD CONDITION

Flours and meals are fit to use if:

- free from infestation
- free from physical contamination (for example, metal objects)
- free from excess moisture
- free from rancidity
- used within the recommended period.

ACCURATE WEIGHING

Flour must be weighed accurately to ensure that:

- the recipe remains balanced
- a uniform product is obtained
- the correct yield is obtained
- faults are prevented.

Note: Flour can be used within limits to adjust the consistency of fermented doughs, short pastry and powder aerated products.

PREPARATION FOR USE

All flours and meals must be sieved prior to use, using a fine sieve for white flour and a coarse sieve for meals. The reasons for sieving flours and meals are:

- to remove lumps
- to remove physical contamination (for example, metal objects)

- to blend with other dry ingredients
- to lighten and assist the mixing process.

SUITABLE STORAGE CONDITIONS

Flours and meals should be stored in the following appropriate conditions to prevent deterioration, leading to wastage:

1 Temperature: 10–16°C (50–60°F).
2 Environment: dry conditions.
3 Time limit:
 White flours – 3 to 6 months.
 Brown flours – 3 months.
 Meals – 2 weeks.

Use strict stock rotation.

LEGISLATION

The contents of raw materials and bakery products are governed by the Food Safety Act 1990. Extracts from the Act state the following standards for flours and meals:

1 Food must be of the nature, substance or quality demanded.
2 Food must not present any risk to health, and must be fit for human consumption.

Rye flour

SOURCE

Rye flour is obtained from the cereal *rye*.

INSOLUBLE GLUTEN FORMING PROTEINS

Rye is the only cereal apart from wheat which contains insoluble gluten forming proteins. However, the gluten-forming proteins of rye flour do not possess the quality or quantity of flour milled from wheat. Therefore a dough made from milled rye flour has a sticky dense consistency, and the final baked product displays little oven spring and low volume.

TYPES

Available as light, medium and dark rye.

PROPERTIES

Rye flour is a structural agent and has an important effect upon the following characteristics of a product:

- volume
- colour
- eating qualities
- texture
- flavour
- nutritional value.

SUITABILITY FOR THE PRODUCT

The colour and flavour of rye bread can range from light and mild, to dark and strong, depending upon the type of rye flour used.

FEATURES OF GOOD CONDITION

Rye flours are fit to use if:

- free from infestation
- free from physical contamination (for example, metal objects)
- free from excess moisture
- used within the recommended period.

ACCURATE WEIGHING

Rye flour must be weighed accurately to ensure that:

- the recipe remains balanced
- a uniform product is obtained
- the correct yield is obtained
- faults are prevented.

PREPARATION FOR USE

Rye flour must be sieved prior to use, in order to blend with other ingredients and to remove any physical contamination.

SUITABLE STORAGE CONDITIONS

Rye flour should be stored in the following appropriate conditions to prevent deterioration leading to wastage:

1 Temperature: 10–16°C (50–61°F).
2 Environment: dry conditions.
3 Time limit: up to 3 months.

Use strict stock rotation.

LEGISLATION

The contents of raw materials and bakery products are governed by the Food Safety Act 1990. Extracts from the Act state the following standards should be met.

1 Food must be of the nature, substance or quality demanded.
2 Food must not present any risk to health and be fit for human consumption.

Cornflour

SOURCE

Cornflour is obtained from the cereal *maize*.

Constituents: Cornflour is almost 100% starch and does not contain any insoluble gluten forming proteins.

TYPES

Cornflour is available in one form – a white flour with a powdery nature.

PROPERTIES

Cornflour has an effect upon the following characteristics of products and fillings:

- setting the structure
- eating qualities
- texture
- nutritional value.

SUITABILITY FOR THE PRODUCT

It is used mainly as a thickening agent for custards, sauces, fillings and jellies. It can also be used to dilute strong flours.

FEATURES OF GOOD CONDITION

Cornflour is fit to use if:

- free from physical contamination (for example, metal objects)
- free from excess moisture
- used within the recommended period.

ACCURATE WEIGHING

Cornflour must be weighed accurately to ensure that:

- the recipe remains balanced

- a uniform product is obtained
- the correct yield is obtained
- faults are prevented.

PREPARATION FOR USE

The method of preparing cornflour for addition to a recipe, depends upon the product or filling to which it is to be added. For addition to:

- mixings – sieve with other dry ingredients
- fillings – mix together with a sufficient amount of liquid to form a smooth solution immediately before addition.

SUITABLE STORAGE CONDITIONS

Cornflour should be stored in the following appropriate conditions to prevent deterioration leading to wastage:

1 Temperature: 10–16°C (50–61°F).
2 Environment: dry, airtight conditions.
3 Time limit: 3 to 6 months.

Use strict stock rotation.

LEGISLATION

The contents of raw materials and bakery products are governed by the Food Safety Act 1990. Extracts from the Act state the following standards should be met.

1 Food must be of the nature, substance or quality demanded.
2 Food must not present any risk to health and be fit for human consumption.

Rice flour

SOURCE

Rice flour is obtained from the cereal *rice.*

Constituents: Rice flour is almost 100% starch and does not contain any insoluble gluten forming proteins.

TYPES

Rice and rice materials are available in these forms:

- flour
- ground rice
- rice paper.

PROPERTIES

Rice flour and ground rice have an effect upon the following characteristics of a product:

- texture
- flavour
- eating qualities
- nutritional value.

SUITABILITY FOR THE PRODUCT

Rice and rice materials can be used as follows:

1 Rice flour is added to cake recipes.
2 Ground rice is added to cakes and biscuits and is also a useful dusting material for oven bottom breads and shortbread biscuits.
3 Rice paper is used in the production of macaroon biscuits.

FEATURES OF GOOD CONDITION

Rice materials are fit to use if:

- free from infestation
- free from physical contamination (for example, metal objects)
- free from excess moisture
- the rice paper is clean
- used within the recommended period.

ACCURATE WEIGHING

Rice flour must be weighed accurately to ensure that:

- the recipe remains balanced
- a uniform product is obtained
- the correct yield is obtained
- faults are prevented.

PREPARATION FOR USE

Rice flour and ground rice must be sieved prior to use in order to remove any physical contamination, and to blend with other dry ingredients.

SUITABLE STORAGE CONDITIONS

Rice flour and ground rice should be stored in the following appropriate conditions to prevent deterioration leading to wastage:

1 Temperature: 10–16°C (50–61°F).
2 Environment: dry conditions.
3 Time limit: 3 to 6 months.

Use in strict stock rotation.

LEGISLATION

The contents of raw materials and bakery products are governed by the Food Safety Act 1990. Extracts from the Act state the following standards should be met:

1 Food must be of the nature, substance or quality demanded.
2 Food must not present any risk to health and be fit for human consumption.

Soya flour

SOURCE

Soya flour is obtained from the *soya bean.*

Constituents: Soya flour does not contain any insoluble gluten forming proteins but is very rich in protein and fat as stated below:

- 40% protein
- 26% carbohydrates
- 20% fat
- 7% moisture
- 5% minerals
- 2% lecithin.

TYPES

There are two types of soya flour available:

1 Processed – heat treated.
2 Unprocessed – unrefined state.

PROPERTIES

Soya flour has a beneficial effect on the following characteristics of a product:

- volume
- texture
- colour
- flavour

- eating qualities
- shelf life
- nutritional value.

SUITABILITY FOR THE PRODUCT

The versatility of soya flour is demonstrated by its use in the production of bread, pastries, cakes and sponges.

FEATURES OF GOOD CONDITION

Soya flour is fit to use if:

- free from physical contamination (for example, metal objects)
- free from excess moisture
- free from rancidity
- used within the recommended period.

ACCURATE WEIGHING

Soya flour must be weighed accurately to ensure that:

- the recipe remains balanced
- a uniform product is obtained
- the correct yield is obtained
- faults are prevented.

PREPARATION FOR USE

Soya flour must be sieved prior to use, in order to:

- remove lumps
- remove any physical contamination
- blend with other dry ingredients.

SUITABLE STORAGE CONDITIONS

Soya flour should be stored in the following appropriate conditions to prevent deterioration leading to wastage:

1 Temperature: 10–16°C (50–61°F).
2 Environment: dry, airtight conditions.
3 Time limit: up to 3 months.

Use in strict stock rotation.

LEGISLATION

The contents of raw materials and bakery products are governed by the Food Safety Act 1990. Extracts from the Act state the following standards should be met:

1 Food must be of the nature, substance or quality demanded.
2 Food must not present any risk to health and be fit for human consumption.

Salt

SOURCE

Salt is a natural mineral that is found in many parts of the world.

Constituents:

- 40% sodium
- 60% chlorine.

The chemical name for salt is sodium chloride.

TYPES

There are two types of salt:

1 Vacuum salt.
2 Sea salt.

PROPERTIES

Salt possesses the following properties and benefits for use in bakery products:

- controls the rate of fermentation within doughs and the final volume
- strengthens the gluten
- enhances the flavour and eating quality
- improves crust and crumb colour
- improves crumb stability
- improves the shelf life.

SUITABILITY FOR THE PRODUCT

Small percentages of salt are used in the production of bread and fermented goods, savoury paste and fillings, puff paste, powder aerated products and some cakes.

FEATURES OF GOOD CONDITION

Salt is fit to use if:

- free from physical contamination (for example, metal objects)
- free from excess moisture and free running.

ACCURATE WEIGHING

Salt must be weighed accurately to ensure that:

- the recipe remains balanced
- a uniform product is obtained
- the correct yield is obtained
- faults are prevented.

Note: Excess salt in a dough or filling can have a disastrous effect upon the final product, rendering it inedible.

PREPARATION FOR USE

Salt must be sieved prior to use in order to blend with other dry ingredients and to remove any physical contamination.

SUITABLE STORAGE CONDITIONS

Salt is hygroscopic and should be stored in the following appropriate conditions to prevent the retention of moisture:

1 Temperature: 14–21°C (57–70°F).
2 Environment: dry, airtight conditions.
3 Time limit: keeps indefinitely.

LEGISLATION

The contents of raw materials and bakery products are governed by the Food Safety Act 1990. Extracts from the Act state the following standards should be met:

1 Food must be of the nature, substance or quality demanded.
2 Food must not present any risk to health and be fit for human consumption.

Sugar

SOURCE

Sugar is obtained from two sources: *cane* and *beet* sugar. They are natural substances and belong to the chemical group of carbohydrates which consist of carbon, hydrogen and oxygen. During and after the refining of sugar, it can be categorised into two divisions:

- grains
- syrups.

TYPES

1 Grains:
- caster sugar – fine crystals
- granulated – coarse crystals
- nib sugar – large crystals
- cube sugar
- brown sugars – fine to coarse crystals
- icing sugars – fine powder.

2 Syrups:
- golden syrup
- treacle
- glucose.

PROPERTIES

Sugar and syrups possess the following properties and benefits for use in bakery products:

- sweeten
- shorten, lift and lighten the crumb
- enhance the flavour and eating quality
- caramelise and provide crust colour
- improve the shelf life
- important yeast food during the fermentation of doughs.

SUITABILITY FOR THE PRODUCT

The importance and versatility of sugar to the baker is demonstrated by its use in the production of fermented products, sweet pastries, enriched pastes, powder aerated products, cakes, sponges, almond products, meringues and japonaise.

FEATURES OF GOOD CONDITION

Sugar and syrups are fit to use if:

- free from physical contamination
- free from excess moisture.

ACCURATE WEIGHING

Sugar and syrup must be weighed accurately to ensure that:

- the recipe remains balanced.
- a uniform product is obtained
- the correct yield is obtained
- faults are prevented.

PREPARATION FOR USE

The method of preparing sugar for addition to a recipe depends upon the mixing process. It can be added in the following ways:

- dissolved in liquid prior to addition
- sieved with dry ingredients.

SUITABLE STORAGE CONDITIONS

Sugar is hygroscopic and should be stored in the appropriate conditions below to prevent the retention of moisture:

1 Temperature: 14–21°C (57–70°F).
2 Environment: dry, airtight conditions.
3 Time limit: keeps indefinitely.

LEGISLATION

The contents of raw materials and bakery products are governed by the Food Safety Act 1990. Extracts from the Act state the following standards should be met:

1 Food must be of the nature, substance or quality demanded.
2 Food must not present any risk to health and be fit for human consumption.

Baking powder

SOURCE

Baking powder is a mixture of *acid* and *alkali*. The acid content can be Cream of Tartar or Cream Powder and the alkali content is Bicarbonate of Soda. They are mixed together in the following ratios:

- 2.25 parts of Cream of Tartar with 1 part Bicarbonate of Soda
- 2 parts of Cream Powder with 1 part Bicarbonate of Soda.

Preparation involves sieving together the two chemicals several times to ensure thorough dispersal. Of course, ready-made baking powder is available and preferred by most bakers.

TYPES

Generally, baking powder is a standard raw material.

PROPERTIES

Baking powder is responsible for the aeration, final volume and crumb structure of a product. When baking powder becomes moist during the mixing process and heated in the oven, there is a reaction between the acid and alkali which produces carbon dioxide gas. The gas is present and retained throughout the fabric of the mixture. It lifts the product to its final volume which is maintained until the baking process is complete.

Note: The generation of gas from the reaction between the acid and alkali when subjected to moisture and heat only occurs once – it cannot be repeated. For this reason, mixtures containing baking powder must be kept cool (21°C (70°F) and below) prior to baking. This will ensure that the production of carbon dioxide gas following the reaction will happen in the oven, and this will result in the aeration of the product.

SUITABILITY FOR THE PRODUCT

Small percentages of baking powder are used in the production of sweet pastry, enriched pastes, powder aerated products and cakes, sponges and almond products.

FEATURES OF GOOD CONDITION

Baking powder is fit to use if:

- acid and alkali content are thoroughly dispersed
- free from physical contamination (for example, metal objects)
- free from excess moisture
- used within the recommended period.

ACCURATE WEIGHING

Baking powder must be weighed accurately to ensure that:

- the recipe remains balanced
- a uniform product is obtained
- the correct yield is obtained
- faults are prevented.

Note: Excess baking powder in a mixture can have a disastrous effect upon the final product, rendering it inedible.

PREPARATION FOR USE

Baking powder may require sieving several times prior to weighing, to ensure that the contents are thoroughly dispersed. The reasons for sieving baking powder are:

- to remove lumps
- to remove any physical contamination (for example, metal objects)
- to blend with other dry ingredients.

SUITABLE STORAGE CONDITIONS

Baking powder is hygroscopic and should be stored in the appropriate conditions below to prevent the retention of moisture:

1 Temperature: 10–16°C (50–61°F).
2 Environment: dry, airtight conditions.
3 Time limit: 6 to 12 months.

Use in strict stock rotation.

LEGISLATION

The contents of raw materials and bakery products are governed by the Food Safety Act 1990. Extracts from the Act state the following standards should be met:

1 Food must be of the nature, substance or quality demanded.
2 Food must not present any risk to health and be fit for human consumption.

Milk powder

SOURCE

Milk powder is produced by removing the moisture content from cows milk.

TYPES

Milk powder is available as:

1 Full cream.
2 Semi-skimmed.
3 Skimmed.

Table 2 Constituents of milk powder

Full cream %	Constituents	Skimmed %
27.50	fat	1.00
26.50	proteins	36.00
2.50	moisture	3.00
37.50	lactose	52.00
6.00	minerals	8.00

PROPERTIES

Milk powder has a beneficial effect on the following characteristics of a product:

- texture
- colour
- flavour
- eating qualities
- shelf life
- nutritional value.

Crust colour on bread and fermented products

The sugar naturally present in milk powder is known as lactose. Yeast is unable to use lactose as a food, therefore, when milk powder is included in a dough, it remains present for the baking process. During the baking process, the heat caramelises the lactose on the surface of the product and a golden brown colour is obtained.

Note: Milk powder can be reconstituted to return to liquid milk.

SUITABILITY FOR THE PRODUCT

The versatility of milk powder to the baker is demonstrated by its use in the production of bread and fermented products, sweet pastry, enriched pastes, powder aerated products and cakes and sponges.

FEATURES OF GOOD CONDITION

Milk powders are fit to use if:

- free from infestation
- free from physical contamination (for example, metal objects)
- free from excess moisture

- free from rancidity
- used within the recommended period.

ACCURATE WEIGHING

Milk powder must be weighed accurately to ensure that:

- the recipe remains balanced
- a uniform product is obtained
- the correct yield is obtained
- faults are prevented.

PREPARATION FOR USE

Milk powder must be sieved prior to use:

- to remove lumps
- to remove any physical contamination (for example, metal objects)
- to blend with other dry ingredients.

Reconstitution of milk powders

Milk powder can be returned into liquid milk by adding water. The correct ratios are:

- full cream milk:
  8 parts water to 1 part powder
  1 litre (2 lb 3.75 oz) water to 125 g (4.5 oz) powder.
- skimmed milk:
  10 parts water to 1 part powder
  1 litre (2 lb 3.75 oz) water to 100 g (3.5 oz) powder.

Reconstitute as follows using warm water:

1. Add the milk powder to a small amount of the water content and mix to a paste.
2. Using a whisk, add the remaining water slowly. Whisk continuously until all of the water has been added.
3. Whisk thoroughly to ensure thoroughly dispersed.
4. Chill to reduce the temperature to 4°C (39°F) and treat as fresh milk.

Reconstitution should be done at least 1 hour before use.

SUITABLE STORAGE CONDITIONS

Milk powder is hygroscopic and should be stored in the appropriate conditions below to prevent the retention of moisture:

1 Temperature: 4–10°C (40–50°F).
2 Environment: dry, airtight conditions.
3 Time limit:
full cream – up to 2 months
skimmed – up to 6 months.

Use in strict stock rotation.

LEGISLATION

The contents of raw materials and bakery products are governed by the Food Safety Act 1990. Extracts from the Act state the following standards should be met:

1 Food must be of the nature, substance or quality demanded.
2 Food must not present any risk to health and be fit for human consumption.

Dough conditioners

SOURCE

Dough conditioners contain a mixture of natural and chemical substances. These substances include:

- L-Cysteine – a powerful chemical which modifies and relaxes gluten
- Soya flour – can be used alone for its general improving qualities or as a carrier for other substances that are used in very small quantities
- Ascorbic acid – an oxidising agent that stabilises the gas cells in a dough which results in a baked crumb with uniform cell size
- Fat – assists in the retention of gas within a dough which helps to achieve maximum volume in the baked product
- Yeast foods – simple sugars such as dextrose can be included as food for the yeast to help it produce carbon dioxide gas
- Mould inhibitors – acids such as Proprionic acid and Calcium Proprionate can be included to prevent premature development of mould
- Emulsifiers – produce a softer crumb and increase the shelf life
- Gypsum – keeps a dough conditioner free-flowing.

TYPES

There are a wide range of dough conditioners available to use in the production of bread and fermented products. Many are given the term 'general purpose' because they are suitable to make all kinds of fermented products, from standard tin bread to hot cross buns. Other conditioners are developed for specific purposes:

- to assist the processing method (for example, frozen dough)
- to achieve a pronounced characteristic (for example, crusty bread).

PROPERTIES

Dough conditioners have a beneficial effect on the following characteristics of a product:

- volume
- texture
- colour
- eating qualities
- shelf life.

Elimination of bulk fermentation time

Dough conditioners are popular because they eliminate the need for a dough to ferment for a long period of time, which holds many advantages. For more information refer to p. 117, Activated Dough Development in Breadmaking Processes.

SUITABILITY FOR THE PRODUCT

Dough conditioners are used in the production of bread and fermented products.

FEATURES OF GOOD CONDITION

Dough conditioners are fit to use if:

- free from physical contamination (for example, metal objects)
- free from excess moisture
- used within the recommended period.

ACCURATE WEIGHING

Dough conditioners must be weighed accurately to ensure that:

- the recipe remains balanced
- a uniform product is obtained
- the correct yield is obtained
- faults are prevented.

PREPARATION FOR USE

Dough conditioners must be sieved prior to use:

- to remove lumps
- to remove any physical contamination (for example, metal objects)
- to blend with other dry ingredients.

SUITABLE STORAGE CONDITIONS

Dough conditioners should be stored in the appropriate conditions below to prevent deterioration leading to wastage:

1 Temperature: 10–16°C (50–61°F).
2 Environment: dry conditions.
3 Time limit: 6 to 12 months.

Use in strict stock rotation.

LEGISLATION

The contents of raw materials and bakery products are governed by the Food Safety Act 1990. Extracts from the Act state the following standards should be met:

1 Food must be of the nature, substance or quality demanded.
2 Food must not present any risk to health and be fit for human consumption.

Permitted usage levels

The usage level of L-Cysteine and ascorbic acid is controlled by legislation. The maximum levels that can be used are:

- L-Cysteine – 75 parts per million on the flour weight.
- Ascorbic acid – 200 parts per million on the flour weight.

Caution: Ascorbic acid can be present in bread flour as well as dough conditioners. Therefore, it is necessary for the baker to find out the combined level of ascorbic acid between the flour and dough conditioner, to ensure that the maximum usage level is not exceeded.

Malt

SOURCE

Malt flour and malt products are obtained from barley and wheat that have undergone a controlled process known as *malting.*

The malting process

This begins after the grains have been cleaned. Germination now takes place in an environment that has a controlled level of humidity and temperature. During this period, the starch within the grain is converted into simple sugars. The germination process is halted when the grains are subjected to heat during the drying stage of the process.

The malting process can take up to two weeks to complete. After completion, the malted grains are ready to be processed into various malt products.

TYPES

The malt products that are available are:

1 Malt flour.
2 Dried malt extract.
3 Malt extract syrup.

PROPERTIES

Malt products are an important source of food for yeast in fermented doughs, and improve the following characteristics of a product:

- volume
- texture
- colour
- flavour
- eating qualities
- shelf life
- nutritional value.

SUITABILITY FOR THE PRODUCT

Malt products are used in the production of bread and fermented products.

FEATURES OF GOOD CONDITION

Malt products are fit to use if:

- free from physical contamination (for example, metal objects)
- free from excess moisture
- used within the recommended period.

ACCURATE WEIGHING

Malt products must be weighed accurately to ensure that:

- the recipe remains balanced
- a uniform product is obtained
- the correct yield is obtained
- faults are prevented.

PREPARATION FOR USE

1 Malt flour and dried malt flour must be sieved prior to use:
    - to remove lumps
    - to remove any physical contamination (for example, metal objects)
    - to blend with other dry ingredients.
2 Malt extract syrup should be dissolved in the water content of the recipe to ensure thorough dispersal.

SUITABLE STORAGE CONDITIONS

Malt products are hygroscopic and should be stored in the appropriate conditions below to prevent the retention of moisture:

1 Temperature: 10–16°C (50–61°F).
2 Environment: dry, airtight conditions.
3 Time limit: 6 to 12 months.

Use in strict stock rotation.

LEGISLATION

The contents of raw materials and bakery products are governed by the Food Safety Act 1990. Extracts from the Act state the following standards should be met:

1 Food must be of the nature, substance or quality demanded.
2 Food must not present any risk to health and be fit for human consumption.

Nuts

SOURCE

Most of the nuts used by the baker are obtained from the relevant type of tree. The one exception is that of peanuts which are grown in the ground.

TYPES

The most popular nuts are:

- almonds
- hazelnuts
- peanuts
- walnuts
- coconut.

Other nuts used include pecan, pistachio, brazil and cashew.

Example of average constituents

Table 3 Average constituents of nuts

Almonds %	Constituents	Peanuts %
54.50	oil	39.00
20.00	protein	23.00
15.00	carbohydrates	24.50
6.00	water	9.00
2.50	fibre	2.50
2.00	mineral salts	2.00

Nuts are available in the following forms:

- whole
- halves
- strip
- flaked
- nibbed
- ground.

PROPERTIES

Nuts have a beneficial effect upon the following characteristics of a product:

- texture
- colour
- flavour

- eating qualities
- shelf life
- nutritional value.

SUITABILITY FOR THE PRODUCT

Nuts can be used in the production of fermented products, sweet pastry, enriched pastes, puff pastry, cakes, almond products and japonaise.

FEATURES OF GOOD CONDITION

Nuts are fit to use if:

- free from rancidity
- free from infestation
- free from physical contamination (for example, metal objects)
- free from excess moisture
- used within the recommended period.

ACCURATE WEIGHING

Nuts must be weighed accurately to ensure that:

- the recipe remains balanced
- a uniform product is obtained
- the correct yield is obtained
- faults are prevented.

PREPARATION FOR USE

1 Whole, halved and strip nuts are ready to use and do not require any further preparation.
2 The flavour of flaked and nibbed nuts can be enhanced by roasting in the oven at a temperature of 200°C (392°F) for 10–15 minutes, turning occasionally.
3 Ground nuts that are included in a recipe must be sieved and blended with dry ingredients.

SUITABLE STORAGE CONDITIONS

Nuts should be stored in the appropriate conditions below to prevent deterioration leading to wastage:

1 Temperature: 10–16°C (50–61°F).
2 Environment: dry, airtight conditions.
3 Time limit: 3 to 6 months.

Use strict stock rotation.

LEGISLATION

The contents of raw materials and bakery products are governed by the Food Safety Act 1990. Extracts from the Act state the following standards should be met:

1 Food must be of the nature, substance or quality demanded.
2 Food must not present any risk to health and be fit for human consumption.

FERMENTATION INGREDIENT

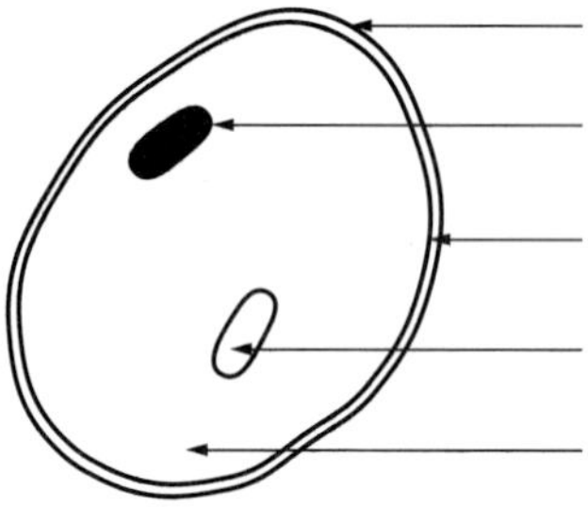

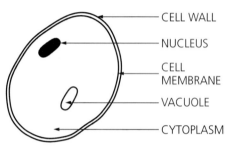

Figure 1 A yeast cell

Yeast

SOURCE

Yeast is a species belonging to the fungi family of plants. The strain used by the baker is called Saccharomyces Cerevisiae.

Structure

Yeast is a living single cell organism, oval in shape that can only be seen under a microscope.

The average composition of a yeast cell is:

- 71% moisture
- 14% protein
- 10% carbohydrates
- 3% mineral matter
- 2% fat.

Reproduction

Yeast has two methods of reproduction:

- Budding – occurs when conditions are favourable
- Sporulation – occurs when conditions are unfavourable.

Budding Under favourable conditions, yeast cells will reproduce by the process of budding. The favourable conditions are:

- sufficient food and simple sugars
- ample moisture
- warmth – 27 to 29°C (80 to 84°F)
- adequate time.

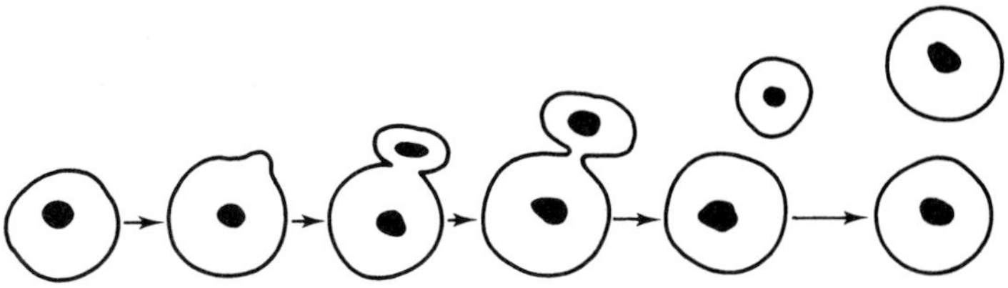

Figure 2 Yeast budding

A small bud appears on the wall of the yeast cell and continues to grow until it becomes equal in size to the original cell. At the same time, the constituents of the cell move towards the new cell, before they divide equally between the original and newly formed cell. When the process has been completed, the new cell breaks away and the reproduction process continues.

Sporulation Under unfavourable conditions, yeast cells will reproduce by sporulation. The unfavourable conditions are:

- insufficient food
- lack of moisture
- unsuitable temperature.

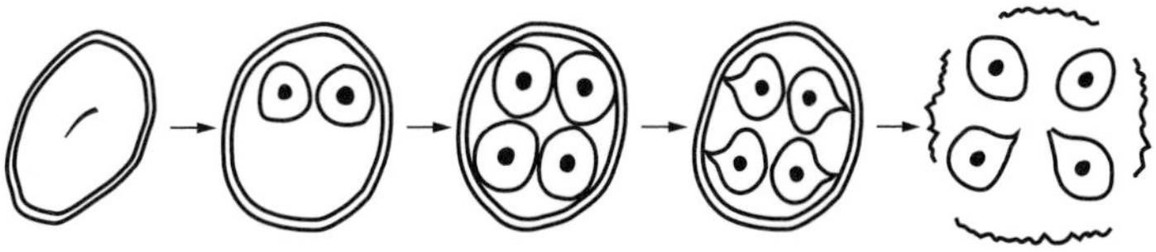

Figure 3 Yeast sporulation

When food and moisture are not available in sufficient quantities, the nucleus will use up all the food that is present within the cytoplasm. The nucleus then divides, usually into four, and the cell wall thickens to offer greater protection to the yeast spores. The yeast spores are able to survive in this condition for very long periods of time until they regain favourable conditions and reproduce by the budding process.

TYPES

Yeast is available in these forms:

1 Compressed.
2 Dried.
3 Liquid.

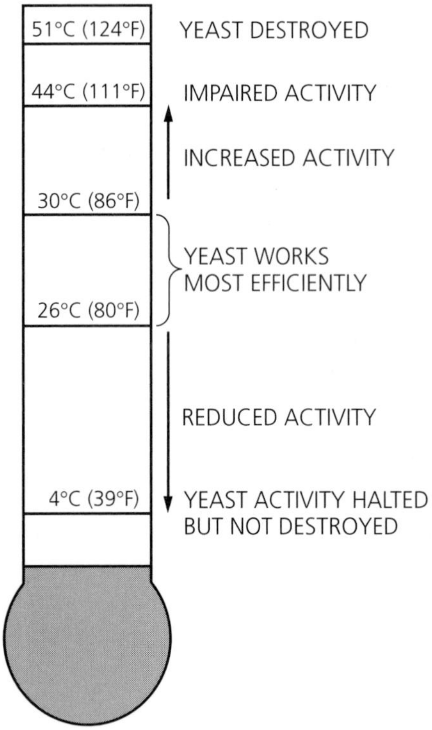

Figure 4 The effects of temperature on yeast

PROPERTIES

The activity of yeast within a dough is called *fermentation.* During fermentation, simple sugars are produced as food for the yeast. The yeast cells are able to absorb and use the food to produce large quantities of carbon dioxide gas and a small amount of alcohol. As a result of the fermentation process, yeast has effect upon the following characteristics of a product:

- the expansion and final volume
- the mellowing of the gluten to obtain a uniform shape and soft crumb
- flavour produced during the fermentation process.

Generally, for yeast to perform effectively during the fermentation process and obtain the product characteristics, the temperature of the dough should be between 26–30°C (79–86°F).

EFFECTS OF TEMPERATURE AND INGREDIENTS

Temperature

See Figure 4.

Ingredients

1 *Salt* Salt slows down the activity of yeast. It therefore controls and stabilises the rate of fermentation within a dough when used at the appropriate level. High levels of salt will retard or destroy the yeast. You should *never* allow yeast to come into direct contact with salt.
2 *Sugar* Yeast works effectively in solutions that contain no more than 13% sugar. Doughs that contain sugar above this level will experience a reduced rate of fermentation. Very high concentrations of sugar will retard or destroy the yeast. You should *never* allow yeast to come into direct contact with sugar.
3 *Fats* High levels of fat have a retarding effect upon the activity of yeast.
4 *Spices* High levels of spices have a retarding effect upon the activity of yeast.

Note: It may be necessary to use the ferment and dough process to make a dough that contains a high level of sugar, fat and spices. This is to encourage and promote the activity of yeast and to avoid the retarding effect that these ingredients have upon the yeast.

SUITABILITY FOR THE PRODUCT

Yeast is used in the production of bread and fermented products.

FEATURES OF GOOD CONDITION

Yeast is fit to use if:

- it is cream-coloured
- the temperature is cool: 4°C (39°F)
- the consistency is firm with a clean break
- used within the recommended period.

ACCURATE WEIGHING

Yeast must be weighed accurately to ensure that:

- the recipe remains balanced
- a uniform product is obtained
- the correct yield is obtained
- faults are prevented.

PREPARATION FOR USE

The most common method of adding yeast to a dough is to disperse it in the tempered water to ensure thorough dispersal. However, yeast can be added in the dry state during the high speed mixing process.

SUITABLE STORAGE CONDITIONS

Yeast should be stored in the appropriate conditions below to prevent deterioration leading to wastage:

1 Temperature: 2–4°C (35–39°F).
2 Environment: dry conditions.
3 Time limit: up to 1 month.

Use in strict stock rotation.

Stacking

As yeast is a living organism, it has the ability to generate heat. To prevent the generation of heat leading to deterioration and reduction in activity, boxes of yeast must be stacked with some space between the boxes. This will allow the cool air to circulate and prevent a rise in temperature.

LEGISLATION

The contents of raw materials and bakery products are governed by the Food Safety Act 1990. Extracts from the Act state the following standards should be met:

1 Food must be of the nature, substance or quality demanded.
2 Food must not present any risk to health and be fit for human consumption.

ENRICHING INGREDIENTS

Fats and oils

SOURCE

Fats and oils are obtained from the following sources:

- vegetables
- animals
- milk
- marine.

TYPES

The most common types of fats and oils are:

- butter
- cake margarine
- shortening
- lard
- pastry margarine
- high ratio shortening
- vegetable oil
- emulsions.

Example of constituents

Table 4 Sample constituents of fats and oils

Butter %	Constituents	Cake margarine %
82.00	fat	83.00
15.00	moisture	14.00
1.60	curd	1.50
1.40	minerals	1.50

PROPERTIES

Fats and oils possess the following properties in the production of bakery products:

1 *Aeration* The ability to incorporate air during the mixing process, which contributes to the aeration and final volume of a product.
2 *Shortening* The ability to surround the insoluble gluten forming proteins of flour during the mixing process. Liquids then have restricted access to the gluten which does not become fully developed; the result is a shortness to the eating quality of the final product.
3 *Laminating* The ability to withstand the rolling and folding process of lamination. They allow layers of dough and fat to be built up which helps to achieve the final volume of the product.
4 *Emulsifying* The ability to assist in the formation of a smooth, clear dough, paste or batter.
5 *Frying* The ability to withstand high temperatures without smoking and igniting during the cooking of a product.
6 *Flavour* The ability to contribute directly to the flavour of a product.
7 *Eating quality* A pleasing effect upon the general eating quality (for example, soft crumb).
8 *Nutritional value* Fats and oils contain a high level of calories and are a good source of energy.

Table 5 Fats and their properties

Fat \ Property	Volume	Shortening	Lamination	Emulsifying	Frying	Flavour	Eating qualities	Nutritional value	Keeping qualities
Butter	●	●	●	●		●	●	●	●
Cake margarine	●	●		●			●	●	●
Shortening	●	●		●			●	●	●
Lard		●				●	●	●	●
Pastry margarine	●		●				●	●	●
High ratio shortening	●	●		●			●	●	●
Vegetable oil		●			●		●	●	●

9 *Keeping qualities* The softening, emulsifying and enriching properties of fats and oils help to extend the shelf life of a product.

See Table 5, for the properties of fats and oils.
Note: Emulsions are mixtures containing water and oil, and are used to grease baking tins and trays to ensure the easy release of baked products.

SUITABILITY FOR THE PRODUCT

The suitability of a fat or oil for a process or product depends upon the properties they possess. Table 6 indicates the suitability of a fat for a product.

Table 6 Suitability for the product

Fat \ Product	Bread	Fermented products	Sweet pastries	Savoury pastries	Puff pastries	Powder aerated products	Cakes	Almond products	Choux pastry
Butter		●	●		●	●	●	●	●
Cake margarine		●	●			●	●	●	●
Shortening	●	●	●	●		●	●		
Lard	●	●		●					
Pastry margarine		●			●				
High ratio shortening							●		
Vegetable oil	●	●				●	●		

FEATURES OF GOOD CONDITION

Fats and oils are fit to use if:

- free from physical contamination (for example, metal objects)
- free from separation and rancidity
- used within the recommended period.

ACCURATE WEIGHING

Fats and oils must be weighed accurately to ensure that:

- the recipe remains balanced
- a uniform product is obtained
- the correct yield is obtained
- faults are prevented.

PREPARATION FOR USE

Generally, most fats are stored at a temperature between 16–21°C (61–70°F) prior to use, to ensure that they are of a suitable consistency for addition to doughs, pastes and batters. However, some notable exceptions are:

1 During warm weather: the fat may need to be stored in a chilled environment to prevent excessive softening and eventual separation.
2 During lamination: butter that is to be used for lamination purposes must be stored at 4°C (39°F) prior to use, to be able to withstand the rolling and folding process.
3 During mixing to create product characteristics: for example, boiled paste for pork pies involves boiling the shortening or lard with water before adding to the flour. The boiling liquor gelatinises starch within the flour and produces a crisp pastry.

SUITABLE STORAGE CONDITIONS

Fats and oils should be stored in the appropriate conditions below to prevent rancidity leading to wastage:

1 Temperature: 10–16°C (50–61°F).
2 Environment: dry conditions.
3 Time limit: up to 1 month.

Use in strict stock rotation.

LEGISLATION

The contents of raw materials and bakery products are governed by the Food Safety Act 1990. Extracts from the Act state the following standards should be met:

1 Food must be of the nature, substance or quality demanded.
2 Food must not present any risk to health and be fit for human consumption.

Fruit

SOURCE

The many fruits used by the baker are grown from the following sources:

- tree (eg apples)
- vine (eg grapes)

- plant (eg strawberries)
- bush (eg blackberries)

After harvesting, the fruits are processed and are available in these forms:

- fresh
- tinned
- dried
- sugar preserved
- frozen.

TYPES

The types of fruits in common use are:

1 *Fresh* apples, strawberries, pears, bananas, grapes, kiwi, raspberries and blackberries.
2 *Tinned* apple, pineapple, mandarin orange, peaches, cherries, raspberries, blackberries, apricots and pears.
3 *Dried* currants, sultanas, raisins and dates.
4 *Sugar preserved* cherries, pineapples, orange and lemon peel.
5 *Frozen* strawberries, raspberries and blackberries.

PROPERTIES

Fruit will confer some of the following properties to bakery products:

- flavour
- colour
- texture
- moisture
- visual appeal
- variety
- eating qualities
- keeping qualities
- nutritional value.

SUITABILITY FOR THE PRODUCT

1 Fresh, tinned and frozen fruit: Most of the types of fruit listed in these categories are suitable to be used as follows:
   - in unbaked mixtures
   - in fillings
   - as a decorative material.
2 Dried fruit: The types of fruit listed in this category are suitable to be used as follows:

- in unbaked mixtures
- in fillings.

3 Sugar preserved fruit: The types of fruit listed in this category are suitable to be used as follows:
- in unbaked mixtures
- as a decorative material.

Fruits are used in the production of most categories of bakery products, with little exception.

FEATURES OF GOOD CONDITION

Fruits are fit to use if:

- free from decomposition
- free from infestation and moulds
- free from physical contamination (for example, metal objects)
- free from excess moisture
- used within the recommended period.

ACCURATE WEIGHING

Fruit must be weighed accurately to ensure:

- the recipe remains balanced
- a uniform product is obtained
- the correct yield is obtained
- faults are prevented.

PREPARATION FOR USE

1 *Fresh fruits* The preparation of fresh fruits may involve:
- peeling
- washing
- drying
- removing stalks, stones and cores
- slicing
- chopping
- pulping

2 *Tinned fruits* The preparation of tinned fruits may involve:
- drying
- slicing
- chopping
- pulping.

3 *Dried fruits* The preparation of dried fruits may involve:
- washing

- drying
- removing stalks, stones and cores
- soaking.

4 *Sugar preserved fruits* The preparation of sugar preserved fruits may involve:
- washing
- drying
- cutting
- chopping.

5 *Frozen fruits* The preparation of frozen fruits may involve:
- defrosting
- drying
- pulping.

SUITABLE STORAGE CONDITIONS

Fruit should be stored in the appropriate conditions below to prevent deterioration leading to wastage: see Table 7.

Table 7 Suitable storage conditions for fruit

	Temperature	Conditions	Time limit
Fresh fruit	10–16°C (50–61°C)	dry and ventilated	1–7 days
Tinned fruit	10–21°C (50–70°F)	avoid sunlight and damage	up to 3 years
Dried fruit	10–16°C (50–61°F)	sealed container	up to 6 months
Sugar preserved fruit	10–16°C (50–61°F)	sealed container	up to 6 months
Frozen fruit	−22°C (−7°F)	sealed packaging	up to 12 months

Use in strict stock rotation.

LEGISLATION

The contents of raw materials and bakery products are governed by the Food Safety Act 1990. Extracts from the Act state the following standards should be met:

1 Food must be of the nature, substance or quality demanded.
2 Food must not present any risk to health and be fit for human consumption.

LIQUID INGREDIENTS

Egg

SOURCE

The egg used by the baker is obtained from chickens.

TYPES

The types of egg in common use are:

1 Shell egg.
2 Chilled liquid egg.
3 Frozen egg.
4 Frozen egg whites.
5 Dried egg white.

Note: Egg whites are known as albumen.

Table 8 Constituents of whole egg, albumen and yolk

Constituents	% Whole egg	% Albumen	% Yolk
Moisture	74	87	50
Protein	12.5	12.25	16
Fat	12	0.25	32
Minerals	1	0.5	1
Organic matter	0.5	nil	1

PROPERTIES

Egg possesses the following properties in the production of bakery products:

1 *Moisturising* Egg contains 74% water and has the ability to moisturise its own weight in flour.
2 *Aeration* Whisked egg can incorporate air and increase in volume. It has the ability to aerate its own weight in flour. A stiff foam is obtained when egg whites and sugar incorporate air during whisking (for example, meringues).
3 *Structural* Egg is distributed throughout the fabric of a mixture. When egg is subjected to heat during the baking process, it expands, the proteins coagulate and the structure is established.
4 *Emulsifying* Egg yolk contains a natural emulsifying agent known as lecithin. The lecithin assists in the formation of a smooth, clear mixture.

5 *Enriching* Egg contains a high level of protein and fat which contribute to the nutritional value of egg.
6 *Flavouring* Egg has its own characteristic flavour which is conferred to bakery products.
7 *Colouring* Egg confers a yellow colour to bakery products. When used alone, egg whites confer a white colour to bakery products.
8 *Glazing* When egg is mixed with an appropriate quantity of milk, it can be used to glaze the top surface of many bakery products.
9 *Eating quality* Egg confers lightness, moisture and flavour to the eating qualities of bakery products.
10 *Keeping qualities* The moisturising, emulsifying, enriching and general softening properties of the egg will help to extend the shelf life of a product.
11 *Nutritional value* Egg contain a high level of calories and is a good source of energy.

SUITABILITY FOR THE PRODUCT

- Whole egg (whether shell, liquid or frozen) is used in the production of bread and fermented products, sweet pastries, enriched pastes, powder aerated products, cakes, sponges, almond goods and choux pastry.
- Frozen egg whites and reconstituted dried egg whites are used in the production of cakes, biscuits, almond goods, meringues, japonaise and royal icing.

FEATURES OF GOOD CONDITION

Egg and egg whites are fit to use if:

- the smell is fresh
- the colour is normal
- free from physical contamination (for example, metal objects)
- used within the recommended period.

ACCURATE WEIGHING

Egg and egg whites must be weighed accurately to ensure that:

- the recipe remains balanced
- a uniform product is obtained
- the correct yield is obtained
- faults are prevented.

PREPARATION FOR USE

Defrosting

Prior to use, frozen egg and egg whites must be defrosted gently. Defrosting can be achieved by standing the containers in a room overnight at a temperature of between 16–21°C (61–70°F).

Tempering

1 To incorporate egg into some mixtures (in particular, cake batters), it must be warmed to 21°C (70°F) to prevent the batter from curdling.
2 Some mixtures need to be cool (in particular, scone doughs) to prevent baking powder from working. The egg must therefore be in a chilled condition, 4°C (39°F).

Vehicle for other ingredients

Ingredients that are used in small quantities can be mixed through the egg content prior to addition, in order to ensure thorough dispersal. Some examples of these ingredients are:

- glycerine
- essences
- colours
- flavours
- compounds.

Reconstitution of dried egg whites

Dried egg whites are returned to liquid form by adding water. The correct ratio of water to dried egg white is:

7 parts water to 1 part powder
1 litre (2 lb 3.5 oz) water to 143 g (5 oz) powder

Reconstitute as follows, using water:

1 Add the dried egg white to a small amount of the water content and mix to a paste.
2 Using a whisk, add the remaining water slowly. Whisk continuously until all the water has been added.
3 Whisk thoroughly to ensure through dispersal.
4 Chill to reduce the temperature to 4°C (39°F) and treat as fresh egg whites.

Reconstitution should be done at least 1 hour before use.

Improving whipping power

The whipping power of egg whites can be improved by using one of the following methods:

1 Allow to stand in the refrigerator to obtain a slight acidic nature.
2 Add a small amount of weak acid. The acids that are suitable are Citric, Acetic and Tartaric.

SUITABLE STORAGE CONDITIONS

Egg is prone to contamination by salmonella bacteria, therefore liquid egg, frozen egg, frozen egg whites and dried egg whites are pasteurised by the supplier. Egg should be stored in the appropriate conditions in Table 9 to prevent premature deterioration leading to wastage.

Table 9 Suitable storage conditions for eggs

Type	Temperature	Conditions	Time limit
Shell	4°C (39°F)	clean container	3–4 weeks
Liquid	4°C (39°F)	sealed container	2–3 days
Frozen	−22°C (−7°F)	sealed container	6–12 months
Frozen egg whites	−22°C (−7°F)	sealed container	6–12 months
Dried egg whites	4–10°C (39–50°F)	dry, airtight	2–3 months

Use in strict stock rotation.

LEGISLATION

The contents of raw materials and bakery products are governed by the Food Safety Act 1990. Extracts from the Act state the following standards should be met:

1 Food must be of the nature, substance or quality demanded.
2 Food must not present any risk to health and be fit for human consumption.

Milk

SOURCE

The milk used by the baker is primarily cow's milk.

TYPES

The types of milk in common use are:

1 Full cream.
2 Semi-skimmed.
3 Skimmed.

Constituents

Table 10 Constituents of milk

Full cream %	Constituents	Skimmed %
87.80	water	90.80
3.50	fat	0.10
3.50	protein	3.80
4.50	lactose	4.60
0.70	minerals	0.70

PROPERTIES

Milk has a beneficial effect upon the following characteristics of a product:

- moistness
- texture
- colour
- flavour
- eating qualities
- shelf life
- nutritional value.

SUITABILITY FOR THE PRODUCT

Milk is used in the production of bread and fermented products, sweet pastries, enriched pastes, powder aerated products and cakes. It is also an important ingredient for the manufacture of custards, sauces and other fillings.

FEATURES OF GOOD CONDITION

Milk is fit to use if:

- the smell is fresh
- the colour is normal and there is no sign of separation
- free from physical contamination (for example, metal objects)
- used within the recommended period.

ACCURATE WEIGHING

Milk must be weighed accurately to ensure that:

- the recipe remains balanced
- a uniform product is obtained
- the correct yield is obtained
- faults are prevented.

PREPARATION FOR USE

Tempering

1 Milk that is to be used in the production of fermented doughs and cake batters should be warmed to 21°C (70°F) to help obtain the required final dough or batter temperature.
2 Some mixtures need to be cool (in particular, scone doughs) to prevent baking powder from working. The milk therefore must be in a chilled condition, 4°C (39°F).

Vehicle for other ingredients

In the manufacture of custards and sauces, dry ingredients such as cornflour can be mixed through the milk to ensure thorough dispersal.

SUITABLE STORAGE CONDITIONS

Milk is prone to contamination by bacteria, so it is either pasteurised or sterilised by the supplier. Milk should be stored in the appropriate conditions below to prevent premature deterioration leading to wastage.

1 Temperature: 4°C (39°F).
2 Conditions: sealed containers.
3 Time limit: 5–6 days.

Use in strict stock rotation.

LEGISLATION

The contents of raw materials and bakery products are governed by the Food Safety Act 1990. Extracts from the Act state the following standards should be met:

1 Food must be of the nature, substance or quality demanded.
2 Food must not present any risk to health and be fit for human consumption.

Fresh cream

SOURCE

Fresh cream is obtained from the fat content of cow's milk.

TYPES

The types of cream in common use are:

1 Single – contains 18% butterfat.
2 Whipping – contains 35% butterfat.
3 Double – contains 48% butterfat.

PROPERTIES

Fresh cream has a beneficial effect upon the following characteristics of a product:

- texture
- colour
- flavour
- eating qualities
- nutritional value.

SUITABILITY FOR THE PRODUCT

1 Single Cream:
   Used in the production of sauces and fillings and as a pouring cream.
   Unable to be whipped to a stiff consistency suitable for spreading or piping because of the low butterfat content.
2 Whipping Cream:
   Used as a filling, coating and finishing material.
3 Double Cream:
   Used in the production of rich fillings.

FEATURES OF GOOD CONDITION

Fresh cream is fit to use if:

- the smell is fresh
- the colour is normal and there is no sign of separation
- free from physical contamination (for example, metal objects)
- used within the recommended period.

HYGIENIC HANDLING

Fresh cream is prone to contamination by bacteria and is therefore pasteurised by the supplier. It is essential to observe strict hygiene measures when fresh cream is involved during the production process. Some of those measures are:

- staff training on hygiene
- a separate area for the production of fresh cream products
- a cool environment 14°C (57°F)
- to use only sterile equipment, for example, whipping equipment, savoy bags, piping tubes
- to use clean packaging
- transport and display under refrigerated conditions.

ACCURATE WEIGHING

Fresh cream must be weighed accurately to ensure that:

- the recipe remains balanced
- a uniform product is obtained
- the correct yield is obtained
- faults are prevented.

PREPARATION FOR USE

Single cream does not require any preparation prior to use.

Whipping cream

As the name suggests, this cream can be whipped to a stiff consistency that is suitable for spreading and piping.

Whipping Process:
Prior to whipping, ensure the cream is at a temperature of 4°C (39°F). Using a whisk, the cream must be whipped on medium or top speed until a stiff consistency is obtained. During whipping the cream will more than almost double in volume; this is known as the over-run. Care must be taken during the final stages of the whipping process to prevent the cream from over-mixing. Over-mixing will lead to separation and seeping, and eventually the cream will become butter.

Additives:
Two materials can be added to whipping cream, they are:

- sugar – up to a maximum of 13% = 130 g per litre
- stabiliser – up to a maximum of 0.3% = 3 g per litre.

Note:
1 Some stabilisers can be mixed through the sugar, prior to addition to ensure thorough dispersal.
2 On request, suppliers will add stabilisers at source.

SUITABLE STORAGE CONDITIONS

Fresh cream should be stored in the appropriate conditions below to prevent premature deterioration leading to wastage:

1 Temperature: 4°C (39°F).
2 Conditions: sealed container.
3 Time limit: 5–6 days.

Use in strict stock rotation.

LEGISLATION

The contents of raw materials and bakery products are governed by the Food Safety Act 1990. Extracts from the Act state the following standards should be met:

1 Food must be of the nature, substance or quality demanded.
2 Food must not present any risk to health and be fit for human consumption.

IMITATION CREAM

This provides an alternative to fresh cream. Imitation cream is an emulsion which includes water, vegetable oils, sugar and stabiliser. While containers remain unopened, they have a long storage life, but once the seal is broken they must be handled with the same hygienic measures as for fresh cream. The preparation and use is the same as fresh cream with an increased over-run.

FINISHING MATERIALS

Jams and curds

CONTENTS

Jams

Jams are prepared from the following ingredients:

- fruits
- sugar
- pectin
- colouring matter
- acid.

Curds

Curds are prepared from the following ingredients:

- citrus fruits
- sugar
- glucose
- fat
- flavour
- cornflour.

TYPES

- *Jams* raspberry, strawberry, blackcurrant, apple and raspberry, pineapple etc.
- *Curds* lemon and orange.

PROPERTIES

Jams and curds confer the following properties to bakery products:

- flavour
- moisture
- colour
- visual appeal
- variety
- eating qualities
- nutritional value.

FEATURES OF GOOD CONDITION

Jams and curds are fit to use if:

- free from mould and fermentation
- free from physical contamination (for example, metal objects)
- free from excess moisture
- used within the recommended period.

PREPARATION

Blend jams and curds slowly until a smooth consistency is obtained.

APPLICATION

Jams and curds can be applied to fill and decorate bakery products using a palette knife, scraper, piping bag or depositing machine.

SUITABILITY FOR THE PRODUCT

Jams and curds are used in the production of fermented products, sweet pastries, enriched pastes, puff pastries, cakes, sponges and almond goods.

SUITABLE STORAGE CONDITIONS

Jams and curds should be stored in the appropriate conditions below to prevent deterioration leading to wastage:

1 Temperature: 10–16°C (50–61°F).
2 Environment: out of sunlight, sealed container.
3 Time limit: 12–18 months.

Use in strict stock rotation.

LEGISLATION

The contents of raw materials and bakery products are governed by the Food Safety Act 1990. Extracts from the Act state the following standards should be met:

1 Food must be of the nature, substance or quality demanded.
2 Food must not present any risk to health and be fit for human consumption.

Fondant

CONTENTS

Fondant is prepared from the following ingredients:

- sugar
- water
- glucose.

TYPES

The main type of fondant used by bakers is available in a dense solid form which requires preparation prior to use.

PROPERTIES

Fondant confers the following properties to bakery products:

- colour
- gloss and visual appeal
- variety
- moisture

- flavour
- eating qualities
- keeping qualities.

FEATURES OF GOOD CONDITION

Fondants are fit to use if:

- free from hardness
- free from fermentation
- free from physical contamination (for example, metal objects)
- used within the recommended period.

PREPARATION

Using a bain-marie, follow this sequence:

1 Place sufficient fondant into the bain-marie.
2 Add a small amount of stock syrup to the fondant.
3 Heat slowly, stirring continuously until the fondant reaches a temperature of 37°C (99°F).
4 Add colour and flavour as required.
5 Using stock syrup, adjust to the required consistency and use immediately.

Note:

- When not in use, fondant should be kept covered with a thin film of water or syrup.
- Fondant that is heated above the recommend temperature will set hard with a dull appearance.
- Fondant that is not heated sufficiently will remain runny and sticky.

APPLICATION

Fondant can be applied to coat, enrobe and decorate bakery products using a palette knife, dipping fork, enrober or piping bag.

SUITABILITY FOR THE PRODUCT

Fondant is used in the production of fermented products, sweet pastry, enriched pastes, puff pastry, cakes, sponges, almond goods and choux pastry.

SUITABLE STORAGE CONDITIONS

Fondant should be stored in the appropriate conditions to prevent deterioration leading to wastage. The appropriate storage conditions are:

1 Temperature: 10–16°C (50–61°F).
2 Environment: dry and sealed containers.
3 Time limit: up to 2 years.

Use in strict stock rotation.

LEGISLATION

The contents of raw materials and bakery products are governed by the Food Safety Act 1990. Extracts from the Act state the following standards should be met:

1 Food must be of the nature, substance or quality demanded.
2 Food must not present any risk to health and be fit for human consumption.

Buttercream

CONTENTS

Buttercreams are prepared from the following ingredients:

- butter
- sugar
- flavouring
- colours
- a minimum of 22.5% butterfat.

TYPES

There are many recipes for buttercream. The basic recipe is to use equal quantities of butter and sugar to produce a buttercream that can be coloured and flavoured.

PROPERTIES

Buttercreams confer the following properties to bakery products:

- flavour
- moisture
- colour
- visual appeal
- variety
- eating qualities
- keeping qualities
- nutritional value.

FEATURES OF GOOD CONDITION

Buttercream is fit to use if:

- free from physical contamination (for example, metal objects)
- free from separation and rancidity
- used within the recommended period.

PREPARATION

Using a mixing bowl and beater, blend the butter and sugar together, then beat until a light consistency is obtained. Add colour and flavour as required.

APPLICATION

Buttercream can be applied to fill, coat and decorate bakery products using a palette knife, scraper or piping bag.

SUITABILITY FOR THE PRODUCT

Buttercream is used in the production of enriched pastries, puff pastries, cakes, almond goods and japonaise.

SUITABLE STORAGE CONDITIONS

Buttercream should be stored in the appropriate conditions below to prevent deterioration leading to wastage:

1 Temperature: 10–16°C (50–61°F).
2 Environment: dry and sealed containers.
3 Time limit: up to 1 month.

Use in strict stock rotation.

LEGISLATION

The contents of raw materials and bakery products are governed by the Food Safety Act 1990. Extracts from the Act state the following standards should be met:

1 Food must be of the nature, substance or quality demanded.
2 Food must not present any risk to health and be fit for human consumption.

ALTERNATIVE FILLINGS TO BUTTERCREAM

There are fillings that provide an economical alternative to buttercream. The butter is replaced with margarine, shortening and milk powder. The properties, features of good condition, preparation for use, application, suitability for the product, storage conditions and legislation are all as for buttercream.

Custard

CONTENTS

Custard is prepared from the following ingredients:

- milk
- sugar
- egg
- cornflour
- vanilla flavour
- egg colour.

TYPES

There are many recipes for custard that will provide a smooth, firm setting filling.

PROPERTIES

Custard confers the following properties to bakery products:

- flavour
- moisture
- colour
- visual appeal
- eating qualities
- nutritional value.

FEATURES OF GOOD CONDITION

Custard is fit to use if:

- the smell is fresh
- the colour is normal
- free from physical contamination (for example, metal objects)
- used within the recommended period.

PREPARATION

To prepare custard, follow this sequence:

1 Add the cornflour to a small amount of the milk, all of the egg, vanilla flavour and egg colour. Mix to a paste.
2 Add the sugar to the remaining milk and bring to the boil.

3 Pour the boiling solution onto the paste, stirring vigorously to avoid lumps.
4 Return to the heat and bring to the boil, stirring continuously until a thick, smooth custard is obtained. Remove from the heat.
5 Cover and allow to cool if necessary.

APPLICATION

Custard can be applied to fill and decorate bakery products using a savoy bag or depositing mechanism.

SUITABILITY FOR THE PRODUCT

Custard is used in the production of fermented products, sweet pastries, puff pastries, sponges and choux pastry.

SUITABLE STORAGE CONDITIONS

Custard should be stored in the appropriate conditions below to prevent deterioration leading to wastage:

1 Temperature: 4°C (39°F).
2 Environment: sealed container.
3 Time limit: 24 hours.

Use in strict stock rotation.

Note: Custard should be prepared and used within the same day.

LEGISLATION

The contents of raw materials and bakery products are governed by the Food Safety Act 1990. Extracts from the Act state the following standards should be met:

1 Food must be of the nature, substance or quality demanded.
2 Food must not present any risk to health and be fit for human consumption.

Chocolate flavoured coating

CONTENTS

Chocolate flavoured coatings are prepared from the following ingredients:

- vegetable fats
- cocoa powder

- sugar
- milk solids
- emulsifier.

TYPES

The types of chocolate flavoured coatings are:

1 Plain.
2 Milk.
3 White.

PROPERTIES

Chocolate flavoured coatings confer the following properties to bakery products:

- flavour
- colour
- visual appeal
- variety
- eating quality
- keeping qualities
- nutritional value.

FEATURES OF GOOD CONDITION

Chocolate flavoured coatings are fit to use if:

- free from physical contamination (for example, metal objects)
- free from moisture
- used within the recommended period.

PREPARATION

Using a bain-marie, gently heat and melt the chocolate flavoured coating until a temperature of between 37–45°C (99–113°F) is obtained. It is recommended to use the coatings at the lower end of the temperature range for piping, and the higher for coating and enrobing.

Caution: Water or steam must not be allowed to come into contact with the coating because it will thicken and become unusable.

APPLICATION

Chocolate flavoured coatings can be applied to coat, enrobe and decorate bakery products using a palette knife, dipping fork, enrober or piping bag.

SUITABILITY FOR THE PRODUCT

Chocolate flavoured coatings are used in the production of enriched pastries, cakes, sponges, almond goods, meringues, japonaise and choux pastry.

SUITABLE STORAGE CONDITIONS

Chocolate flavoured coatings should be stored in the appropriate conditions below to prevent deterioration leading to wastage:

1 Temperature: 10–16°C (50–61°F).
2 Environment: dry conditions.
3 Time limit: 6–12 months.

Use in strict stock rotation.

LEGISLATION

The contents of raw materials and bakery products are governed by the Food Safety Act 1990. Extracts from the Act state the following standards should be met:

1 Food must be of the nature, substance or quality demanded.
2 Food must not present any risk to health and be fit for human consumption.

Food colours

SOURCE

Food colours are obtained from natural and artificial sources, for example:

1 Natural:
   - yellow from egg yolk
   - red from insects known as cochineal
   - chocolate from the cocoa bean.
2 Artificial: Water soluble preparations produced from chemicals.

TYPES

A full range of food colours are available from lemon to black in liquid, paste and powder form.

Note: A colour can be combined with an appropriate flavour; this is known as a compound.

PROPERTIES

Food colours have a beneficial effect upon the following characteristics of a product:

- crumb colour
- crust colour
- overall appearance.

SUITABILITY FOR THE PRODUCT

Food colours can be used in the production of fermented products, sweet pastries, enriched pastries, cakes and sponges, powder aerated products and almond products.

FEATURES OF GOOD CONDITION

Food colours are fit to use if:

- free from fermentation and mould
- free from physical contamination (for example, metal objects)
- used within the recommended period.

ACCURATE WEIGHING

Food colours must be weighed accurately to ensure that:

- the correct shade is obtained
- a uniform product is obtained
- there is no unnecessary wastage of food colours and products.

PREPARATION FOR USE

Dough, paste and batter

To ensure food colours are thoroughly dispersed, they should be mixed through one of the other ingredients in the recipe, eg egg, prior to addition to the dough, paste or batter.

Finishing materials

Food colours can be added directly to finishing materials such as fondant and buttercream.

SUITABLE STORAGE CONDITIONS

Food colours should be stored in the appropriate conditions below to prevent deterioration leading to wastage:

1 Temperature: 10–16°C (50–61°F).

2 Environment: dark, dry, airtight conditions.
3 Time limit: up to 12 months.

LEGISLATION

The contents of raw materials and bakery products are governed by the Food Safety Act 1990. Extracts from the Act state the following standards should be met:

1 Food must be of the nature, substance or quality demanded.
2 Food must not present any risk to health and be fit for human consumption.

Colour regulations

New regulations on the use of colour came into force on 1 January 1996. The regulations state:

- the type of colours used
- the maximum usage levels for each colour.

For more details, refer to the Colour Regulations (Dir 94/96/EC).

Food flavourings

SOURCE

Food flavourings are obtained from natural and artificial sources, eg:

1 Natural:
   - fruit
   - plants
   - herbs
   - spices.
2 Artificial: Organic acids are combined with alcohol to form esters that taste just like the real thing.
3 Nature identical: Produced from chemicals to obtain a flavouring which is chemically identical to the natural material.

TYPES

A full range of food flavourings are available from vanilla to savoury and spicy in these forms:

1 Liquid.

2 Paste.
3 Powder.

Note: A flavour can be combined with an appropriate colour; this is known as a compound.

PROPERTIES

Food flavourings have a beneficial effect upon the following characteristics of a product:

- flavour
- eating qualities
- colour.

SUITABILITY FOR THE PRODUCT

Food flavourings can be used in the production of fermented products, sweet pastries, short pastries, enriched pastries, cakes and sponges, powder aerated products, almond products and sandwiches.

FEATURES OF GOOD CONDITION

Food flavourings are fit to use if:

- free from fermentation and mould
- free from physical contamination (for example, metal objects)
- used within the recommended period.

ACCURATE WEIGHING

Food flavourings must be weighed accurately to ensure that:

- a palatable taste is obtained
- a uniform product is obtained
- there is no unnecessary wastage of food flavourings and products.

PREPARATION FOR USE

Dough, paste and batter

To ensure food flavourings are thoroughly dispersed, they should be mixed through one of the other ingredients in the recipe, eg egg, flour, etc, prior to addition to the dough, paste or batter.

Finishing materials

Food flavourings can be added directly to finishing materials such as fondant and buttercream.

SUITABLE STORAGE CONDITIONS

Food flavourings should be stored in the appropriate conditions below to prevent deterioration leading to wastage:

1 Temperature: 10–16°C (50–61°F).
2 Environment: dark, dry, airtight conditions.
3 Time limit: up to 12 months.

LEGISLATION

The contents of raw materials and bakery products are governed by the Food Safety Act 1990. Extracts from the Act state the following standards should be met:

1 Food must be of the nature, substance or quality demanded.
2 Food must not present any risk to health and be fit for human consumption.

C H A P T E R

three

Breadmaking processes

For many people, bread is a major part of their diet, because it is a valuable source of nutrition and fibre. As a result, a wide range of bread and fermented products are produced by the modern baker. Products can cross borders, and local favourites become popular nationally and sometimes internationally.

CHARACTERISTICS OF BREAD AND FERMENTED PRODUCTS

Bread and fermented products should have some of the following characteristics:

1 A bold volume and uniform shape.
2 An even crust colour with a glazed appearance known as the *bloom*.
3 An even oven spring or expansion, giving the product a wholesome appearance.
4 A clean and bright crumb colour.
5 Regular and evenly distributed cells to form a resilient crumb structure.
6 Sufficient moisture to the crumb to make a product enjoyable to the palate.
7 A fine flavour and aroma.

Categories of bread and fermented products

Bread and fermented products can be broadly divided into five categories:

1 White bread – eg Farmhouse, Sandwich, Cottage and Bloomer.
2 Brown bread – eg Small Brown, Country Cereal.
3 Rolls – eg Scotch Baps, Vienna, Bridge Rolls and Brown Fancy Rolls.
4 Enriched Rolls – eg Teacakes, Chelsea Buns, Hot Cross Buns and Cream Buns (Cookies).
5 Speciality Bread – eg Sun Dried Tomato Bread, Tiger Bread, Stollen and Malt Bread.

THE PROCESSES

Breadmaking is an old craft which has made many advances due to new technology. However, today's baker still needs to acquire the skills, knowledge and judgment of the craft of breadmaking. There are five major processes used to produce bread and fermented products:

1 The Bulk Fermentation Process.
2 The Mechanical Dough Development Process.
3 The Activated Dough Development Process.

4 The Sponge and Dough Process.
5 The Ferment and Dough Process.

The aim of mixing

Whichever breadmaking process is used, there are three stages to the mixing process:

Stage 1 – to disperse and dissolve the ingredients.
Stage 2 – to hydrate and develop the gluten forming proteins.
Stage 3 – to form a smooth clear dough.

Basic ingredients

The basic ingredients required to make successful bread are:

- strong flour
- salt
- shortening
- yeast
- water.

All other ingredients used to produce bread and fermented products are known as improvers; eg, sugar, egg etc.

The recipe

A recipe is a list of ingredients and quantities that has been tried and tested for its reliability. A recipe that has been weighed and prepared carefully, and has followed the mixing process, will produce a quality product.

Dough temperature

The dough temperature will depend upon:

- the mixing process
- type of product
- the temperature of the water.

The dough temperature range is between 21–31°C (70–88°F). The formula to calculate the water temperature is:

$$2 \times \text{dough temperature} - \text{flour temperature} = \text{water temperature}$$

The dough temperature is stated for each recipe, and the

flour temperature should be obtained using a thermometer during production.

Dough consistency

The consistency of a fermented dough will depend upon the type of product and the level of liquid. The range of dough consistencies are described as slack through to tight. As a guide, small fermented products are slack, tin breads are slightly tighter and breads without the support of a tin are tight. It is difficult to discuss the variations of dough consistencies, as it is through practice and experience that a baker will develop a feel for dough consistencies.

Points to consider when processing bread and fermented products

1 Accurate scaling of dough pieces is essential to
   - comply with legislation governing the weight of bread
   - obtain the specified yield and maintain profit levels
   - obtain a uniform product.
2 Gentle but firm moulding is necessary to obtain the correct shape and smooth unbroken skin.
3 It is essential to allow dough pieces a rest period known as *intermediate proof* after initial moulding. This rest period allows gluten-forming proteins to recover and become relaxed, ready for the final shaping.

Final proof

Generally, the ideal conditions to prepare dough pieces for the baking process are in an enclosed chamber known as a *final prover*. The final prover should be at a temperature of 38–40°C (100–104°F) with a relative humidity of 85%. The warmth and moisture provided within the final prover allow the dough pieces to expand evenly and prevent the surface of the dough from skinning.

There are two measures which can be used to determine when a dough piece is ready for the baking process:

1 Assessment of the volume using a measuring guide.
2 By pressing the surface of the dough with the finger – when the impression remains in the dough, the dough piece is ready to be baked. The length of the final proving

can vary, therefore experience plays a vital role in judging this part of the production process.

During the baking process

During the early stages of the baking process, rapid expansion occurs which produces an increase in volume known as oven spring. Once the heat has penetrated the dough piece and the partially baked bread has reached a temperature of 54–60°C (129–140°F), the yeast is killed and the final volume is obtained. As the baking process continues, the proteins begin to coagulate until the structure becomes set at a temperature of 78°C (172°F). Crust colour emerges as the sugar begins to caramelise at a temperature of 130°C (266°F). Fully loaded ovens are beneficial to the baking process as the humidity generated from the dough pieces assists in obtaining a good shape and an even bake. Each dough piece will lose approximately 10% of its original weight due to the evaporation of moisture. Finally, the appropriate baking temperature for a product depends upon its:

- shape, size and depth
- density
- sugar content
- characteristics.

Cooling

It is vital that all bread and fermented products are removed from the baking tins and tray immediately on withdrawal from the oven and placed onto a cooling wire. This will prevent the product from becoming soggy by a process known as sweating. Before slicing, wrapping and finishing can begin, all bread and fermented products must be allowed to cool to a temperature of 27°C (81°F).

C H A P T E R

four

The Bulk Fermentation Process

This process was used before the introduction of high speed mixing and dough conditioners which both eliminate the need for bulk fermentation time. Some bakers still prefer this breadmaking process because of the fine flavour produced during fermentation and evident in the final product.

MIXING METHOD

An outline of the mixing method follows, but each recipe contains a more detailed description of the method.

1 Sieve together the dry ingredients.
2 Add the fat content and rub through the dry ingredients.
3 Disperse the yeast into tempered water and add to the above ingredients.
4 Form a dough.
5 Check consistency.
6 Mix until a smooth clear dough is obtained and the gluten forming proteins are developed.
7 Cover the dough and keep warm during the Bulk Fermentation Time.

BULK FERMENTATION TIME (BFT)

This term is used to describe the length of time that the dough is allowed to ferment in bulk. BFT is measured from the end of the mixing method to the beginning of the scaling process. The length of BFT can be from 1–16 hours, and is related to the level of salt and yeast in the recipe, as well as the dough temperature.

Maintaining ideal conditions

During the BFT, the following conditions must be observed:

1 Keep the dough covered to prevent the dough surface from skinning.
2 Maintain the appropriate temperature to control the rate of fermentation. This will ensure that the dough is ripe in time to maintain the production schedule.

Changes that occur during fermentation

During fermentation, the following physical and chemical changes take place within the dough:

1 The yeast produces large quantities of carbon dioxide (CO_2) and a small amount of alcohol.
2 Action by enzymes ripens the gluten forming proteins.

3 The gluten forming proteins become extensible and develop the ability to retain carbon dioxide.
4 The ripening process of the gluten produces flavour.

Knock back

This involves manipulation of the dough after a half to two thirds of the BFT. Knocking back is given for the following reasons:

- to expel the carbon dioxide gas
- to even out the dough temperature because the outside of the dough can become cooler than the inside
- to stimulate and help develop the gluten.

ADVANTAGES AND DISADVANTAGES

Advantages

1 The mixing method is completed in one operation.
2 There is no need for a special mixing machine.
3 The dough has a greater tolerance of fermentation.
4 The baked product has a finer flavour.

Disadvantages

1 Expensive flours are required.
2 Fermentation and production time is increased.
3 The dough requires more attention by staff.
4 The fermenting dough requires space.
5 It may be necessary to start production early.

OVEN CHART

Product	Baking temperature in °C (°F)	Baking time in minutes	Additional control procedures
Sm White Tin Bread	232 (450)	25	Open damper for final 10 mins
Sm Brown Tin Bread	232 (450)	25	" " " "
Sm Brown Farmhouse	232 (450)	25	" " " "
Sm Wholemeal Tin Bread	232 (450)	25	" " " "
Tin and Plaited Milk Bread	226 (440)	25	" " " "
Stotties	240 (464)	15	None
Cottage Bread	232 (450)	25	Open damper for final 10 mins
Festival Bread	216 (420)	60	" " " " 20 mins
Hufflers	232 (450)	20–25	" " " " 10 mins
Huffkins	232 (450)	12–15	" " " " 5 mins
Jewish Cholla Bread	225 (437)	25	" " " " 10 mins
Cheese Bread	204 (400)	30	" " " "
Sun Dried Tomato Bread	225 (437)	25–30	" " " "
Rye Bread	225 (437)	40–45	Use steam during first 10 mins then release
Vienna Bread	240–250 (464–482)	25	" " " " " " "
Soft Fancy Rolls	250 (482)	10–12	Open damper for final 5 mins
Brown Rolls	250 (482)	10–12	" " " "
Iced Fingers	225 (437)	10–12	" " " "
Teacakes	220 (428)	12–15	" " " "
Hot Cross Buns	232 (450)	12–15	" " " "
Malt Bread	180 (356)	60	" " " " 10 mins
Crumpets	Moderate hot plate	8–10	None
Muffins	Moderate hot plate	10–12	None
Pizzas	225 (437)	15–20	None
Brioche	232 (450)	10–12	Open damper for final 5 mins

RECIPES USING THE BULK FERMENTATION PROCESS

SMALL WHITE TIN BREAD AND FARMHOUSE

(See colour plate 1.)

Ingredients

Kilo	Gram	%	Ingredients	lb	oz
1	100	100.00	bread flour	2	7.00
	25	2.27	salt		1.00
	20	1.82	skimmed milk powder		0.75
	25	2.27	shortening		1.00
	45	4.00	yeast		1.75
	630	57.20	water	1	7.00
1	845		Gross weight	4	2.50
1	798		Net weight	4	1.25

Production Points

Dough temperature	**27°C (81°F)**
Bulk Fermentation Time	**1 hour**
Knock back	**30–40 mins**
Scaling weight	**450 g (1 lb)**
Yield	**4**
Baking temperature	**232°C (450°F)**
Baking time	**25 mins**

Note: This recipe is also suitable for the production of Coburgs, Sandwich Bread, Large White Bread and Multi-Piece Bread.

Mixing method

1. Sieve together the flour, salt and skimmed milk powder.
2. Add the shortening and rub through the dry ingredients on speed 1, using a dough hook.
3. Disperse the yeast into the tempered water and add to the above ingredients.
4. Mix on speed 1 for 2 minutes until a dough is formed.
5. Check for extremes in consistency and adjust as necessary.
6. Mix on speed 1 for 15 minutes or speed 2 for 10 minutes.
7. Cover the dough and keep warm during the BFT.
8. After 30–40 minutes of the BFT, knock back the dough.
9. After the completion of the BFT, the dough is ready to be scaled and processed.

Processing methods

SMALL WHITE TIN BREAD

1. Scale 4 at 450 g (1 lb) and mould round.
2. Rest for 8 to 10 minutes to allow the dough pieces to recover.
3. Re-mould the dough pieces and form them into a cylinder shape.
4. Place the dough pieces into warm, greased, small bread tins.
5. Prove at 38–40°C (100–104°F) in humid conditions.
6. Bake at 232°C (450°F) for 25 minutes.
7. After baking, remove the bread from the tins immediately and place on a cooling wire.

WHITE FARMHOUSE BREAD

1. Follow stages 1, 2 and 3 of Small White Tin Bread.
2. Place the dough pieces into warm, greased, farmhouse tins.
3. Prove at 38–40°C (100–104°F) in humid conditions.
4. After three-quarters of the final proof, dust with bread flour and cut down the centre of the dough piece. Note, this cut should be approximately 1 cm (0.5") deep.

5 Return the dough pieces to the final prover for the remaining proving time.
6 Follow stages 6 and 7 of Small White Tin Bread.

SMALL BROWN TIN BREAD AND FARMHOUSE

(See colour plate 6.)

Ingredients

Kilo	Gram	%	Ingredients	lb	oz
1	100	100.00	brown flour	2	7.00
	25	2.27	salt		1.00
	10	0.90	skimmed milk powder		0.50
	25	2.27	shortening		1.00
	40	3.63	yeast		1.50
	660	60.00	water	1	7.50
1	860		Gross weight	4	2.50
1	813		Net weight	4	0.75

Production Points

Dough temperature	**26°C (79°F)**
Bulk Fermentation Time	**30 mins**
Knock back	**N/A**
Scaling weight	**450 g (1 lb)**
Yield	**4**
Baking temperature	**232°C (450°F)**
Baking time	**25 mins**

Note: This recipe is also suitable for the production of Small Brown Coburgs and Large Brown Bread.

Mixing method

1 Using a coarse sieve, sieve together the flour, salt and skimmed milk powder.
2 Add the shortening and rub through the dry ingredients on speed 1, using a dough hook.
3 Disperse the yeast into the tempered water and add to the above ingredients.
4 Mix on speed 1 for 2 minutes until a dough is formed.
5 Check for extremes in consistency and adjust as necessary.
6 Mix on speed 1 for 15 minutes or speed 2 for 10 minutes.
7 Cover the dough and keep warm during the BFT.
8 After the completion of the BFT, the dough is ready to be scaled and processed.

Processing methods

SMALL BROWN TIN BREAD

1 Scale 4 at 450 g (1 lb) and mould round.
2 Rest for 8 to 10 minutes to allow the dough pieces to recover.
3 Re-mould the dough pieces and form them into a cylinder shape.
4 Place the dough pieces into warm, greased, small bread tins.
5 Prove at 38–40°C (100–104°F) in humid conditions.
6 Bake at 232°C (450°F) for 25 minutes.
7 After baking, remove the bread from the tins immediately and place on a cooling wire.

BROWN FARMHOUSE BREAD

1 Follow stages 1, 2 and 3 of Small Brown Tin Bread.
2 Place the dough pieces into warm, well greased, farmhouse tins.
3 Prove at 38–40°C (100–104°F) in humid conditions.
4 After three-quarters of the final proof, dust with brown flour and cut down the centre of the dough piece. This cut should be approximately 1 cm (0.50") deep.

5 Return the dough pieces to the final prover for the remaining proving time.
6 Follow stages 6 and 7 of Small Brown Tin Bread.

SMALL WHOLEMEAL TIN BREAD AND COBURG

Ingredients

Kilo	Gram	%	Ingredients	lb	oz
1	100	100.00	wholemeal flour	2	7.00
	25	2.27	salt		1.00
	20	1.82	shortening		0.75
	40	3.63	yeast		1.50
	705	64.00	water	1	8.00
1	890		Gross weight	4	2.25
1	843		Net weight	4	0.50

Production Points

Dough temperature	**26°C (79°F)**
Bulk Fermentation Time	**30 mins**
Knock back	**N/A**
Scaling weight	**450 g (1 lb)**
Yield	**4**
Baking temperature	**232°C (450°F)**
Baking time	**25 mins**

Note: This recipe is also suitable for the production of Large Wholemeal Bread.

Mixing method

1 Using a coarse sieve, sieve together the flour and salt.
2 Add the shortening and rub through on speed 1 using a dough hook.
3 Disperse the yeast into the tempered water and add to the above ingredients.
4 Mix on speed 1 for 2 minutes until a dough is formed.
5 Check for extremes in consistency and adjust as necessary.
6 Mix on speed 1 for 15 minutes or speed 2 for 10 minutes.
7 Cover the dough and keep warm during the BFT.
8 After the completion of the BFT the dough is ready to be scaled and processed.

Processing methods

SMALL WHOLEMEAL TIN BREAD

1 Scale 4 at 450 g (1 lb) and mould round.
2 Rest for 8 to 10 minutes to allow the dough pieces to recover.
3 Re-mould the dough pieces and form them into a cylinder shape.
4 Place the dough pieces into warm, greased, small bread tins.
5 Prove at 38–40°C (100–104°F) in humid conditions.
6 Bake at 232°C (450°F) for 25 minutes.
7 After baking, remove the bread from the tins immediately and place on a cooling wire.

SMALL WHOLEMEAL TIN COBURG

1 Follow stages 1, 2 and 3 of Small Wholemeal Tin Bread.
2 Re-mould the dough pieces into a ball shape.
3 Place the dough pieces into warm, greased, Coburg tins.
4 Now follow stages 5, 6 and 7 of Small Wholemeal Tin Bread.

TIN AND PLAITED MILK BREAD

Ingredients

Kilo	Gram	%	Ingredients	lb	oz
1	100	100.00	bread flour	2	7.00
	25	2.27	salt		1.00
	55	5.00	skimmed milk powder		2.00
	35	3.18	butter		1.25
	45	4.00	yeast		1.75
	640	58.00	water	1	7.25
1	900		Gross weight	4	4.25
1	852		Net weight	4	2.50

Production Points

Dough temperature	**26°C (79°F)**
Bulk Fermentation Time	**1 hour**
Knock back	**30–40 mins**
Scaling weight	**450 g (1 lb)**
Yield	**4**
Baking temperature	**226°C (440°F)**
Baking time	**25 mins**

Note: This recipe is also suitable for the production of Milk Bread Rolls.

(See colour plate 2.)

Mixing method

1 Sieve together the flour, salt and skimmed milk powder.
2 Add the butter and rub through the dry ingredients on speed 1, using a dough hook.
3 Disperse the yeast into the tempered water and add to the above ingredients.
4 Mix on speed 1 for 2 minutes until a dough is formed.
5 Check for extremes in consistency and adjust as necessary.
6 Mix on speed 1 for 15 minutes or speed 2 for 10 minutes.
7 Cover the dough and keep warm during the BFT.
8 After 30–40 minutes of the BFT, knock back the dough.
9 After the completion of the BFT, the dough is ready to be scaled and processed.

Processing method

TINNED MILK BREAD

1 See Figure 5 below: for (a) and (c), scale 4 at 450g (1 lb); for (b), scale 24 at 75g (2.75oz). Mould round.
2 Rest for 8 to 10 minutes to allow the dough pieces to recover.
3 Re-mould the dough pieces and form them into any one of the shapes in Figure 5.
4 Place the shaped dough pieces into warm, greased round or oval shaped tins as illustrated.
5 Eggwash the tops of the dough pieces.
6 Prove at 38–40°C (100–104°F) in humid conditions.
7 Bake at 226°C (440°F) for 25 minutes.
8 After baking, remove the bread from the tins immediately and place on a cooling wire.

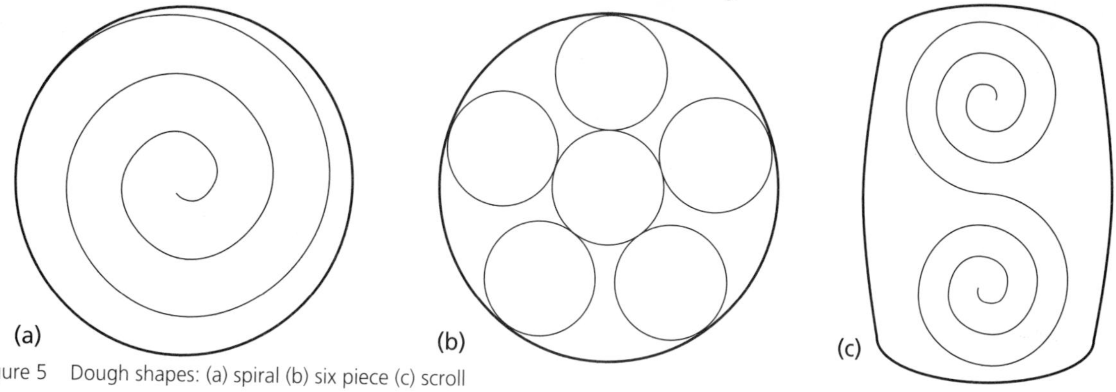

Figure 5 Dough shapes: (a) spiral (b) six piece (c) scroll

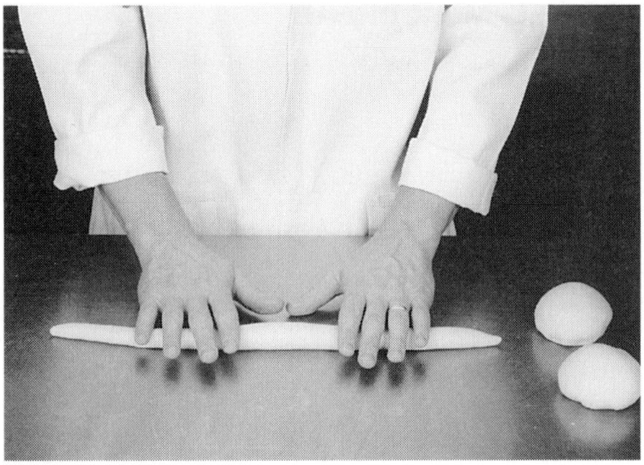

a Roll the dough pieces to a long strand

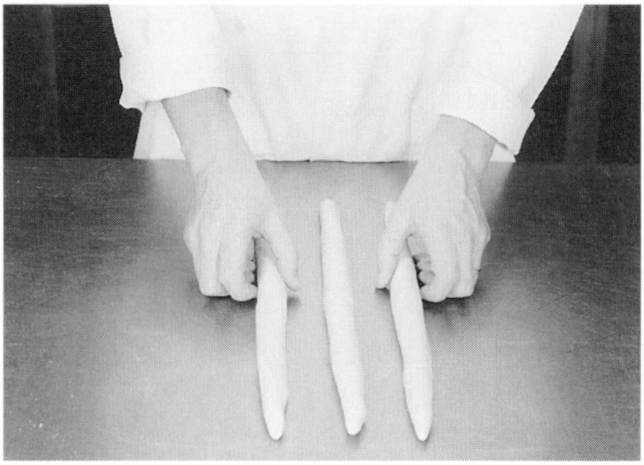

b Place three strands side by side

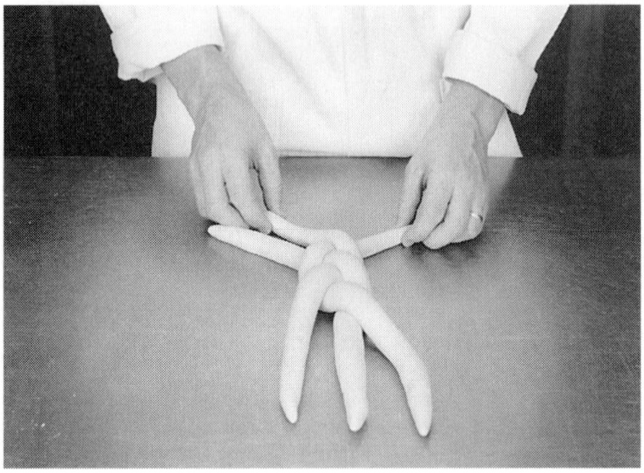

c Plait the strands in sequence

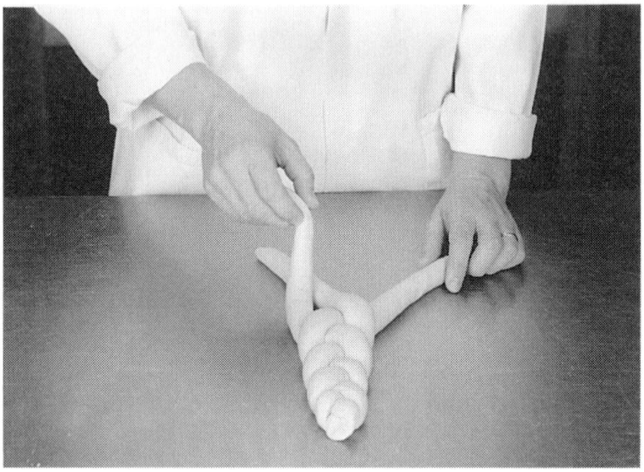

d Turn dough piece over and complete plait

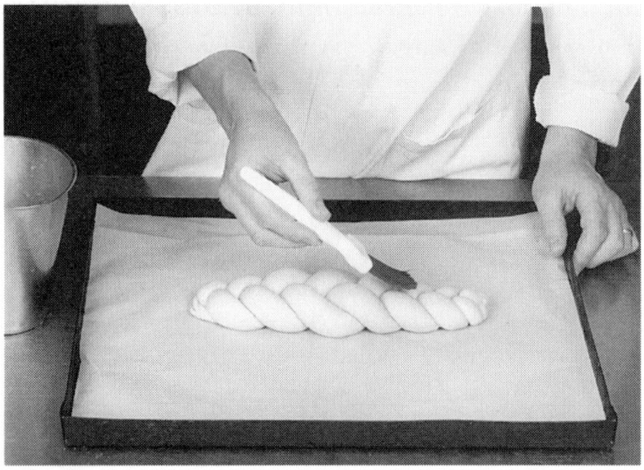

e Eggwash top surface of plait

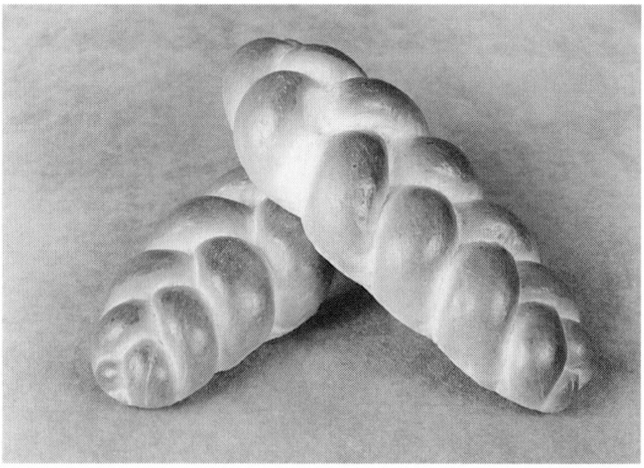

f Plaited Milk Bread

PLAITED MILK BREAD

1. Scale 12 at 150g (5.25oz) and mould round.
2. Rest for 8 to 10 minutes to allow the dough pieces to recover.
3. Roll the dough pieces to a long strand measuring approximately 30cm (12") in length (see p.80, a).
4. Place three strands side by side in a vertical position (see b).
5. Begin in the centre and plait the strands in this sequence until you reach the end of the strands: 1 over 2 then 3 over 2 (see c).
6. Turn the dough piece over and repeat stage 5 (see d).

Note: ensure that both ends of the plait are securely bound together.

7. Place the plait on a warm, greased baking tray.
8. Eggwash the top surface of the plait (see e).
9. Prove at 38–40°C (100–104°F) in humid conditions.
10. Bake at 226°C (440°F) for 25–30 mins.
11. After baking remove the bread from the tray immediately, and place on a cooling wire.

STOTTIES

Ingredients

Kilo	Gram	%	Ingredients	lb	oz
1	100	100.00	bread flour	2	7.00
	25	2.27	salt		1.00
	10	0.90	skimmed milk powder		0.50
	45	4.00	shortening		1.75
	45	4.00	yeast		1.75
	640	58.00	water	1	6.50
1	865		Gross weight	4	2.50
1	818		Net weight	4	1.25

Mixing method

1. Sieve together the flour, salt and skimmed milk powder.
2. Add the shortening and rub through the dry ingredients on speed 1, using a dough hook.
3. Disperse the yeast into the tempered water and add to the above ingredients.
4. Mix on speed 1 for 2 minutes until a dough is formed.
5. Check for extremes in consistency and adjust as necessary.
6. Mix on speed 1 for 15 minutes or speed 2 for 10 minutes.
7. Cover the dough and keep warm during the BFT.
8. After 30–40 minutes of the BFT, knock back the dough.
9. After the completion of the BFT, the dough is ready to be scaled and processed.

Processing method

1. Scale 6 at 300 g (11 oz) and mould round.
2. Rest for 10 to 12 minutes to allow the dough pieces to recover.
3. Pin the dough pieces to approximately 22.5 cm (9") in diameter.

Now follow one of these production methods.

Stotties

Production Points

Dough temperature	**28–29°C (83–85°F)**
Bulk Fermentation Time	**1 hour**
Knock back	**30–40 mins**
Scaling weight	**300 g (11 oz)**
Yield	**6**
Baking temperature	**240°C (464°F)**
Baking time	**15 mins**

Note: This recipe is also suitable for the production of Divider Buns, Bread Rolls and Bridge Rolls.

TRADITIONAL – OVEN BOTTOM

1 Place on to dusted, proving boards and cover.
2 Allow to prove in a warm environment.
3 For ease of handling and to obtain the best result, stotties should be baked in a slightly under-proved condition.
4 Using your middle finger, make a hole in the centre of each stottie to ensure the dough pieces rise evenly during the baking process.
5 Place the dough pieces directly onto the oven sole using a peel.
6 After 6 to 8 minutes, carefully turn the stotties over using a peel. Bake for a further 6 to 8 minutes.
7 Draw from the oven using a peel and place on a cooling wire.

Note:

- The traditional method of baking stotties does require some practice to perfect.
- The bottom heat should be 50 per cent higher than the top heat when baking stotties.

CONVENIENT – TRAY METHOD

1 Place onto a warm, greased baking tray.
2 Dock the centre of each stottie.
3 Prove at 38–40°C (100–104°F) in humid conditions.
4 After full proof, place into the oven.
5 After 6 to 8 minutes, draw from the oven and carefully turn the stotties over.

6 Return the tray of stotties to the oven and complete the baking process.
7 On withdrawal from the oven place the stotties on a cooling wire.

Note: An improved flavour and appearance is obtained from the Traditional – Oven Bottom method.

COTTAGE BREAD

Ingredients

Kilo	Gram	%	Ingredients	lb	oz
1	120	100.00	bread flour	2	8.00
	25	2.23	salt		1.00
	20	1.78	skimmed milk powder		0.75
	25	2.23	shortening		1.00
	45	4.00	yeast		1.75
	625	56.00	water	1	6.00
1	860		Total gross weight	4	2.50
1	813		Net weight	4	0.75

Production Points

Dough temperature	**27°C (81°F)**
Bulk Fermentation Time	**1 hour**
Knock back	**30–40 mins**
Scaling weight	**450 g (1 lb)**
Yield	**4**
Baking temperature	**232°C (450°F)**
Baking time	**25 mins**

Note: This recipe is also suitable for the production of Danish Bread, Bloomers, Tiger Bread and Coburgs.

Mixing method

1 Sieve together the flour, salt and skimmed milk powder.
2 Add the shortening and rub through the dry ingredients on speed 1 using a dough hook.
3 Disperse the yeast into the tempered water and add to the above ingredients.
4 Mix on speed 1 for 2 minutes until a dough is formed.
5 Check for extremes in consistency and adjust as necessary.
6 Mix on speed 1 for 15 minutes or speed 2 for 10 minutes.
7 Cover the dough and keep warm during the BFT.
8 After 30–40 minutes of the BFT, knock back the dough.
9 After the completion of the BFT the dough is ready to be scaled and processed.

Processing method

1 Scale 4 at 300 g (11 oz) and 4 at 150 g (5 oz) and mould round.
2 Rest for 10 minutes to allow the dough pieces to recover.
3 Pin out both pieces slightly and dampen the top surface of the large dough piece.
4 Assemble by placing the small dough piece directly on top of the large dough piece. Secure the two dough pieces together using the fingers or a rolling pin to make a hole in the centre and form the correct shape, place on a warm well greased tray.
5 Using a sharp knife, notch the side of the dough pieces.
6 Prove at 38–40°C (100–104°F) in humid conditions.
7 Bake at 232°C (450°F) for 25 minutes.
8 After baking, remove the bread from the tray immediately and place on a cooling wire.

FESTIVAL BREAD

Ingredients

Kilo	Gram	%	Ingredients	lb	oz
1	000	100.00	strong bread flour	2	3.50
	15	1.50	salt		0.50
	15	1.50	skimmed milk powder		0.50
	5	0.50	non diastatic malt flour		0.25
	15	1.50	yeast		0.50
	500	50.00	water	1	1.75
1	550		Gross weight	3	6.25
1	511		Net weight	3	4.75

Mixing method

1. Sieve together the flour, salt, skimmed milk powder and non-diastatic malt flour.
2. Disperse the yeast into the tempered water and add to the above ingredients.
3. Mix on speed 1 for 2 minutes until a dough is formed.
4. Check for extremes in consistency and adjust as necessary.
5. Mix on speed 1 for 15 minutes.
6. Cover the dough and keep warm during the BFT.
7. After 30–40 minutes of the BFT, knock back the dough.
8. After the completion of the BFT the dough is ready to be scaled and processed.

Note: It is sometimes advisable to reduce the BFT because of the lengthy processing method.

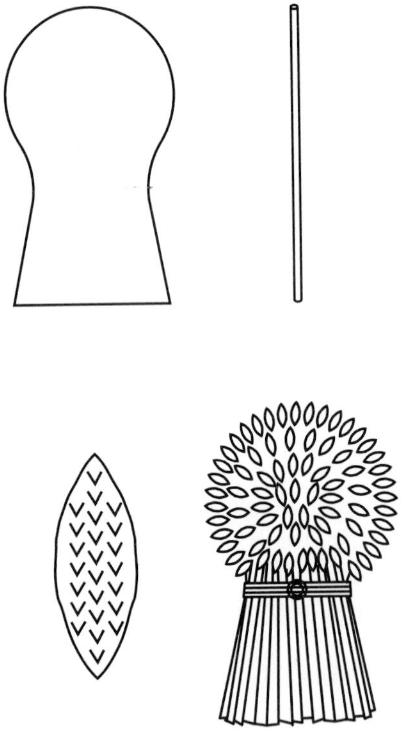

Figure 6 Wheatsheaf: (a) template – stage 2 (b) stalks – stage 5 (c) ears of wheat – stage 7 (d) final product

Processing method

WHEATSHEAF

1. Using 650 g (1 lb 8 oz) of dough, roll out the dough to 1.25 cm (0.50") thick.
2. Using a template, cut out the shape illustrated in Figure 6, the edge to be cut at an angle. Place onto a greased tray.
3. Dock the base heavily.
4. Wash the base with water to prevent skinning.
5. Using approximately 250 g (9 oz) of dough, divide and form long thin strings for stalks and place on bottom half of base.
6. Using the remaining dough, scale at 15 g. Mould round and then mould to a tapered finger shape.
7. Using scissors make three rows of cuts as illustrated to form the ears of wheat.
8. Place the ears of wheat onto the base, beginning on the outer edge of the base. Work your way in towards the centre, until the base is fully covered.
9. Use the remaining dough to form stalks which can be placed and knotted around the waist of the wheatsheaf.
10. Brush all of the wheatsheaf with eggwash.
11. Prove at 32–34°C (89–93°F) in humid conditions for approximately 15 minutes.
12. Bake at 216°C (420°F) for approximately 1 hour.

Production Points

Dough temperature	**23°C (73°F)**
Bulk Fermentation Time	**1 hour**
Knock back	**30–40 mins**
Scaling weight	**As required**
Baking temperature	**216°C (420°F)**
Baking time	**1 hour**

Note:

- Place some stalks and ears in a haphazard manner for a more natural appearance.
- Eggwash the dough pieces throughout the process, to prevent the dough from skinning.

HUFFLERS AND HUFFKINS

Ingredients

Kilo	Gram	%	Ingredients	lb	oz
1	100	100.00	strong bread flour	2	7.00
	25	2.27	salt		1.00
	35	3.18	skimmed milk powder		1.25
	40	3.63	shortening		1.50
	35	3.18	yeast		1.25
	725	66.00	water	1	10.00
	10	1.00	sugar		0.50
1	970		Gross weight	4	6.50
1	920		Net weight	4	4.75

Production Points

Dough temperature	**23°C (73°F)**
Bulk Fermentation Time	**2 hours**
Knock back	**$1^1/_2$ hours**
Scaling weight:	
Hufflers	**900 g (2 lb)**
Huffkins	**60 g (2 oz)**
Yield:	
Hufflers	**2**
Huffkins	**30**
Baking temperature	**232°C (450°F)**
Baking time:	
Hufflers	**20–25 mins**
Huffkins	**12–15 mins**

Mixing method

1. Sieve together the flour, salt and skimmed milk powder.
2. Add the shortening and rub through the dry ingredients on speed 1 using a dough hook.
3. Disperse the yeast into the tempered water. Add and dissolve the sugar, then add to the above ingredients.
4. Mix on speed 1 for 2 minutes until a dough is formed.
5. Check for extremes in consistency and adjust as necessary.
6. Mix on speed 1 for 15 minutes.
7. Cover the dough and keep warm during the BFT.
8. After $1^1/_2$ hours of the BFT, knock back the dough.
9. After the completion of the BFT, the dough is ready to be scaled and processed.

Processing methods

HUFFLERS

1. Scale 2 at 900 g (2 lb) and mould round.
2. Rest for 8 to 10 minutes to allow the dough pieces to recover.
3. Pin the dough out to approximately 30 cm (12") in diameter, taking care to maintain a round shape and place on a warm, greased tray.
4. Eggwash and dredge the top with flour.
5. Using a scotch scraper cut the dough piece into 8 equal segments.
6. Prove at 38–40°C (100–104°F) in humid conditions.
7. Bake at 232°C (450°F) for 25 minutes.
8. After baking, place the Hufflers on a cooling wire.

Huffler

HUFFKINS

1 Scale 30 at 60 g (2 oz) and mould round.
2 Rest for 8 to 10 minutes to allow the dough pieces to recover.
3 Using a rolling pin, pin out slightly and place on a warm, greased tray.
4 Eggwash and dust with flour.
5 Prove at 38–40°C (100–104°F) in humid conditions.
6 Bake at 232°C (450°F) for 12–15 minutes.
7 After baking, place the Huffkins on a cooling wire.

JEWISH CHOLLA BREAD

Ingredients

Kilo	Gram	%	Ingredients	lb	oz
1	000	100.00	bread flour	2	3.50
	20	2.00	salt		0.75
	90	9.00	egg		3.25
	60	6.00	sugar		2.00
	45	4.50	yeast		1.50
	535	53.50	water	1	3.00
	100	10.00	vegetable oil		3.50
1	850		Gross weight	4	1.50
1	803		Net weight	4	0.00

Mixing method

1 Sieve together the flour and salt.
2 Dissolve the sugar in egg at 21°C.
3 Disperse the yeast into the tempered water. Now add this at the same time as the egg and sugar to the dry ingredients.
4 Mix on speed 1 for 2 minutes until a dough is formed.
5 Now add the vegetable oil slowly over 2–3 minutes using speed 1 and 2.
6 Mix on speed 2 for 5 minutes, then check for extremes in the consistency. Adjust as necessary.
7 Mix on speed 2 for a further 5 minutes.
8 Cover the dough and keep warm during the BFT.

Production Points	
Dough temperature	**27°C (81°F)**
Bulk Fermentation Time	**1 hour**
Knock back	**30–40 mins**
Scaling weight	**450 g (1 lb)**
Yield	**4**
Baking temperature	**225°C (437°F)**
Baking time	**25 mins**

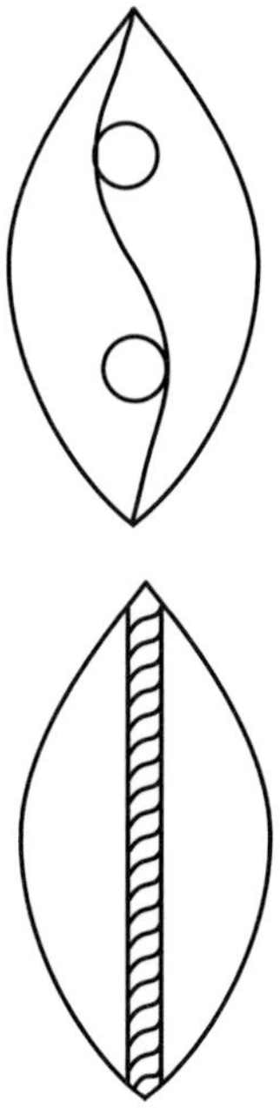

(a)

(b)

Figure 7 Jewish Cholla Bread: (a) Type A, stage 6 (b) Type B, stage 3

(See overleaf for ingredients)

9 After 30–40 minutes of the BFT, knock back the dough.
10 After completion of the BFT the dough is ready to be scaled and processed.

Processing method

TYPE A

1 Scale 4 at 420 g (15 oz) and 4 at 30 g (1 oz) and mould round.
2 Rest for 8 to 10 minutes to allow the dough pieces to recover.
3 Re-mould the large dough pieces and form them into a tapered cylinder shape.
4 Eggwash the large dough piece.
5 Roll out the small dough pieces into long strands.
6 Place one strand on top of the large dough piece with two loops as illustrated (Figure 7a).
7 Eggwash all of the dough pieces.
8 Prove at 38–40°C (100–104°F) in humid conditions.
9 Bake at 225°C (437°F) for 25 minutes.
10 After baking, place the bread on a cooling wire.

TYPE B

1 Scale 4 at 400 g (14 oz) and 8 at 25 g (1 oz) and mould round.
2 Follow stages 2, 3, 4 and 5 of Type A.
3 Using two strands, form a thin plait and place this on top of the large dough piece as illustrated (Figure 7b).
4 Follow stages 7, 8, 9 and 10 of Type A.

CHEESE BREAD

Mixing method

1 Sieve together the flour, salt and skimmed milk powder.
2 Add the shortening and rub through the dry ingredients on speed 1 using a dough hook.
3 Disperse the yeast into the tempered water, add and dissolve the sugar. Add to the above ingredients.
4 Mix on speed 1 for 2 minutes until a dough is formed.
5 Check for extremes in consistency and adjust as necessary.
6 Mix on speed 1 for 15 minutes or speed 2 for 10 minutes.
7 Cover the dough and keep warm during the BFT.

Ingredients

Kilo	Gram	%	Ingredients	lb	oz
1	000	100.00	bread flour	2	3.50
	20	2.00	salt		0.75
	20	2.00	skimmed milk powder		0.75
	30	3.00	shortening		1.00
	40	4.00	yeast		1.50
	580	58.00	water	1	4.75
	15	1.50	sugar		0.50
	200	20.00	grated cheese		7.25
1	905		Gross weight	4	4.00
1	857		Net weight	4	2.25

Production Points

Dough temperature	**27°C (81°F)**
Bulk Fermentation Time	**1 hour**
Knock back	**30–40 mins**
Scaling weight	**460 g (1 lb 0.5 oz)**
Yield	**4**
Baking temperature	**204°C (400°F)**
Baking time	**30 mins**

8 After 30–40 minutes of the BFT, knock back the dough. At this stage, mix the grated cheese through the dough.
9 After the remaining BFT, the dough is ready to be scaled and processed.

Processing method

1 Scale 4 at 460 g (1 lb 0.5oz) and mould round.
2 Rest for 8 to 10 minutes to allow the dough pieces to recover.
3 Re-mould the dough pieces and form them into a cylinder shape.
4 Place the dough pieces into warm, greased, small bread tins.
5 Prove at 38–40°C (100–104°F) in humid conditions.
6 Bake at 204°C (400°F) for 30 minutes.
7 After baking, remove the bread from the tins immediately and place on a cooling wire.

Note:

- This product requires a lower baking temperature because of the high crust colour obtained from the cheese content.
- A higher scaling weight is required because of the greater weight loss during an extended baking time.

SUN DRIED TOMATO BREAD

Note: Soak the sun dried tomatoes in boiling water for 30 minutes.

Ingredients

Kilo	Gram	%	Ingredients	lb	oz
1	000	100.00	bread flour	2	3.50
	20	2.00	salt		0.75
	25	2.50	skimmed milk powder		1.00
	25	2.50	shortening		1.00
	40	4.00	yeast		1.50
	600	60.00	water	1	5.50
	25	2.50	sugar		1.00
	200	20.00	chopped sun dried tomatoes		7.25
1	935		Gross weight	4	5.50
1	886		Net weight	4	3.75

Mixing method

1 Sieve together the flour, salt and skimmed milk powder.
2 Add the shortening and rub through the dry ingredients on speed 1 using a dough hook.
3 Disperse the yeast into the tempered water. Add and dissolve the sugar, and add to the above ingredients.
4 Mix on speed 1 for 2 minutes until a dough is formed.
5 Check for extremes in consistency and adjust as necessary.
6 Mix on speed 1 for 15 minutes or speed 2 for 10 minutes.
7 Cover the dough and keep warm during BFT.
8 After 30–40 minutes of the BFT, knock back the dough. At this stage, mix the chopped sun dried tomatoes through the dough.

Production Points	
Dough temperature	**27°C (81°F)**
Bulk Fermentation Time	**1 hour**
Knock back	**30–40 mins**
Scaling weight	**450 g (1 lb)**
Yield	**4**
Baking temperature	**225°C (437°F)**
Baking time	**25–30 mins**

9 After the remaining BFT the dough is ready to be scaled and processed.

Processing method

1 Scale 4 at 450 g (1 lb) and mould round.
2 Rest for 8 to 10 minutes to allow the dough pieces to recover.
3 Re-mould the dough pieces into a ball shape.
4 Place the dough pieces into 15 cm (6") diameter hoops that are laid out on a baking tray. The hoops and tray should be warm and greased.
5 Using the back of the hand flatten the dough pieces.
6 Prove at 38–40°C (100–104°F) in humid conditions.
7 Bake at 225°C (437°F) for 25–30 minutes.
8 After baking, remove the bread from the tins immediately and place on a cooling wire.

RYE BREAD

Ingredients

Kilo	Gram	%	Ingredients	lb	oz
	825	100.00	strong bread flour	1	13.50
	275	33.30	rye flour		10.00
	20	1.80	salt		0.75
	25	2.27	shortening		0.75
	40	3.60	yeast		1.50
	625	57.00	water	1	6.25
	40	3.60	black treacle		1.50
1	850		Gross weight	4	0.25
1	803		Net weight	3	14.50

Production Points	
Dough temperature	**26°C (79°F)**
Bulk Fermentation Time	**1 hour**
Knock back	**30–40 mins**
Scaling weight	**450 g (1 lb)**
Yield	**4**
Baking temperature	**225°C (437°F)**
Baking time	**40–45 mins**

Mixing method

1 Sieve together the flour, rye flour and salt.
2 Add the shortening and rub through the dry ingredients on speed 1 using a dough hook.
3 Disperse the yeast into the tempered water. Add the black treacle and dissolve, then add to the above ingredients.
4 Mix on speed 1 for 2 minutes until a dough is formed.
5 Check for extremes in consistency and adjust as necessary.
6 Mix on speed 1 for 15 minutes or speed 2 for 10 minutes.
7 Cover the dough and keep warm during BFT.
8 After 30–40 minutes of the BFT, knock back the dough.
9 After the completion of the BFT the dough is ready to be scaled and processed.

Processing method

1 Scale 4 at 450 g (1 lb) and mould round.
2 Rest for 10 to 15 minutes to allow the dough pieces to recover.
3 Re-mould the dough pieces as follows:
- ball shape for a round wicker basket
- cylinder shape for an oblong wicker basket.

4 Place the dough pieces into the appropriate basket that has been dredged with rye flour.

5 Prove at 34–38°C (93–100°F) in humid conditions.
6 Carefully turn the dough pieces onto a warm, greased tray.
7 Bake at 225°C (437°F) for 40–45 minutes using steam during the first 10 minutes of the baking process.
8 After baking, remove the bread from the tray immediately and place onto a cooling wire.

VIENNA BREAD

Ingredients

Kilo	Gram	%	Ingredients	lb	oz
1	100	100.00	strong bread flour	2	7.00
	30	2.72	salt		1.00
	25	2.27	skimmed milk powder		1.00
	5	0.45	high diastatic malt flour		0.25
	20	1.81	shortening		0.75
	45	4.00	yeast		1.50
	630	57.20	water	1	6.50
1	855		Gross weight	4	2.00
1	808		Net weight	4	0.25

Production Points

Dough temperature	**24°C (75°F)**
Bulk Fermentation Time	**1 hour**
Knock back	**30–40 mins**
Scaling weight	**300 g (10.75 oz)**
Yield	**6**
Baking temperature	**240–250°C (464–482°F)**
Baking time	**approx 25 mins**

Note: This recipe is also suitable for the production of Vienna Rolls.

Mixing method

1 Sieve together the flour, salt, skimmed milk powder and high diastatic malt flour.
2 Add the shortening and rub through the dry ingredients on speed 1 using a dough hook.
3 Disperse the yeast into the tempered water and add to the above ingredients.
4 Mix on speed 1 for 2 minutes until a dough is formed.
5 Check for extremes in consistency and adjust as necessary.
6 Mix on speed 1 for 15 minutes or speed 2 for 10 minutes.
7 Cover the dough and keep warm during the BFT.
8 After 30–40 minutes of the BFT, knock back the dough.
9 After the completion of the BFT the dough is ready to be scaled and processed.

Vienna Bread

Processing method

1. Scale 6 at 300 g (10.75 oz) and mould round.
2. Rest for 8 to 10 minutes to allow the dough pieces to recover.
3. Re-mould the dough pieces into a baton shape, place the dough pieces onto a warm oiled perforated tray.
4. Prove at 38–40°C (100–104°F) in humid conditions.
5. After three-quarters of the final proof, cut the batons three times across the top of the dough piece.
6. Return the dough pieces to the final prover for the remaining proving time.
7. Bake at 240–250°C (464–482°F) using steam. Baking time approximately 20 minutes.

   Note: To obtain the appropriate characteristics of Vienna breads, steam should be used in the following sequence.
   - Prior to loading the oven, inject steam for 3 minutes.
   - Continue to inject steam whilst loading the oven.
   - After 8–10 minutes the steam must be released from the oven chamber. However, the method of steaming will depend upon the type of ovens. Some ovens do not have the capacity to inject steam for this period of time or retain steam during setting.
   - Complete the baking process in a dry atmosphere to obtain a thin, glossy, crisp crust.

8. After baking remove the bread from the trays immediately and place on a cooling wire.

SOFT FANCY ROLLS

Ingredients

Kilo	Gram	%	Ingredients	lb	oz
1	000	100.00	bread flour	2	3.50
	25	2.50	salt		1.00
	20	2.00	skimmed milk powder		0.75
	50	5.00	shortening		2.00
	40	4.00	yeast		1.50
	590	59.00	water	1	5.00
1	725		Gross weight	3	13.75
1	681		Net weight	3	12.25

Mixing method

1. Sieve together the flour, salt and skimmed milk powder.
2. Add the shortening and rub through the dry ingredients on speed 1 using a dough hook.
3. Disperse the yeast into the tempered water and add to the above ingredients.
4. Mix on speed 1 for 2 minutes until a dough is formed.
5. Check for extremes in consistency and adjust as necessary.
6. Mix on speed 1 for 15 minutes or speed 2 for 10 minutes.
7. Cover the dough and keep warm during the BFT.
8. After 30–40 minutes of the BFT, knock back the dough.
9. After the completion of the BFT the dough is ready to be scaled and processed.

Production Points

Dough temperature	**26°C (79°F)**
Bulk Fermentation Time	**1 hour**
Knock back	**30–40 mins**
Scaling weight	**50 g (1.75 oz)**
Yield	**33**
Baking temperature	**250°C (482°F)**
Baking time	**10–12 mins**

Note: This recipe is also suitable for the production of

Processing method

1 Scale 33 at 50 g (1.75 oz) and mould round.
2 Rest for 8 to 10 minutes to allow the dough pieces to recover.
3 Re-mould the dough pieces, and form them into any one of the following shapes.

Knot:
i Roll the dough piece to a long thin strand measuring approximately 16 cm (6.5") in length.
ii Form the shape of a number six and from this position complete a single knot.

Spiral:
i Roll the dough piece to a long thin strand measuring approximately 16 cm (6.5") in length.
ii Starting at one end roll the dough up to form a spiral.

Rosette:
i Roll the dough piece to a long thin strand measuring approximately 20 cm (8") in length.
ii Tie a knot leaving long tails.
iii Take one tail over and one tail under and secure into the centre.

One Strand Plait:
i Roll the dough piece to a long thin strand measuring approximately 20 cm (8") in length.
ii Form the shape of a number six.
iii Bring the long tail under and through the loop.
iv Twist the bottom of the loop, from left to right. Now bring the remainder of the tail under and through the bottom loop.

4 Place the dough pieces onto a warm, greased baking tray.
5 Prove at 38–40°C (100–104°F) in humid conditions.
6 Bake at 250°C (482°F) for 10–12 minutes.
7 After baking remove the rolls from the tray immediately and place on a cooling wire.

Note:
- The appearance of these rolls can be enhanced by the use of eggwash and various seeds.
- The shapes given for Milk Bread Rolls are also suitable for Soft Fancy Rolls.

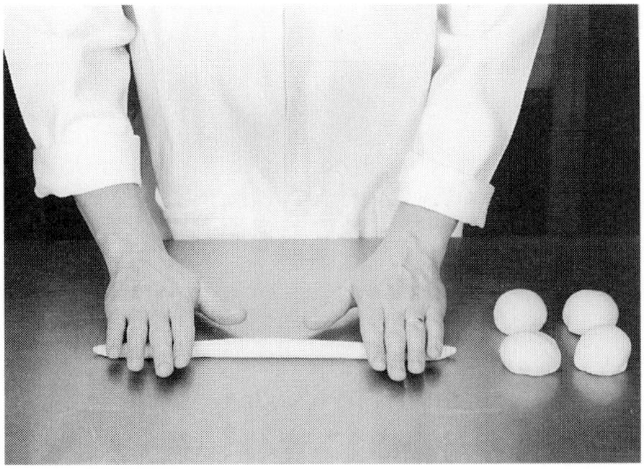

To make a one strand plait, roll the dough piece to a long thin strand

Form the shape of a number six

Bring the long tail under and through the loop

Twist the bottom of the loop, from left to right. Now bring the remainder of the tail under and through the bottom loop

Soft Fancy Rolls

BROWN ROLLS

Ingredients

Kilo	Gram	%	Ingredients	lb	oz
1	000	100.00	brown flour	2	3.50
	25	2.27	salt		1.00
	20	2.00	skimmed milk powder		0.75
	50	5.00	shortening		1.75
	35	3.50	yeast		1.25
	600	60.00	water	1	5.50
1	730		Gross weight	3	13.75
1	686		Net weight	3	12.25

Production Points

Dough temperature	**26°C (79°F)**
Bulk Fermentation Time	**30 mins**
Knock back	**N/A**
Scaling weight	**50 g (1.75 oz)**
Yield	**33**
Baking temperature	**250°C (482°F)**
Baking time	**10–12 mins**

Note: This recipe is also suitable for the production of Brown Fancy Rolls.

Mixing method

1 Using a coarse sieve, sieve together the flour, salt and skimmed milk powder.
2 Add the shortening and rub through the dry ingredients on speed 1 using a dough hook.
3 Disperse the yeast into the tempered water and add to the above ingredients.
4 Mix on speed 1 for 2 minutes until a dough is formed.
5 Check for extremes in consistency and adjust as necessary.
6 Mix on speed 1 for 15 minutes or speed 2 for 10 minutes.
7 Cover the dough and keep warm during the BFT.
8 After the completion of the BFT the dough is ready to be scaled and processed.

Processing method

1 Scale 33 at 50 g (1.75 oz) and mould round.
2 Rest for 8 to 10 minutes to allow the dough pieces to recover.
3 Pin out the dough pieces to a flat round shape.
4 Place the dough pieces onto a warm, greased tray.
5 Prove at 38–40°C (100–104°F) in humid conditions.
6 Bake at 250°C (482°F) for 10–12 minutes.
7 After baking, remove the rolls from the tray immediately and place on a cooling wire.

ICED FINGERS

Ingredients

Kilo	Gram	%	Ingredients	lb	oz
1	000	100.00	bread flour	2	3.50
	10	1.00	salt		0.50
	50	5.00	skimmed milk powder		2.00
	100	10.00	shortening		3.50
	100	10.00	egg		3.50
	100	10.00	sugar		3.50
	70	7.00	yeast		2.50
	490	49.00	water	1	1.50
1	920		Gross weight	4	4.50
1	872		Net weight	4	2.75

Production Points

Dough temperature	**27°C (81°F)**
Bulk Fermentation Time	**1 hour**
Knock back	**30–40 mins**
Scaling weight	**50 g (1.75 oz)**
Yield	**36**
Baking temperature	**225°C (437°F)**
Baking time	**10–12 mins**

Note: This recipe is also suitable for the production of Cream Buns (Cookies), Belgian Buns, Devon Splits, Parisian Buns, Chelsea Buns, Butter Buns.

Mixing method

1 Sieve together the flour, salt and skimmed milk powder.
2 Add the shortening and rub through the dry ingredients on speed 1 using a dough hook.
3 Mix the egg and sugar together, and disperse the yeast into the tempered water. Now add both of these solutions to the above ingredients.
4 Mix on speed 1 for 2 minutes until a dough is formed.
5 Check for extremes in consistency and adjust as necessary.
6 Mix on speed 1 for 15 minutes or speed 2 for 10 minutes.
7 Cover the dough and keep warm during the BFT.
8 After 30–40 minutes of the BFT, knock back the dough.
9 After the completion of the BFT the dough is ready to be scaled and processed.

Iced Fingers and Cookies

Processing method

1 Scale 36 at 50 g (1.75 oz) and mould round.
2 Rest for 8 to 10 minutes to allow the dough pieces to recover.
3 Re-mould the dough pieces and roll them into a finger shape measuring approximately 10 cm (4") in length.
4 Place the dough pieces onto a warm, greased tray.
5 Prove at 38–40°C (100–104°F) in humid conditions.
6 Bake at 225°C (437°F) 10–12 minutes.

7 After baking remove the fingers from the tray immediately and allow to cool on a wire.
8 When cool, dip the top of the fingers into water icing or fondant, and remove the excess with a palette knife.
9 Allow the icing to set.

Note: The water icing and fondant may be coloured and flavoured.

TEACAKES

(See colour plate 3.)

Ingredients

Kilo	Gram	%	Ingredients	lb	oz
1	000	100.00	bread flour	2	3.50
	10	1.00	salt		0.50
	50	5.00	skimmed milk powder		2.00
	100	10.00	shortening		3.50
	100	10.00	egg		3.50
	100	10.00	sugar		3.50
	70	7.00	yeast		2.50
	490	49.00	water	1	1.50
	150	15.00	currants		5.50
	50	5.00	mixed peel		2.00
2	120		Gross weight	4	12.00
2	067		Net weight	4	10.00

Production Points

Dough temperature	**27°C (81°F)**
Bulk Fermentation Time	**1 hour**
Knock back	**30–40 mins**
Scaling weight	**100 g (3.5 oz)**
Yield	**20**
Baking temperature	**220°C (428°F)**
Baking time	**12–15 mins**

Note: This recipe is also suitable for the production of Currant Buns (omit mixed peel) and Tea Loaves.

Mixing method

1 Sieve together the flour, salt and skimmed milk powder.
2 Add the shortening and rub through the dry ingredients on speed 1 using a dough hook.
3 Mix the egg and sugar together, and disperse the yeast into the tempered water. Now add both of these solutions to the above ingredients.
4 Mix on speed 1 for 2 minutes until a dough is formed.
5 Check for extremes in consistency and adjust as necessary.
6 Mix on speed 1 for 15 minutes or speed 2 for 10 minutes.
7 Cover the dough and keep warm during the BFT.
8 After 30–40 minutes of the BFT, knock back the dough. At this stage, mix the currants and mixed peel through the dough.
9 After the remaining BFT the dough is ready to be scaled and processed.

Processing method

1 Scale 20 at 100 g (3.5 oz) and mould round.
2 Rest for 8 to 10 minutes to allow the dough pieces to recover.
3 Pin the dough pieces to approximately 8 cm (3.25") in diameter.
4 Place the dough pieces onto a warm, well-greased tray.
5 Brush the top of the dough piece with eggwash.
6 Prove at 38–40°C (100–104°F) in humid conditions.
7 Bake at 220°C (428°F) 12–15 minutes.
8 After baking, remove the teacakes from the tray immediately and place on a cooling wire.

HOT CROSS BUNS

Ingredients

Kilo	Gram	%	Ingredients	lb	oz
1	000	100.00	strong bread flour	2	3.50
	8	0.70	salt		0.25
	30	3.00	skimmed milk powder		1.00
	20	2.00	mixed spice		0.75
	150	15.00	shortening		5.25
	75	7.50	egg		2.75
	150	15.00	sugar		5.25
	90	9.00	yeast		3.25
	460	46.00	water	1	0.25
	200	20.00	currants		7.00
	100	10.00	sultanas		3.50
	50	5.00	mixed peel		1.75
2	333		Gross weight	5	2.25
2	274		Net weight	5	0.25

Production Points

Dough temperature	**26°C (79°F)**
Bulk Fermentation Time	**1 hour**
Knock back	**30–40 mins**
Scaling weight	**60 g (2 oz)**
Yield	**37**
Baking temperature	**232°C (450°F)**
Baking time	**12–15 mins**

Mixing method

1 Sieve together the flour, salt, skimmed milk powder and mixed spice.
2 Add the shortening and rub through the dry ingredients on speed 1 using a dough hook.
3 Mix the egg and sugar together, and disperse the yeast into the tempered water. Now add both of these solutions to the above ingredients.
4 Mix on speed 1 for 2 minutes until a dough is formed.
5 Check for extremes in consistency and adjust as necessary.
6 Mix on speed 1 for 15 minutes or speed 2 for 10 minutes.
7 Cover the dough and keep warm during the BFT.
8 After 30–40 minutes of the BFT, knock back the dough. At this stage, mix the fruit through the dough.
9 After the remaining BFT the dough is ready to be scaled and processed.

Processing method

1 Scale 37 at 60 g (2 oz) and mould round.
2 Rest for 8 to 10 minutes to allow the dough pieces to recover.
3 Re-mould the dough pieces and place them onto a warm, greased tray. At this stage, ensure the dough pieces are placed in straight rows to facilitate easy piping of the crosses at stage 5.
4 Prove at 38–40°C (100–104°F) in humid conditions.
5 Using the cross batter, pipe lines across the rows of dough pieces to form a cross on each dough piece as illustrated (page 98).

Note: After the piping of the crosses, the dough pieces must be placed in the oven immediately. This will prevent the crosses from flowing.

6 Bake at 232°C (450°F) for 12–15 minutes.
7 After withdrawal from the oven, brush with the after bake glaze.
8 Now place the Hot Cross Buns onto a cooling wire.

Pipe horizontal lines across the dough

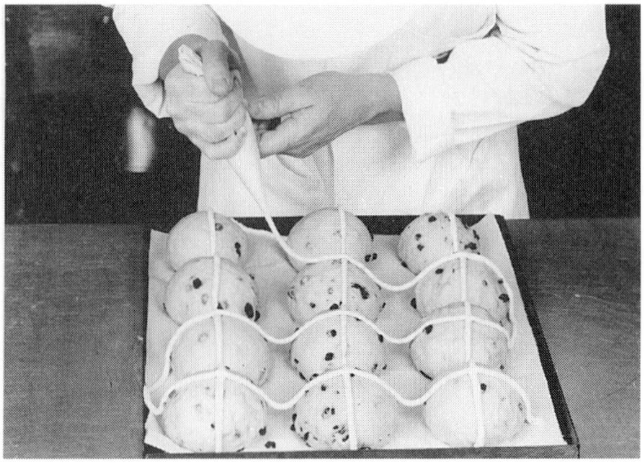

Turn the tray 90°; pipe horizontal lines across the dough again, to form a cross on each dough piece

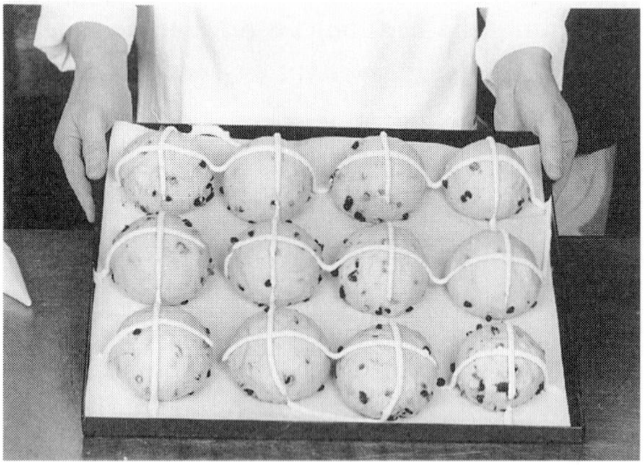

Place the dough pieces in the oven immediately

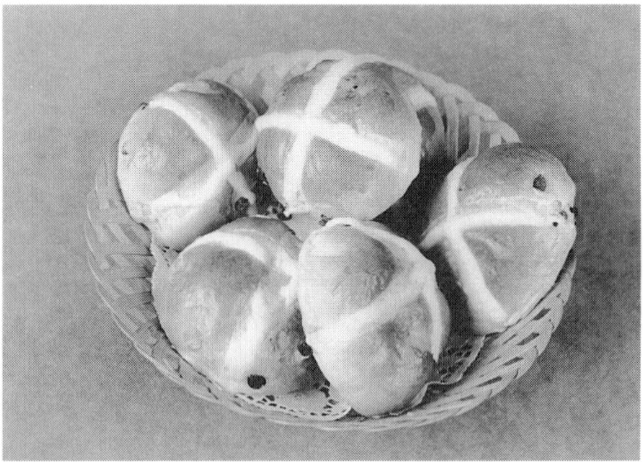

Hot Cross Buns

HOT CROSS BUNS BATTER

Ingredients

Kilo	Gram	%	Ingredients	lb	oz
	100	100.00	medium strength flour		3.50
	1	1.00	baking powder		pinch
	10	10.00	skimmed milk powder		0.25
	1	1.00	salt		pinch
	20	20.00	shortening		0.75
	110	11.00	water		4.00
	242		Gross weight		8.50
	236		Net weight		8.25

Mixing method

1 Sieve together the flour, baking powder, skimmed milk powder and salt.
2 Add the shortening and rub through the dry ingredients.
3 Add the water slowly until a paste is formed using a beater.
4 Now add the remaining water slowly until a smooth batter, or a suitable consistency for piping is obtained.

AFTER BAKE GLAZE

Ingredients

Kilo	Gram	%	Ingredients	lb	oz
	100	100.00	fresh milk		3.50
	15	15.00	shell egg		0.50
	10	10.00	sugar		0.25
	125		Gross weight		4.25
	122		Net weight		4.00

Mixing method

1 Whisk all of the ingredients together. The glaze is now ready for use.

Note: If the glaze is allowed to stand for a period of time, re-whisk before using.

MALT BREAD

Ingredients

Kilo	Gram	%	Ingredients	lb	oz
	700	100.00	bread flour	1	9.00
	15	2.10	salt		0.50
	40	14.30	dried malt extract		0.75
	350	50.00	low diastatic malt flour		12.5
	15	2.10	shortening		0.50
	70	10.00	yeast		2.50
	540	77.10	water	1	3.75
	25	3.50	treacle		1.00
	250	35.70	sultanas		9.00
2	005		Gross weight	4	9.75
1	954		Net weight	4	7.75

Mixing method

1 Sieve together the flour, salt, dried malt extract and low diastatic malt flour.
2 Add the shortening and rub through the dry ingredients on speed 1 using a dough hook.
3 Disperse the yeast into the tempered water. Add and disperse the treacle. Add this solution to the above ingredients.
4 Mix on speed 1 for 2 minutes until a dough is formed.
5 Check for extremes in consistency and adjust as necessary.
6 Mix on speed 1 for 15 minutes or speed 2 for 10 minutes.
7 At the end of stage 6, mix the sultanas through the dough on speed 1.
8 Cover the dough and keep warm during the BFT.
9 After the BFT the dough is ready to be scaled and processed.

Production Points

Dough temperature	**27°C (81°F)**
Bulk Fermentation Time	**30 mins**
Knock back	**N/A**
Scaling weight	**325 g (11.5 oz)**
Yield	**6**
Baking temperature	**180°C (356°F)**
Baking time	**approx 1 hour**

Processing method

1 Scale 6 at 325 g (11.50 oz) and mould round.
2 Rest for 8 to 10 minutes to allow the dough pieces to recover.
3 Re-mould the dough pieces and form them into a cylinder shape.
4 Place the dough pieces into warm, greased pup tins, which must be on a greased tray. The dough pieces must be placed into the tins with the seam facing upwards.
5 Prove at 38–40°C (100–104°F) in humid conditions.
6 Prior to baking, turn the tins over onto the greased tray and bake at 180°C (356°F) for approximately 1 hour.
7 On withdrawal from the oven remove the tins and glaze the tops of the malt bread with after bake glaze.
8 Now place the malt bread on a cooling wire.

CRUMPETS

Ingredients

Kilo	Gram	%	Ingredients	lb	oz
1	000	100.00	bread flour	2	3.500
	30	3.00	salt		1.000
	55	5.50	yeast		2.000
1	110	111.00	water	2	7.500
	10	1.00	sugar		0.500
	3	0.30	bicarbonate of soda		0.125
	280	28.00	cold water		10.000
2	488		Gross weight	5	8.50
2	425		Net weight	5	6.25

Production Points

Dough temperature	**26°C (79°F)**
Bulk Fermentation Time	**1 hour**
Knock back	**N/A**
Scaling weight	**approx 60 g (2 oz)**
Yield	**approx 40**
Baking temperature	**Moderate hot-plate**
Baking time	**8–10 mins**

Mixing method

1 Sieve the flour and salt together.
2 Disperse the yeast into the tempered water. Now dissolve the sugar into the yeast/water solution. Add this solution to the above ingredients.
3 Mix on speed 1 for 2 minutes using a beater to form a batter.
4 Mix on speed 1 for 10 minutes or speed 2 for 5 minutes.
5 Cover the batter and keep warm during the BFT.
6 After the completion of the BFT, dissolve the bicarbonate of soda in the cold water and mix it well through the batter.

The batter must be used immediately.

Processing method

1 The hot-plate must be clean, polished and free from grease and set at the correct temperature.
2 Now place lightly greased crumpet rings onto the hot-plate.

Note: Begin at the left hand side of the hot-plate and place the first row of crumpet rings one ring width in from the end of the hot-plate. This will leave sufficient space for each crumpet to be turned during the baking process.

3 Using a ladle or funnel shaped dropper fill each ring to approximately two-thirds full.

4 During this stage of the baking process, bubbles will appear on the surface. These will set and form the open, rubbery character of the crumpet.
5 When the top of the crumpets are firm, remove the rings and turn the crumpets over until the tops are lightly coloured.
6 Remove the crumpets from the hot-plate and place them on a cooling wire.

MUFFINS

Ingredients

Kilo	Gram	%	Ingredients	lb	oz
1	000	100.00	strong bread flour	2	3.50
	20	2.00	salt		0.75
	20	2.00	skimmed milk powder		0.75
	20	2.00	shortening		0.75
	35	3.50	yeast		1.25
	700	70.00	water	1	9.00
	10	1.00	sugar		0.25
1	805		Gross weight	4	0.25
1	760		Net weight	3	14.75

Production Points

Dough temperature	**27°C (81°F)**
Bulk Fermentation Time	**1 hour**
Knock back	**30–40 mins**
Scaling weight	**50–60 g (2 oz)**
Yield	**29–35**
Baking temperature	**Moderate hot-plate**
Baking time	**10–12 mins**

Mixing method

1 Sieve together the flour, salt and skimmed milk powder.
2 Add the shortening and rub through the dry ingredients on speed 1 using a dough hook.
3 Disperse the yeast into the tempered water, add and dissolve the sugar and add to the above ingredients.
4 Mix on speed 1 for 2 minutes until a dough is formed.
5 Check for extremes in consistency and adjust as necessary.
6 Mix on speed 1 for 15 minutes or speed 2 for 10 minutes.
7 Cover the dough and keep warm during the BFT.
8 After 30–40 minutes of the BFT, knock back the dough.
9 After the completion of the BFT the dough is ready to be scaled and processed.

Processing method

1 Scale 29 at 60 g (2 oz) or 35 at 50 g (1.75 oz) and mould round.
2 Rest for 8 to 10 minutes to allow the dough pieces to recover.
3 Slightly flatten the dough pieces.
4 Place the flattened dough pieces onto a board that has been dusted with ground rice.
5 Keep the dough pieces covered and allow sufficient proving time prior to baking.
6 Place lightly greased muffin hoops onto the hot-plate to warm.
7 Transfer the dough pieces into the hoops on the hot-plate and bake one side to a golden brown colour.
8 Turn the muffins over and complete the baking process.
9 Remove the hoops and muffins from the hot-plate, and place the muffins on a cooling wire.

PIZZA BASES

Ingredients

Kilo	Gram	%	Ingredients	lb	oz
1	000	100.00	bread flour	2	3.50
	10	1.00	salt		0.50
	50	5.00	yeast		1.75
	500	50.00	milk	1	1.75
	250	25.00	vegetable or olive oil		9.00
1	810		Gross weight	4	0.50
1	765		Net weight	3	15.00

Production Points

Dough temperature	**27°C (81°F)**
Bulk Fermentation Time	**15 mins**
Knock back	**N/A**
Scaling weight	**170 g (6 oz)**
Yield	**10**
Baking temperature	**225°C (437°F)**
Baking time	**15–20 mins**

(See colour plate 4.)

Mixing method

1 Sieve together the flour and salt.
2 Disperse the yeast into tempered milk and add to the above ingredients.
3 Mix on speed 1 until a dough is formed.
4 Add the vegetable oil or olive oil slowly to the dough on speed 1.
5 When the dough has absorbed the oil, mix on speed 1 for 15 minutes or speed 2 for 10 minutes.
6 Cover the dough and keep warm during the BFT.
7 After the completion of the BFT the dough is ready to be scaled and processed.

Processing method

1 Scale 10 at 170 g (6 oz) and mould round.
2 Rest for 8 to 10 minutes to allow the dough pieces to recover.
3 Pin the dough pieces to approximately 22.5 cm (9") in diameter, and place onto a warm greased tray or a pizza pan.
4 Spread approximately 85 g (3 oz) of pizza topping over the surface of the dough piece. Stay within 1.25 cm (0.5") of the edge of the dough piece to allow for the flow of the pizza topping.
5 Sprinkle the base with approximately 110 g (4 oz) of grated Mozzarella cheese.
6 Apply further combinations of topping such as:
- ham and pineapple
- tuna and sweetcorn
- salami and peppers
- tandoori chicken
- seafood, prawns, cockles and mussels
- chilli mince.

7 For a *crisp* base, bake immediately at 225°C (437°F) for 15–20 minutes.
For a *softer* pizza base, allow a final proof of approximately 15 minutes prior to baking as above.
8 After baking remove the pizza from the tray or pan ready for consumption.

Note: Pizza production can be organised to ensure that they are freshly baked and hot at the point of sale.

PIZZA TOPPING

Ingredients

Kilo	Gram	%	Ingredients	lb	oz
	825	100.00	tinned tomatoes	1	13.50
	45	5.50	tomato puree		1.50
	10	1.20	salt		0.25
	2.5	0.30	oregano		pinch
	2.5	0.30	pepper		pinch
	885		Gross weight	1	15.25
	862		Net weight	1	14.50

Production Points

Scaling weight	**85 g (6 oz)**
Yield	**10 for 22.5 cm (9") diameter pizza base**

Mixing method

1 Remove the core from the tinned tomatoes and chop into small pieces.
2 Add the remaining ingredients to the tinned tomatoes and mix them all together.
3 The topping is now ready to use.

BRIOCHE

Ingredients

Kilo	Gram	%	Ingredients	lb	oz
1	000	100.00	bread flour	2	3.50
	30	3.00	salt		1.00
	110	11.00	sugar		4.00
	550	55.00	egg	1	3.50
	110	11.00	yeast		4.00
	110	11.00	milk	1	4.00
	280	28.00	butter		10.00
2	190		Gross weight	4	14.00
2	135		Net weight	4	12.00

Mixing method

1 Sieve the flour and salt together.
2 Mix the sugar and egg together. Disperse the yeast into tempered milk. Now add both these solutions to the flour and salt.
3 Mix on speed 1 for 2 minutes until a dough is formed.
4 Check for extremes in consistency and adjust as necessary.
5 Mix on speed 1 for 15 minutes or speed 2 for 10 minutes.
6 Now add and beat the butter through on speed 2 until a smooth dough is obtained.
7 Cover the dough and keep warm during the BFT.
8 After 30–40 minutes of the BFT, knock back the dough.
9 After the completion of the BFT the dough is ready to be scaled and processed.

Processing method

1 Scale 85 at 25 g (1 oz) and mould round.
2 Rest for 5 minutes to allow the dough pieces to recover.
3 Re-mould the dough pieces and form them into the shape of a small cottage loaf. This shape is obtained by pressing

Production Points

Dough temperature	**23°C (73°F)**
Bulk Fermentation Time	**1 hour**
Knock back	**30–40 mins**
Scaling weight	**25 g (1 oz)**
Yield	**85**
Baking temperature	**232°C (450°F)**
Baking time	**10–12 mins**

and rolling the dough piece with your middle finger. This action will form a small and a large piece of dough, which can now be assembled and secured into the shape of a small cottage loaf.

4 Place the dough pieces into warm, well-greased, fluted patty tins.
5 Prove at 32–34°C (89–93°F) in humid conditions.
6 Bake at 232°C (450°F) for 10–12 minutes.
7 After baking, remove the brioche from the tins immediately and place on a cooling wire.

CHAPTER *five*

The Mechanical Dough Development Process

After many years of research and development, the Mechanical Dough Development process (MDD) was introduced to the baking industry at the London Bakery Exhibition in 1963. There are two aspects of this process that were of special interest to the baker:

1. A mixing time of only 2–4 minutes, yet the dough was fully developed.
2. The elimination of Bulk Fermentation Time, which was usually a period of 2–3 hours.

Bakers within the UK quickly accepted and adopted the MDD process for the advantages that this new technology offered. Within a very short period of time the breadmaking industry had been revolutionised.

MIXING METHOD

This is an outline of the mixing method, but each recipe contains a more detailed description of the method.

1 Place the ingredients into the mixing chamber in the following order:
   - cold water
   - dry ingredients
   - fat and yeast.
2 Mix to the required watt hour input.
3 The dough is now ready to be scaled and processed.

Alterations to the recipe

- Ascorbic acid must be included in the recipe to a maximum of 200 parts per million (ppm) based on the flour weight. Therefore it is important that the baker is aware of the level of ascorbic acid present in the flour added by the miller.
- The level of water must be increased by approximately 2% of the flour weight. This is because the flour is able to absorb more water during mixing.
- Fat must be included at the rate of approximately 1% of the flour weight to ensure that oven spring takes place during the baking process.

Energy input

The mixing time is determined by the amount of energy the dough absorbs during mixing. The energy input is measured in watt hours. The formula for calculation of the required number of watt hours is 11 watt hours per kilo of dough; for example:

Total weight of ingredients	=	15 kilos, 500 grams
Energy input	=	11×15.5
Required watt hours	=	170.5

CHANGES WHICH OCCUR DURING MIXING

Bonds and proteins

It is understood that the intense mechanical action of the mixing plate upon the dough, has an effect on the bonds holding the proteins responsible for the structure and volume of the bread. At the end of the mixing time, the links between the bonds and proteins have been effectively rearranged to produce a ripe dough which is ready for processing. To encourage this speedy development of the dough, ascorbic acid (Vitamin C) must be included in the recipe.

Finally, the addition of fat will also assist with the development of the dough and its ability to retain gas during the latter stages of breadmaking.

Dough temperature

The intensity of the mixing process creates friction within the mixing chamber. The friction produces heat which increases the dough temperature by approximately 14°C (57°F). To control the dough temperature, it is necessary to use cold water and sometimes crushed ice during the hot weather. Normal dough temperatures for dough mixed on a high speed machine are 29–31°C (85–88°F).

Addition of fruit

Dried fruit should be added and mixed through the dough, during the final 15 seconds of mixing.

Dividing

Dividing should take place within 8 minutes of the dough leaving the mixer. This is to ensure accurate scaling weights are obtained.

ADVANTAGES AND DISADVANTAGES

Advantages

1 The mixing time is considerably reduced from up to 20 minutes to 3–4 minutes.
2 The elimination of a bulk fermentation period:
- saves production time
- removes the need for fermentation space
- saves labour time (eg knock back).

3 An increased yield is obtained because of:
- the increased water level
- reduced fermentation losses.

4 Consistent results are obtained.
5 Allows for the organisation of sociable working hours.

Disadvantages

1 A special high speed mixer is required for this process.
2 The need for crushed ice during hot weather can cause difficulty.
3 Mechanical breakdowns cause havoc with the production schedules.
4 Costs are increased because of the need to add ascorbic acid.
5 There is some loss in the flavour because the dough does not have a fermentation period.

OVEN CHART

Product	Baking temperature in °C (°F)	Baking time in minutes	Additional control procedures
Lge White	232 (450)	35–40	Open damper for final 10 mins
Multi-Piece Bread	232 (450)	35–40	" " " "
Lge Brown	232 (450)	35–40	" " " "
Lge Wholemeal Tin Bread	232 (450)	35–40	" " " "
Bloomers and Danish Bread	232 (450)	20–25	Use steam during first 10 mins then release
Burger Buns	238 (460)	10–12	Open damper for final 5 mins
Barm Cakes	232 (450)	10–12	" " " "
Cream Buns (Cookies)	232 (450)	10–15	" " " "
Devon Splits	232 (450)	10–15	" " " "
Parisian Buns	232 (450)	10–15	" " " "
Germ Meal Bread	237 (458)	25	" " " " 10 mins

RECIPES USING THE MECHANICAL DOUGH DEVELOPMENT PROCESS

LARGE WHITE AND MULTI-PIECE BREAD

Ingredients

Kilo	Gram	%	Ingredients	lb	oz
10	000	100.00	bread flour	22	0.00
	225	2.25	salt		8.00
	180	1.80	skimmed milk powder		6.50
	100	1.00	dough conditioner		3.50
	225	2.25	shortening		8.00
	400	4.00	yeast		14.25
5	900	59.00	cold water	13	1.25
17	030		Gross weight	37	9.50
16	604		Net weight	36	9.00

Production Points

Required watt hours	**187**
Dough temperature	**29–31°C (85–88°F)**
Bulk Fermentation Time	**Nil**
Knock back	**N/A**
Scaling weight	**900 g (2 lbs)**
Yield	**18**
Baking temperature	**232°C (450°F)**
Baking time	**35–40 mins**

Note: This recipe is also suitable for the production of Small White, Farmhouse, Sandwich Bread, Tinned Coburgs and Long Cut Tin

Mixing method

1 Place the ingredients into the mixing chamber in the following order:
- cold water
- flour, salt, skimmed milk powder and dough conditioner
- shortening and yeast.

2 Mix to the required watt hour input.
3 The dough is now ready to be scaled and processed.

Processing methods

LARGE WHITE BREAD

1 Scale 18 at 900 g (2 lb) and mould round.
2 Rest for 8–10 minutes to allow the dough pieces to recover.
3 Re-mould the dough pieces and form them into a cylinder shape.
4 Place the dough pieces into warm, greased, large bread tins.
5 Prove at 38–40°C (100–104°F) in humid conditions.
6 Bake at 232°C (450°F) for 35–40 minutes.
7 After baking, remove the bread from the tins immediately and place onto a cooling wire.

MULTI-PIECE BREAD

1 Follow stages 1 and 2 of Large White.
2 Rest for 8–10 minutes to allow the dough pieces to recover.
3 Re-mould the dough pieces to a long cylinder measuring 36 cm (14") in length.
4 Cut the dough piece using a scraper into three, and fold as illustrated on page 110.
5 Place into a warm, greased large bread tin.
6 Now follow stages 5, 6 and 7 of Large White Bread.

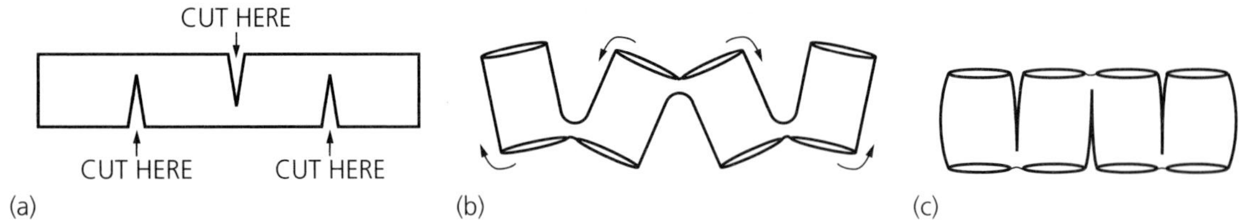

Figure 8 Multipiece bread (a) make three cuts (b) twist the dough (c) ready for the oven

LARGE BROWN

Ingredients

Kilo	Gram	%	Ingredients	lb	oz
10	000	100.00	brown flour	22	0.00
	250	2.50	salt		9.00
	100	1.00	skimmed milk powder		3.50
	100	1.00	dough conditioner		3.50
	225	2.25	shortening		8.00
	350	3.50	yeast		12.50
6	200	62.00	cold water	13	11.00
17	225		Gross weight	37	15.50
16	796		Net weight	37	0.00

Production Points

Required watt hours	**189**
Dough temperature	**29–31°C (85–88°F)**
Bulk Fermentation Time	**Nil**
Knock back	**N/A**
Scaling weight	**900 g (2 lb)**
Yield	**18**
Baking temperature	**232°C (450°F)**
Baking time	**35–40 mins**

Note: This recipe is also suitable for the production of Small Brown, Brown Farmhouse, and Brown Coburgs.

Mixing method

1. Place the ingredients into the mixing chamber in the following order:
   - cold water
   - flour, salt, skimmed milk powder and dough conditioner
   - shortening and yeast.
2. Mix to the required watt hour input.
3. The dough is now ready to be scaled and processed.

Processing method

1. Scale 18 at 900 g (2 lb) and mould round.
2. Rest for 8–10 minutes to allow the dough pieces to recover.
3. Re-mould the dough pieces and form them into a cylinder shape.
4. Place the dough pieces into warm, greased, large bread tins.
5. Prove at 38–40°C (100–104°F) in humid conditions.
6. Bake at 232°C (450°F) for 35–40 minutes.
7. After baking, remove the bread from the tins immediately and place onto a cooling wire.

LARGE WHOLEMEAL TIN BREAD

Ingredients

Kilo	Gram	%	Ingredients	lb	oz
10	000	100.00	wholemeal flour	22	0.00
	250	2.50	salt		9.00
	100	1.00	dough conditioner		3.50
	200	2.00	shortening		7.25
	365	3.65	yeast		13.00
6	400	64.00	cold water	14	2.25
17	315		Gross weight	38	3.50
16	882		Net weight	37	3.50

Production Points

Required watt hours	**189**
Dough temperature	**29–31°C (85–88°F)**
Bulk Fermentation Time	**Nil**
Knock back	**N/A**
Scaling weight	**900 g (2 lb)**
Yield	**18**
Baking temperature	**232°C (450°F)**
Baking time	**35–40 mins**

Note: This recipe is also suitable for the production of Small Wholemeal Tin Bread and Coburgs.

Mixing method

1 Place the ingredients into the mixing chamber in the following order:
- cold water
- flour, salt and dough conditioner
- shortening and yeast.

2 Mix to the required watt hour input.
3 The dough is now ready to be scaled and processed.

Processing method

1 Scale 18 at 900 g (2 lb) and mould round.
2 Rest for 8–10 minutes to allow the dough pieces to recover.
3 Re-mould the dough pieces and form them into a cylinder shape.
4 Place the dough pieces into warm, large, greased bread tins.
5 Prove at 38–40°C (100–104°F) in humid conditions.
6 Bake at 232°C (450°F) for 35–40 minutes.
7 After baking, remove the bread from the tins immediately and place onto a cooling wire.

BLOOMERS AND DANISH BREAD

Ingredients

Kilo	Gram	%	Ingredients	lb	oz
10	000	100.00	bread flour	22	0.00
	225	2.25	salt		8.00
	180	1.80	skimmed milk powder		6.50
	100	1.00	dough conditioner		3.50
	200	2.00	shortening		7.25
	400	4.00	yeast		14.25
5	600	56.00	cold water	12	8.00
16	705		Gross weight	36	15.50
16	287		Net weight	36	0.00

Mixing method

1 Place the ingredients into the mixing chamber in the following order:
- cold water
- flour, salt, skimmed milk powder and dough conditioner
- shortening and yeast.

2 Mix to the required watt hour input.
3 The dough is now ready to be scaled and processed.

Processing method

1 Scale 36 at 455 g (1 lb) and mould round.
2 Rest for 8–10 minutes to allow the dough pieces to recover.

Bloomers and Danish

Production Points

Required watt hours	**184**
Dough temperature	**29–31°C (85–88°F)**
Bulk Fermentation Time	**Nil**
Knock back	**N/A**
Scaling weight	**455 g (1 lb)**
Yield	**36**
Baking temperature	**232°C (450°F)**
Baking time	**20–25 mins**

Note: This recipe is also suitable for the production of Cottage Bread, Tiger Bread and Coburgs.

Ingredients

Kilo	Gram	%	Ingredients	lb	oz
10	000	100.00	bread flour	22	0.00
	200	2.00	salt		7.25
	200	2.00	skimmed milk powder		7.25
	100	1.00	dough conditioner		3.50
	400	4.00	shortening		14.50
	400	4.00	yeast		14.50
5	900	59.00	cold water	13	1.25
17	200		Gross weight	38	0.25
16	770		Net weight	37	1.00

3 Re-mould the dough pieces and form them into a long baton shape.
4 Place the dough pieces onto a warm, greased tray.
5 Prove at 38–40°C (100–104°F) in humid conditions.
6 After three quarters of the final proof, cut in the following way and return to the prover.
   - *Bloomers* Make approximately 10 cuts 1 cm (0.5") deep across the top of the dough piece.
   - *Danish* Dust with bread flour, then make one cut down the side of the dough piece with the knife held at an angle.
7 Bake at 232°C (450°F) for 20–25 minutes. For the Bloomers only, use steam in the oven chamber for the first 10 minutes of the baking process.
8 After baking, remove from the trays immediately and place on a cooling wire.

FINGER ROLLS

Mixing method

1 Place the ingredients into the mixing chamber in the following order:
   - cold water
   - flour, salt, skimmed milk powder and dough conditioner
   - shortening and yeast.
2 Mix to the required watt hour input.
3 The dough is now ready to be scaled and processed.

Production Points

Required watt hours	**189**
Dough temperature	**29–31°C (85–88°F)**
Bulk Fermentation Time	**Nil**
Knock back	**N/A**
Scaling weight	**50 g (1.75 oz)**
Yield	**335**
Baking temperature	**245°C (470°F)**
Baking time	**10–12 mins**

Note: This recipe is also suitable for the production of Bread Rolls, Scotch Baps, Stotties, Soft Fancy Rolls, Divider Buns and Bridge Rolls.

Processing method

1 Scale 335 at 50 g (1.75 oz) and mould round.
2 Rest for 8–10 minutes to allow the dough pieces to recover.
3 Re-mould the dough pieces and form them into a finger shape approximately 10 cm (4") long.
4 Place the dough pieces onto a warm, greased tray.
5 Prove at 38–40°C (100–104°F) in humid conditions.
6 Bake at 245°C (470°F) for 10–12 minutes.
7 After baking, remove the rolls from the tray immediately and place on a cooling wire.

BURGER BUNS

Mixing method

1 Place the ingredients into the mixing chamber in the following order:
- cold water
- flour, salt, skimmed milk powder, dough conditioner and sugar
- shortening and yeast.

2 Mix to the required watt hour input.
3 The dough is now ready to be scaled and processed.

Ingredients

Kilo	Gram	%	Ingredients	lb	oz
10	000	100.00	bread flour	22	0.00
	200	2.00	salt		7.25
	300	3.00	skimmed milk powder		10.75
	100	1.00	dough conditioner		3.50
	360	3.60	sugar		10.75
	500	5.00	shortening	1	2.00
	300	3.00	yeast		10.75
5	900	59.00	cold water	13	1.25
17	600		Gross weight	38	14.25
17	160		Net weight	37	14.00

Production Points

Required watt hours	**194**
Dough temperature	**29–31°C (85–88°F)**
Bulk Fermentation Time	**Nil**
Knock back	**N/A**
Scaling weight	**60 g (2 oz)**
Yield	**286**
Baking temperature	**238°C (460°F)**
Baking time	**10–12 mins**

Burger Buns and Barm Cakes

Processing method

1 Scale 286 at 60 g (2 oz) and mould round.
2 Rest for 8–10 minutes to allow the dough pieces to recover.
3 Pin out the dough pieces to a flat round shape to fit the indentation of the burger tray.
4 Place the dough pieces onto a warm, greased burger tray.
5 Brush the top of the dough pieces with water, then sprinkle with sesame seeds.
6 Prove at 38–40°C (100–104°F) in humid conditions.
7 Bake at 238°C (460°F) for 10–12 minutes.
8 After baking, remove the buns from the tray immediately and place them onto a cooling wire.

BARM CAKES

Ingredients

Kilo	Gram	%	Ingredients	lb	oz
10	000	100.00	bread flour	22	0.00
	200	2.00	salt		7.25
	200	2.00	skimmed milk powder		7.25
	100	1.00	dough conditioner		3.50
	800	8.00	shortening	1	12.50
	400	4.00	yeast		14.25
5	800	58.00	cold water	12	15.25
17	500		Gross weight	38	12.00
17	062		Net weight	37	12.50

Production Points

Required watt hours	**192**
Dough temperature	**29–31°C (85–88°F)**
Bulk Fermentation Time	**Nil**
Knock back	**N/A**
Scaling weight	**60 g (2 oz)**
Yield	**284**
Baking temperature	**232°C (450°F)**
Baking time	**10–12 mins**

Mixing method

1 Place the ingredients into the mixing chamber in the following order:
- cold water
- flour, salt, skimmed milk powder and dough conditioner
- shortening and yeast.

2 Mix to the required watt hour input.
3 The dough is now ready to be scaled and processed.

Processing method

1 Scale 284 at 60 g (2 oz) and mould round.
2 Rest for 8–10 minutes to allow the dough pieces to recover.
3 Pin out the dough pieces to a flat round shape.
4 Place the dough pieces onto a warm silicone lined tray.
5 Prove at 38–40°C (100–104°F) in humid conditions.
6 Bake at 232°C (450°F) for 4–5 minutes.
7 Remove the tray from the oven and quickly turn over each dough piece and return to the oven to complete the baking process.

Note: Ensure the dough pieces are baked sufficiently prior to turning to maintain the volume and character of a Barm Cake.

8 After baking, remove the Barm Cakes from the tray immediately and place onto a cooling wire.

CREAM BUNS (COOKIES), DEVON SPLITS AND PARISIAN BUNS

Note: This recipe is also suitable for the production of Iced Fingers, Teacakes, Chelsea Buns, Currant Buns, Butter Buns, Tea Loaf, Bath Buns and Belgian Buns.

Ingredients

Kilo	Gram	%	Ingredients	lb	oz
10	000	100.00	bread flour	22	0.00
	100	1.00	salt		3.50
	400	4.00	skimmed milk powder		14.25
	100	1.00	dough conditioner		3.50
1	000	10.00	shortening	2	3.75
1	000	10.00	sugar	2	3.75
1	000	10.00	egg	2	3.75
	900	9.00	yeast	2	0.00
4	900	49.00	cold water	10	15.00
19	400		Gross weight	42	15.50
18	915		Net weight	41	14.00

Production Points

Required watt hours	**213**
Dough temperature	**29–31°C (85–88°F)**
Bulk Fermentation Time	**Nil**
Knock back	**N/A**
Scaling weight:	
Cream Buns (Cookies)	**60 g (2 oz)**
Parisian buns	**60 g (2 oz)**
Devon Split	**180 g (6.50 oz)**
Yield	**315 at 60 g (2 oz)**
	105 at 180 g (6.50 oz)
Baking temperature	**232°C (450°F)**
Baking time	**10–15 mins**

Mixing method

1 Place the ingredients into the mixing chamber in the following order:
- cold water and egg
- flour, salt, skimmed milk powder, dough conditioner and sugar
- shortening and yeast.

2 Mix to the required watt hour input.
3 The dough is now ready to be scaled and processed.

Processing method

1 Scale 315 at 60 g (2 oz) or 105 at 180 g (6.50 oz) and mould round.
2 Rest for 8–10 minutes to allow the dough pieces to recover.
3 Re-mould the dough pieces as described below.
- *Cream Buns (Cookies)* re-mould the dough piece into a ball shape.
- *Devon Splits* re-mould the dough piece to a long baton shape.
- *Parisian Buns* Roll the dough piece to a long thin strand measuring approximately 16 cm (6.50") in length. Form the shape of a number six, and from this position, complete a single knot.

4 Place the dough pieces onto a warm greased tray.
5 Prove at 38–40°C (100–104°F) in humid conditions.
6 Bake at 232°C (450°F) for 10–15 minutes.
7 After baking remove the items from the tray and place on a cooling wire.

Finishing method

CREAM BUNS (COOKIES)
- Split the bun horizontally through the centre without cutting all the way through.
- Pipe a small amount of jam onto the base of the bun.

- Fill the bun with a piped rosette of cream.
- Dredge the bun top with icing sugar.

DEVON SPLIT

- Split the baton vertically down the side without cutting all the way through.
- Pipe a line of jam down the middle.
- Fill the baton with a piped rope of cream.
- Dredge the baton with icing sugar.

PARISIAN BUNS

- Dip the bun into white fondant.
- Sprinkle the bun with roasted flaked almonds before the fondant sets.

GERM MEAL BREAD

Ingredients

Kilo	Gram	%	Ingredients	lb	oz
10	000	100.00	germ meal flour	22	0.00
	100	1.00	dough conditioner		3.50
	125	1.25	shortening		4.50
	310	3.10	yeast		11.00
6	750	67.50	cold water	15	0.00
17	285		Gross weight	38	3.00
16	852		Net weight	37	4.00

Production Points

Dough temperature	**30°C (86°F)**
Bulk Fermentation Time	**Nil**
Knock back	**N/A**
Scaling weight	**450 g (1 lb)**
Yield	**37**
Baking temperature	**237°C (458°F)**
Baking time	**25 mins**

Mixing method

1. Place the ingredients into the mixing chamber in the following order:
   - cold water
   - flour and dough conditioner
   - shortening and yeast.
2. Mix to the required watt hour input.
3. The dough is now ready to be scaled and processed.

Processing method

1. Scale 37 at 450 g (1 lb) and mould round.
2. Rest for 8–10 minutes to allow the dough pieces to recover.
3. Re-mould the dough pieces and form them into a cylinder shape.
4. Place the dough pieces into warm, greased small bread tins.
5. Prove at 38–40°C (100–104°F) in humid conditions.
6. Bake at 237°C (458°F) for 25 minutes.
7. After baking, remove the bread from the tins immediately and place onto a cooling wire.

CHAPTER *six*

The Activated Dough Development Process

The Activated Dough Development process (ADD) was developed during the 1960s, but was not available to the UK baker until the 1970s. This followed amendments to the Bread and Flour (Amendment) Regulations 1972 which allowed the use of L-Cysteine up to 75 ppm of the flour weight.

Since its introduction, this process has increased in popularity among bakers from all sectors of the industry. There are two reasons why this process is favoured by bakers:

1. No special mixing machine is required.
2. Bulk Fermentation Time is eliminated.

MIXING METHOD

This is an outline of the mixing method. Each recipe contains a more detailed description of the method.

1 Sieve together the dry ingredients.
2 Add the fat content and rub through the dry ingredients.
3 Disperse the yeast into tempered water and add to the above ingredients.
4 Form a dough.
5 Check consistency.
6 Mix until a smooth and clear dough is obtained and the gluten forming proteins are fully developed.
7 The dough is now ready to be scaled and processed.

Changes which occur during mixing

When the chemical L-Cysteine is used in conjunction with an oxidising agent and fat to make a dough, rapid dough development takes place. At the end of the mixing time, all the necessary changes have taken place which normally occur during long periods of fermentation. L-Cysteine is included in general purpose dough conditioners with other substances which also accelerate the fermentation process.

Main points to be observed

To ensure that doughs made by the ADD process are fully developed, the following points must be observed:

1 Choose a dough conditioner which is suitable for your needs.
2 The amount of dough conditioner you need to use, varies according to the type of conditioner. Generally, use dough conditioners at a rate of 1–3% of the flour weight. It is advisable to follow the manufacturers' recommendations. Furthermore, the baker must know how much ascorbic acid is present in the flour and the dough conditioner, to ensure that the level does not exceed 200 ppm of the flour weight.
3 Allow the appropriate mixing time to ensure the dough is fully developed.
4 Obtain a dough temperature between 27–30°C (81–86°F).

Processing

After mixing, doughs made by ADD must be processed immediately. They must reach the final prover no more than 30 minutes after being removed from the mixing machine.

ADVANTAGES AND DISADVANTAGES

Advantages

1 A special mixer is not required. The majority of mixing machines within the industry are suitable for this process.
2 There are no fermentation losses, so that an increased yield is obtained.
3 The mixing method is completed in one operation.
4 The elimination of a bulk fermentation period:
 - saves production time
 - removes the need for fermentation space
 - saves labour time, for example knock back.
5 Consistent results are obtained.
6 Allows for the organisation of sociable working hours, for example, a later start in the morning.

Disadvantages

1 There is some loss of flavour because the dough does not have a fermentation period.
2 Dough conditioners are an added expense, therefore costs are increased.

OVEN CHART

Product	Baking temperature in °C (°F)	Baking time in minutes	Additional control procedures
Sandwich Bread	232 (450)	35–40	Open damper for final 10 mins
Tinned Coburgs	232 (450)	25	" " " "
Sm Tinned Brown Coburgs	232 (450)	25	" " " "
Lge Tinned Brown Coburgs	232 (450)	35	" " " "
Small Granary	232 (450)	25	Use steam during first 10 mins then release
Lge Granary	232 (450)	35	" " " " " " "
Sm Country Cereal Bread	232 (450)	25	Open damper for final 10 mins
Lge Country Cereal Bread	232 (450)	35	" " " "
Sm Coburgs	232 (450)	25	Use steam during first 10 mins then release
Lge Coburgs	232 (450)	30–35	" " " " " " "
French Sticks	245 (470)	25	" " " " " " "
Baguettes	245 (470)	20	" " " " " " "
Petit Pain	245 (470)	15	" " " " " " "
Tiger Bread	232 (450)	25	" " " " " " "
Divider Buns	245 (470)	10	Open damper for final 5 mins
Bridge Rolls	245 (470)	10	" " " "
Milk Bread Rolls	226 (440)	10–15	" " " "
Vienna Rolls	240–250 (464–482)	10–15	Use steam during first 10 mins then release
Brown Fancy Rolls	250 (482)	10–12	Open damper for final 5 mins
Chelsea Buns	232 (450)	10–15	" " " "
Currant Buns	232 (450)	10–15	" " " "
Butter Buns	232 (450)	10–15	" " " "
Doughnuts	190 (374)	2–4	None
Croissants	238 (460)	12–15	Open damper for final 5 mins
Danish Pastries	238 (460)	10–15	" " " "
Farls	226 (440)	20–25	" " " 10 mins

RECIPES USING THE ACTIVATED DOUGH DEVELOPMENT PROCESS

SANDWICH BREAD AND TIN COBURGS

Ingredients

Kilo	Gram	%	Ingredients	lb	oz
1	100	100.00	bread flour	2	7.00
	25	2.27	salt		1.00
	20	1.82	skimmed milk powder		0.75
	10	0.90	dough conditioner		0.50
	25	2.27	shortening		1.00
	40	3.60	yeast		1.50
	630	57.20	water	1	6.50
1	850		Gross weight	4	2.25
1	803		Net weight	4	0.75

Production Points

Dough temperature	**26°C (79°F)**
Bulk Fermentation Time	**Nil**
Knock back	**N/A**
Scaling weight:	
small	**450 g (1 lb)**
large	**900 g (2 lb)**
Yield:	
small	**4**
large	**2**
Baking temperature	**232°C (450°F)**
Baking time:	
small	**25 mins**
large	**35–40 mins**

Note: This recipe is also suitable for the production of Small White Farmhouse, Large White, Multi-Piece and Long Cut Tin.

Mixing method

1 Sieve together the flour, salt, skimmed milk powder and dough conditioner.
2 Using a spiral or conventional mixer, add the shortening and rub through the dry ingredients on slow speed.
3 Disperse the yeast into tempered water and add to the above ingredients.
4 Using a spiral or conventional mixer, mix on slow speed for 2 minutes.
5 Check for extremes in consistency and adjust as necessary.
6 To complete the mixing method follow the appropriate mixing process:
- spiral mixer – mix on fast speed for 6–8 minutes
- conventional mixer – mix on speed 1 for 20 minutes, or speed 2 for 10 minutes.

7 After the completion of the mixing method, the dough is ready to be scaled and processed.

Processing methods

SANDWICH BREAD

1 Scale 2 at 900 g (2 lb) and mould round.
2 Rest for 8–10 minutes to allow the dough pieces to recover.
3 Re-mould the dough pieces and form them into a cylinder shape.
4 Place the dough pieces into warm, greased, sandwich bread tins.
5 Prove at 38–40°C (100–104°F) in humid conditions until the dough piece is within 2.5 cm (1") from the top of the tin.
6 After proving place and secure the tin lids.
7 Bake at 232°C (450°F) for 35–40 minutes.
8 After baking, remove the bread from the tins immediately and place on a cooling wire.

COBURGS

1 Scale 4 at 450 g (1 lb) and mould round.

2 Rest for 8–10 minutes to allow the dough pieces to recover.
3 Re-mould the dough pieces and form them into a ball shape.
4 Place the dough pieces into warm, greased, coburg tins.
5 Prove at 38–40°C (100–104°F) in humid conditions.
6 After three-quarters of the final proof, cut a cross 1 cm (0.5") deep on the top of the dough piece.
7 Return the dough pieces to the final prover for the remaining proving time.
8 Bake at 232°C (450°F) for 25 minutes.
9 After baking, remove the Coburgs from the tins immediately and place onto a cooling wire.

TINNED BROWN COBURGS

Ingredients

Kilo	Gram	%	Ingredients	lb	oz
1	100	100.00	brown flour	2	7.00
	25	2.27	salt		1.00
	10	0.90	skimmed milk powder		0.50
	10	0.90	dough conditioner		0.50
	25	2.27	shortening		1.00
	40	3.63	yeast		1.50
	660	60.00	water	1	7.50
1	870		Gross weight	4	3.00
1	823		Net weight	4	1.25

Production Points

Dough temperature	**26°C (79°F)**
Bulk Fermentation Time	**Nil**
Knock back	**N/A**
Scaling weight:	
small	**450 g (1 lb)**
large	**900 g (2 lb)**

Mixing method

1 Using a coarse sieve, sieve together the flour, salt, skimmed milk powder and dough conditioner.
2 Using a spiral or conventional mixer, add the shortening and rub through the dry ingredients on slow speed.
3 Disperse the yeast into tempered water and add to the above ingredients.
4 Using a spiral or conventional mixer, mix on slow speed for 2 minutes.
5 Check for extremes in consistency and adjust as necessary.
6 To complete the mixing method, follow the appropriate mixing process:
- spiral mixer – mix on fast speed for 6–8 minutes
- conventional mixer – mix on speed 1 for 20 minutes, or speed 2 for 10 minutes.

7 After the completion of the mixing method, the dough is ready to be scaled and processed.

Processing method

1 Scale 4 at 450 g (1 lb) or 2 at 900 g (2 lb) and mould round.
2 Rest for 8–10 minutes to allow the dough pieces to recover.
3 Re-mould the dough pieces into a ball shape.

Yield:	
small	**4**
large	**2**
Baking temperature	**232°C (450°F)**
Baking time:	
small	**25 mins**
large	**35–40 mins**

Note: This recipe is also suitable for the production of Small Brown Tin Bread, Brown Farmhouse and Large Brown Bread.

4 Place the dough pieces into warm, greased coburg tins.
5 Prove at 38–40°C (100–104°F) in humid conditions.
6 After three-quarters of the final proof, cut a cross 1 cm (0.5") deep on the top of the dough piece.
7 Return the dough pieces to the final prover for the remaining proving time.
8 Bake at 232°C (450°F) for:
small – 25 minutes
large – 35–40 minutes
Use steam in the oven chamber for the first 10 minutes of the baking process.
9 After baking, remove the Coburgs from the tins immediately and place onto a cooling wire.

GRANARY BREAD

Ingredients

Kilo	Gram	%	Ingredients	lb	oz
1	100	100.00	granary flour	2	7.00
	30	2.70	salt		1.00
	10	0.90	dough conditioner		0.25
	25	2.27	shortening		1.00
	40	3.60	yeast		1.50
	645	58.60	water	1	7.00
1	850		Gross weight	4	1.75
1	803		Net weight	4	0.25

Production Points

Dough temperature	**26°C (79°F)**
Bulk Fermentation Time	**Nil**
Knock back	**N/A**
Scaling weight:	
small	**450 g (1 lb)**
large	**900 g (2 lb)**
Yield:	
small	**4**
large	**2**
Baking temperature	**232°C (450°F)**
Baking time:	
small	**25 mins**
large	**35–40 mins**

Mixing method

1 Using a coarse sieve, sieve together the flour, salt and dough conditioner.
2 Add the shortening and rub through the dry ingredients on slow speed.
3 Disperse the yeast into tempered water and add to the above ingredients.
4 Using a spiral or conventional mixer, mix on slow speed for 2 minutes.
5 Check for extremes in consistency and adjust as necessary.
6 To complete the mixing method, follow the appropriate mixing process.
- spiral mixer – mix on fast speed for 6–8 minutes
- conventional mixer – mix on speed 1 for 20 minutes, or speed 2 for 10 minutes.

7 After the completion of the mixing method, the dough is ready to be scaled and processed.

Processing method

1 Scale 4 at 450 g (1 lb) or 2 at 900 g (2 lb) and mould round.
2 Rest for 8–10 minutes to allow the dough pieces to recover.
3 Re-mould the dough pieces into a cylinder shape.
4 Place the dough pieces into warm, greased bread tins.

5 Prove at 38–40°C (100–104°F) in humid conditions.
6 Bake at 232°C (450°F) for:
 small – 25 minutes
 large – 35–40 minutes
 Use steam in the oven chamber for the first 10 minutes of the baking process.
7 After baking, remove the granary bread from the tins immediately and place onto a cooling wire.

COUNTRY CEREAL BREAD

Ingredients

Kilo	Gram	%	Ingredients	lb	oz
1	100	100.00	multi grain flour	2	7.00
	25	2.27	salt		1.00
	10	0.90	dough conditioner		0.50
	20	1.82	shortening		0.75
	40	3.63	yeast		1.50
	660	60.00	water	1	7.50
1	855		Gross weight	4	2.25
1	808		Net weight	4	0.75

Production Points

Dough temperature	**26°C (79°F)**
Bulk Fermentation Time	**Nil**
Knock back	**N/A**
Scaling weight:	
small	**450 g (1 lb)**
large	**900 g (2 lb)**
Yield:	
small	**4**
large	**2**
Baking temperature	**232°C (450°F)**
Baking time:	
small	**25 mins**
large	**35–40 mins**

Mixing method

1 Using a coarse sieve, sieve together the flour, salt and dough conditioner.
2 Using a spiral or conventional mixer, add the shortening and rub through the dry ingredients on slow speed.
3 Disperse the yeast into tempered water and add to the above ingredients.
4 Using a spiral or conventional mixer, mix on slow speed for 2 minutes.
5 Check for extremes in consistency and adjust as necessary.
6 To complete the mixing method follow the appropriate mixing process.
 - spiral mixer – mix on fast speed for 6–8 minutes
 - conventional mixer – mix on speed 1 for 20 minutes, or speed 2 for 10 minutes.
7 After the completion of the mixing method, the dough is ready to be scaled and processed.

Processing method

1 Scale 4 at 450 g (1 lb) or 2 at 900 g (2 lb) and mould round.
2 Rest for 8–10 minutes to allow the dough pieces to recover.
3 Re-mould the dough pieces into a cylinder shape.
4 Place the dough pieces into warm, greased bread tins.
5 Prove at 38–40°C (100–104°F) in humid conditions.
6 Bake at 232°C (450°F) for:
 small – 25 minutes
 large – 35–40 minutes.
7 After baking, remove the bread from the tins immediately and place onto a cooling wire.

COBURGS

Ingredients

Kilo	Gram	%	Ingredients	lb	oz
1	100	100.00	bread flour	2	7.00
	25	2.27	salt		1.00
	20	1.82	skimmed milk powder		0.75
	10	0.90	dough conditioner		0.50
	30	2.72	shortening		1.00
	45	4.00	yeast		1.50
	615	56.00	water	1	5.50
1	845		Gross weight	4	1.25
1	800		Net weight	3	15.75

Production Points

Dough temperature	**27°C (81°F)**
Bulk Fermentation Time	**Nil**
Knock back	**N/A**
Scaling weight:	
small	**450 g (1 lb)**
large	**900 g (2 lb)**
Yield:	
small	**4**
large	**2**
Baking temperature	**232°C (450°F)**
Baking time:	
small	**25 mins**
large	**30–35 mins**

Note: This recipe is also suitable for the production of Cottage Bread, Danish Bread and Bloomers.

Mixing method

1. Sieve together the flour, salt, skimmed milk powder and dough conditioner.
2. Using a spiral or conventional mixer, add the shortening and rub through the dry ingredients on slow speed.
3. Disperse the yeast into tempered water and add to the above ingredients.
4. Using a spiral or conventional mixer, mix on slow speed for 2 minutes.
5. Check for extremes in consistency and adjust as necessary.
6. To complete the mixing method follow the appropriate mixing process.
   - spiral mixer – mix on fast speed for 6–8 minutes
   - conventional mixer – mix on speed 1 for 20 minutes or speed 2 for 10 minutes.
7. After the completion of the mixing method the dough is ready to be scaled and processed.

Coburg

Processing method

1 Scale 4 at 450 g (1 lb) or 2 at 900 g (2 lb) and mould round.
2 Rest for 8–10 minutes to allow the dough pieces to recover.
3 Re-mould the dough pieces into a ball shape.
4 Place the dough pieces onto a warm, greased tray. A perforated tray may be used if desired.
5 Prove at 38–40°C (100–104°F) in humid conditions.
6 After three-quarters of the final proof, cut a cross, 1 cm (0.5") deep on the top of the dough piece.
7 Return the dough pieces to the final prover for the remaining proving time.
8 Bake at 232°C (450°F) for:
   small – 25 minutes
   large – 35 minutes
   Use steam in the oven chamber for the first 10 minutes of the baking process.
9 After baking, remove the coburgs from the tray immediately and place on a cooling wire.

FRENCH BREADS

Ingredients

Kilo	Gram	%	Ingredients	lb	oz
1	000	100.00	French bread flour	2	3.50
	20	2.00	salt		0.75
	10	1.00	dough conditioner		0.50
	25	2.50	yeast		0.75
	650	65.00	water	1	7.25
1	705		Gross weight	3	12.50
1	662		Net weight	3	11.50

Mixing method

1 Sieve together the flour, salt and dough conditioner.
2 Disperse the yeast into tempered water and add to the above ingredients.
3 Using a spiral or conventional mixer, mix on slow speed for 2 minutes.
4 Check for extremes in consistency and adjust as necessary.
5 To complete the mixing method follow the appropriate mixing process.
   - spiral mixer – mix on fast speed for 6–8 minutes
   - conventional mixer – mix on speed 1 for 20 minutes or speed 2 for 10 minutes.
6 After the completion of the mixing method the dough is ready to be scaled and processed.

Processing methods

FRENCH STICKS

1 Scale 3 at 525 g (1 lb 2.75 oz) and mould round.

Figure 9 Hold the blade parallel to the length of the dough piece, and cut just under the surface

Production Points	
Dough temperature	**24°C (75°F)**
Bulk Fermentation Time	**Nil**
Knock back	**N/A**
Scaling weight:	
French Sticks	**525 g (1 lb 2.75 oz)**
Baguette	**325 g (11.5 oz)**
Petit Pain	**70 g (2.5 oz)**
Yield:	
French Sticks	**3**
Baguette	**5**
Petit Pain	**24**
Baking temperature	**245°C (470°F)**
Baking time:	
French Sticks	**25 mins**
Baguette	**20 mins**
Petit Pain	**15 mins**

2 Rest for 8–10 minutes to allow the dough pieces to recover.
3 Roll the dough piece into a long stick shape, 65 cm (26") long.
4 Place the dough pieces onto a lightly oiled French Stick tray.
5 Prove at 30–32°C (86–89°F) in humid conditions for 45–60 minutes.
6 After the final proof, make 5 slanting cuts across the top of the dough piece as illustrated in Figure 9.
7 Bake at 245°C (470°F) using steam. Bake for approximately 25 minutes.

Note: To obtain the appropriate characteristics of French Breads, steam should be used in the following sequence:

- prior to loading the oven, inject steam for 3 minutes
- continue to inject steam while loading the oven
- after 8–10 minutes, the steam must be released from the oven chamber. However, the method of steaming will depend upon the type of oven. Some ovens do not have the capacity to inject steam for this period of time or retain steam during setting.

Complete the baking process in a dry atmosphere to obtain a thin, glossy, crisp crust.

8 After baking, remove the French Sticks from the tray immediately and place on a cooling wire.

BAGUETTES

1 Scale 5 at 325 g (11.5 oz) and mould round.
2 Now follow stages 2, 3, 4 and 5 of French Sticks. At stage 6, make 7 slanting cuts across the top of the dough piece.
3 Bake at 245°C (470°F) using steam. Bake for approximately 20 minutes. Follow the sequence for using steam, baking and cooling techniques as for French Sticks.

PETIT PAIN

1 Scale 24 at 70 g (2.5 oz) and mould round.
2 Rest for 8–10 minutes to allow the dough pieces to recover.
3 Roll the dough pieces into a baton shape.

4 Place the dough pieces onto a lightly oiled French Stick tray.
5 Prove at 30–32°C (86–89°F) in humid conditions.
6 After the final proof, make a cut down the centre of the dough piece.
7 Bake at 245°C (470°F) using steam. Bake for approximately 15 minutes. Follow the sequence for using steam, baking and cooling techniques as for French Sticks.

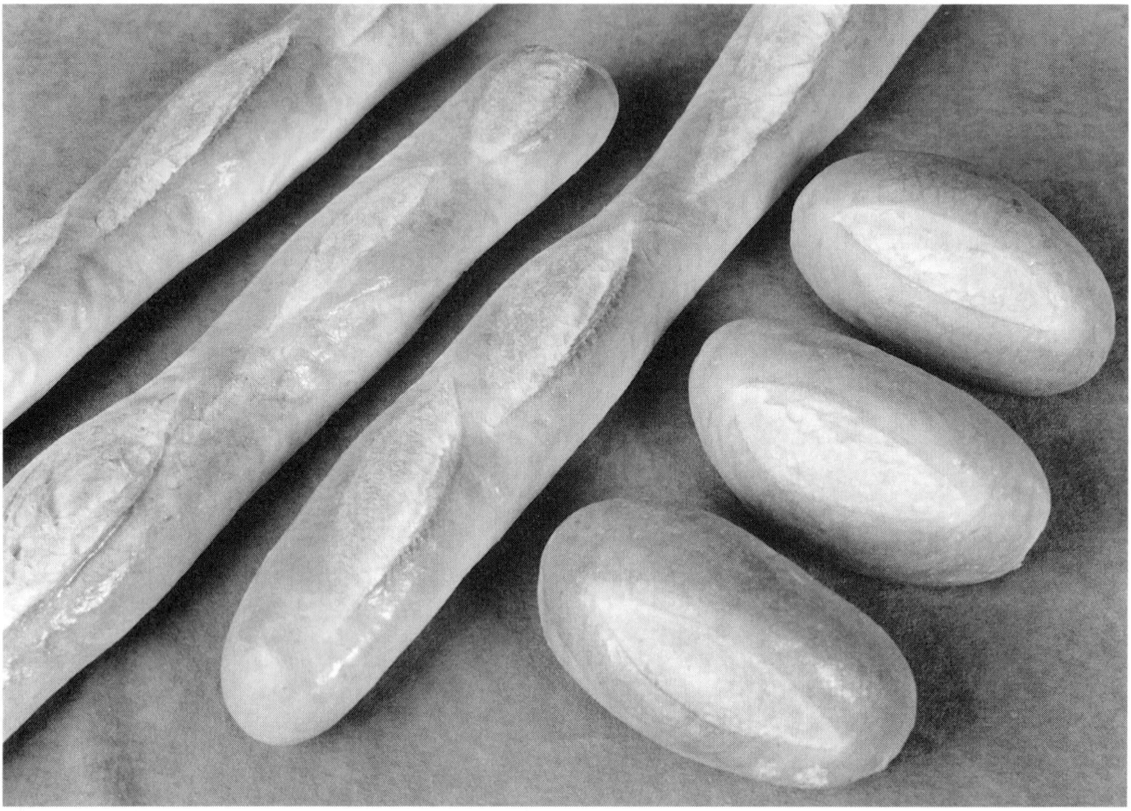

French stick and petit pain

TIGER BREAD

Ingredients

Kilo	Gram	%	Ingredients	lb	oz
1	000	100.00	bread flour	2	3.50
	20	2.00	salt		0.75
	10	1.00	skimmed milk powder		0.25
	10	1.00	dough conditioner		0.25
	30	3.00	shortening		1.00
	35	3.50	yeast		1.25
	615	61.50	water	1	6.00
1	720		Gross weight	3	13.00
1	677		Net weight	3	11.50

Production Points

Dough temperature	**27°C (81°F)**
Bulk Fermentation Time	**Nil**
Knock back	**N/A**
Scaling weight	**420 g (15 oz)**
Yield	**4**
Baking temperature	**232°C (450°F)**
Baking time	**25 mins**

Mixing method

1 Sieve together the flour, salt, skimmed milk powder and dough conditioner.
2 Using a spiral or conventional mixer, add the shortening and rub through the dry ingredients on slow speed.
3 Disperse the yeast into tempered water and add to the above ingredients.
4 Using a spiral or conventional mixer, mix on slow speed for 2 minutes.
5 Check for extremes in consistency and adjust as necessary.
6 To complete the mixing method follow the appropriate mixing process.
- spiral mixer – mix on fast speed for 6–8 minutes
- conventional mixer – mix on speed 1 for 20 minutes or speed 2 for 10 minutes.

7 After the completion of the mixing method, the dough is ready to be scaled and processed.

Tiger Bread

Processing method

1 Scale 4 at 420 g (15 oz) and mould round.
2 Rest for 8–10 minutes to allow the dough pieces to recover.
3 Re-mould the dough pieces into a long baton shape.
4 Place the dough pieces onto a warm, greased tray.

5 Prove at 38–40°C (100–104°F) in humid conditions.
6 After the final proof, brush 30 g of Tiger Paste (see below) onto the top of each dough piece.
7 Bake at 232°C (450°F) for 25 minutes. Use steam in the oven chamber for the first 10 minutes of the baking process.
8 After baking, remove the Tiger Bread from the tray and place on a cooling wire.

TIGER PASTE

Ingredients

Kilo	Gram	%	Ingredients	lb	oz
	15	3.00	yeast		0.50
	500	100.00	water at 38°C	1	1.75
	15	3.00	sugar		0.50
	30	6.00	vegetable oil		1.00
	500	100.00	ground rice	1	1.75
1	060		Gross weight	2	5.50
1	033		Net weight	2	4.50

Mixing method

1 Disperse the yeast into tempered water.
2 Add the sugar and dissolve.
3 Add the vegetable oil and disperse.
4 Add the ground rice and mix to a paste.
5 Allow the paste to ferment for 30 minutes.
6 Stir the paste to eliminate the carbon dioxide gas.

The paste is now ready to use.

Note: This paste confers an interesting decorative surface which cracks and colours during the baking process.

DIVIDER BUNS AND BRIDGE ROLLS

Ingredients

Kilo	Gram	%	Ingredients	lb	oz
1	300	100.00	bread flour	2	14.50
	25	2.00	salt		1.00
	25	2.00	skimmed milk powder		1.00
	15	1.15	dough conditioner		0.50
	50	3.85	shortening		1.75
	60	4.60	yeast		2.00
	760	58.50	water	1	11.25
2	235		Gross weight	5	0.00
2	179		Net weight	4	14.00

Mixing method

1 Sieve together the flour, salt, skimmed milk powder and dough conditioner.
2 Using a spiral or conventional mixer, add the shortening and rub through the dry ingredients on slow speed.
3 Disperse the yeast into tempered water and add to the above ingredients.
4 Using a spiral or conventional mixer, mix on slow speed for 2 minutes.
5 Check for extremes in consistency and adjust as necessary.
6 To complete the mixing method follow the appropriate mixing process.
- spiral mixer – mix on fast speed for 6–8 minutes
- conventional mixer – mix on speed 1 for 20 minutes or speed 2 for 10 minutes.

7 After the completion of the mixing method, the dough is ready to be scaled and processed.

Production Points

Dough temperature	**27°C (81°F)**
Bulk Fermentation Time	**Nil**
Knock back	**N/A**
Scaling weight	**30 g (1 oz)**
Yield	**72**
Baking temperature	**245°C (470°F)**
Baking time	**10 mins**

Note: This recipe is also suitable for the production of Bread Rolls, Scotch Baps, Stotties, Soft Fancy Rolls, Finger Rolls and Burger Buns.

Processing methods

DIVIDER BUNS

1 Scale 2 at 1080 g (2 lb 6.5 oz) and mould round.
2 Rest for 8–10 minutes to allow the dough pieces to recover.
3 Pin out the dough piece to fit inside a hand divider pan. The dough piece should be floured lightly and placed upside down within the divider pan.

Note: This is to ensure the smooth side of the dough pieces are upright when they are tipped out of the divider pan.

4 Position the divider pan and operate the hand divider in the normal manner to cut through and divide the dough piece into 36 equal pieces.
5 Tip the dough pieces from the divider pan and place them onto a warm, greased tray.
6 Prove at 38–40°C (100–104°F) in humid conditions.
7 Bake at 245°C (470°F) for 10 minutes.
8 After baking, remove the Divider Buns from the tray and place onto a cooling wire.

BRIDGE ROLLS

1 Scale 72 at 30 g (1 oz) and mould round.

Note: For quicker scaling, scale 36 at 60 g (2 oz), split the dough piece as evenly as possible and mould round.

2 Rest for 8–10 minutes to allow the dough pieces to recover.
3 Re-mould the dough pieces into a short baton shape.
4 Place the dough pieces onto a warm, greased tray.
5 Prove at 38–40°C (100–104°F) in humid conditions.
6 Bake at 245°C (470°F) for 10 minutes.
7 After baking, remove the Bridge Rolls from the tray and place onto a cooling wire.

MILK BREAD ROLLS

Ingredients

Kilo	Gram	%	Ingredients	lb	oz
1	000	100.00	bread flour	2	3.50
	25	2.50	salt		1.00
	50	5.00	skimmed milk powder		1.75
	10	1.00	dough conditioner		0.50
	35	3.50	butter		1.25
	40	4.00	yeast		1.50
	580	58.00	water	1	4.75
1	740		Gross weight	3	14.25
1	696		Net weight	3	12.75

Production Points

Dough temperature	**26°C (79°F)**
Bulk Fermentation Time	**Nil**
Knock back	**N/A**
Scaling weight	**55 g (2 oz)**
Yield	**30**
Baking temperature	**226°C (440°F)**
Baking time	**10–15 mins**

Note: This recipe is also suitable for the production of Tin and Plaited Milk Bread.

Mixing method

1 Sieve together the flour, salt, skimmed milk powder and dough conditioner.
2 Using a spiral or conventional mixer, add the butter and rub through the dry ingredients on slow speed.
3 Disperse the yeast into tempered water and add to the above ingredients.
4 Using a spiral or conventional mixer, mix on slow speed for 2 minutes.
5 Check for extremes in consistency and adjust as necessary.
6 To complete the mixing method follow the appropriate mixing process.
- spiral mixer – mix on fast speed for 6–8 minutes
- conventional mixer – mix on speed 1 for 20 minutes or speed 2 for 10 minutes.

7 After the completion of the mixing method, the dough is ready to be scaled and processed.

Processing method

1 Scale 30 at 55 g (2 oz) and mould round.
2 Rest for 8–10 minutes to allow the dough pieces to recover.
3 Re-mould the dough pieces and form them into one of the following shapes:

C-Shaped Roll

i Roll the dough piece to a long thin strand measuring approximately 20 cm (8").
ii Roll both ends into the centre to form the shape of the letter C.

Cottage Roll

i This shape is obtained by pressing and rolling the round dough piece with the middle finger. This action will form a small and large piece of dough.
ii Now assemble and secure into the shape of a small cottage loaf.
iii Notch the side of the cottage roll with a sharp knife.

Baton

i Roll the dough piece to a baton shape.
ii Notch the top of the dough piece five times with a sharp knife.

4 Place the dough pieces onto a warm, greased tray.
5 Prove at 38–40°C (100–104°F) in humid conditions.
6 Bake at 226°C (440°F) for 10–15 minutes.
7 After baking remove the rolls from the tray immediately and place on a cooling wire.

Note:
- The appearance of these rolls can be enhanced by the use of eggwash and various seeds.
- The shapes given for Soft Fancy Rolls (p. 92) are also suitable for Milk Bread Rolls.

VIENNA ROLLS

Ingredients

Kilo	Gram	%	Ingredients	lb	oz
1	000	100.00	strong bread flour	2	3.50
	30	3.00	salt		1.00
	25	2.50	skimmed milk powder		1.00
	5	0.50	high diastatic malt flour		0.25
	10	1.00	dough conditioner		0.50
	15	1.50	shortening		0.50
	40	4.00	yeast		1.50
	600	60.00	water	1	5.00
1	725		Gross weight	3	13.25
1	681		Net weight	3	11.75

Production Points

Dough temperature	**24°C (75°F)**
Bulk Fermentation Time	**Nil**
Knock back	**N/A**
Scaling weight	**50 g (1.75 oz)**
Yield	**33**
Baking temperature	**240–250°C (464–482°F)**
Baking time	**10–15 mins**

Note: This recipe is also suitable for Vienna Bread.

Mixing method

1 Sieve together the flour, salt, skimmed milk powder, dough conditioner and high diastatic malt flour.
2 Using a spiral or conventional mixer, add the shortening and rub through the dry ingredients on slow speed.
3 Disperse the yeast into tempered water and add to the above ingredients.
4 Using a spiral or conventional mixer, mix on slow speed for 2 minutes.
5 Check for extremes in consistency and adjust as necessary.
6 To complete the mixing method follow the appropriate mixing process.
- spiral mixer – mix on fast speed for 6–8 minutes
- conventional mixer – mix on speed 1 for 20 minutes or speed 2 for 10 minutes.

7 After the completion of the mixing method, the dough is ready to be scaled and processed.

Processing method

1 Scale 33 at 50 g (1.75 oz) and mould round.
2 Rest for 8–10 minutes to allow the dough pieces to recover.
3 Re-mould the dough pieces and form them into one of the following shapes.

Plain Roll

Re-mould the dough piece into a ball shape.

Split Top Roll

i Re-mould the dough piece into a ball shape.

Vienna Rolls

Note: The processing methods for the Vienna Rolls pictured here can be found in the recipe for Soft Fancy Rolls, on p. 92.

ii Using a sharp knife, make a single cut across the top of the dough piece.

Kaiser

i Pin the dough piece to a flat round shape.

ii Now make five folds. Each fold is made by bringing a section of the edge to the centre of the dough piece.

iii Secure each section in the centre of the dough piece with the thumb.

Note: This roll can be produced very quickly using a Kaiser tool.

Crescent

i Pin out the dough very thinly into a 'V' shape.

ii Hold the pointed end firmly while rolling up the dough piece from the wide end.

iii Keep the dough piece tight during the rolling process, to ensure that a good shape is obtained.

iv Now form the shape of a crescent.

4 Place the dough pieces onto a warm, greased tray.

5 Prove at 38–40°C (100–104°F) in humid conditions.

6 Bake at 240–250°C (464–482°F) for 10–15 minutes.

Note: To obtain the appropriate characteristics of Vienna Rolls, steam should be used in the following sequence:

- prior to loading the oven, inject steam for 3 minutes
- continue to inject steam while loading the oven
- after 8–10 minutes, the steam must be released from the oven chamber. However, the method of steaming will depend upon the type of oven. Some ovens do not have the capacity to inject steam for this period of time or retain steam during setting.
- complete the baking process in a dry atmosphere to obtain a thin, glossy crisp crust.

7 After baking, remove the rolls from the tray and place them onto a cooling wire.

BROWN FANCY ROLLS

Ingredients

Kilo	Gram	%	Ingredients	lb	oz
1	000	100.00	brown flour	2	3.50
	25	2.50	salt		1.00
	20	2.00	skimmed milk powder		0.75
	10	1.00	dough conditioner		0.50
	50	5.00	shortening		1.75
	35	3.50	yeast		1.25
	600	60.00	water	1	5.50
1	740		Gross weight	3	14.25
1	696		Net weight	3	12.75

Production Points

Dough temperature	**26°C (79°F)**
Bulk Fermentation Time	**Nil**
Knock back	**N/A**
Scaling weight	**50 g (1.75 oz)**
Yield	**33**
Baking temperature	**250°C (482°F)**
Baking time	**10–12 mins**

Note: This recipe is also suitable for the production of Brown Rolls.

Brown Fancy Rolls

Mixing method

1 Using a coarse sieve, sieve together the flour, salt, skimmed milk powder and dough conditioner.
2 Using a spiral or conventional mixer, add the shortening and rub through the dry ingredients on slow speed.
3 Disperse the yeast into tempered water and add to the above ingredients.
4 Using a spiral or conventional mixer, mix on slow speed for 2 minutes.
5 Check for extremes in consistency and adjust as necessary.
6 To complete the mixing method follow the appropriate mixing process.
- spiral mixer – mix on fast speed for 6–8 minutes
- conventional mixer – mix on speed 1 for 20 minutes or speed 2 for 10 minutes.

7 After the completion of the mixing method, the dough is ready to be scaled and processed.

Processing methods

1 Scale 33 at 50 g (1.75 oz) and mould round.
2 Rest for 8–10 minutes to allow the dough pieces to recover.
3 Re-mould the dough pieces and form them into one of the following shapes.

Bran Roll

i Slightly flatten the dough piece.
ii Moisten the top surface with water.
iii Dip the dough piece into bran flakes.

Cracked Wheat Roll

Using cracked wheat, follow stages **i**, **ii** and **iii** of Bran Rolls.

Finger Roll

i Roll the dough piece to 10 cm (4") long.
ii Moisten the top surface with water.
iii Dip into bran flakes or cracked wheat.

Note: The shapes given for Soft Fancy Rolls (p. 92) and Milk Bread Rolls (p. 132) are also suitable for Brown Fancy Rolls.

4 Place the dough pieces onto a warm, greased tray.

5 Prove at 38–40°C (100–104°F) in humid conditions.
6 Bake at 250°C (482°F) for 10–12 minutes.
7 After baking, remove the rolls from the tray immediately and place onto a cooling wire.

CHELSEA BUNS, CURRANT BUNS AND BUTTER BUNS

Ingredients

Kilo	Gram	%	Ingredients	lb	oz
1	000	100.00	bread flour	2	3.50
	10	1.00	salt		0.50
	40	4.00	skimmed milk powder		1.50
	10	1.00	dough conditioner		0.50
	100	10.00	shortening		3.50
	100	10.00	sugar		3.50
	100	10.00	egg		3.50
	90	9.00	yeast		3.25
	480	48.00	water	1	1.00
1	930		Gross weight	4	4.75
1	881		Net weight	4	3.00

Production Points

Dough temperature	**27°C (81°F)**
Bulk Fermentation Time	**Nil**
Knock back	**N/A**
Scaling weight	**approx 50 g (1.75 oz) (see processing method)**
Yield	**approx 36**
Baking temperature	**232°C (450°F)**
Baking time	**10–15 mins**

Note: This recipe is also suitable for the production of Iced Fingers, Teacakes, Cream Buns (Cookies), Belgian Buns, Devon Split, Parisian Buns, Tea Loaf and Bath Buns.

Mixing method

1 Sieve together the flour, salt, skimmed milk powder and dough conditioner.
2 Using a spiral or conventional mixer, add the shortening and rub through the dry ingredients on slow speed.
3 Mix the egg and sugar together and disperse the yeast into tempered water. Now add both of these solutions to the above ingredients.
4 Using a spiral or conventional mixer, mix on slow speed for 2 minutes.
5 Check for extremes in consistency and adjust as necessary.
6 To complete the mixing method follow the appropriate mixing process.
- spiral mixer – mix on fast speed for 6–8 minutes
- conventional mixer – mix on speed 1 for 20 minutes or speed 2 for 10 minutes.

7 After completion of the mixing method, the dough is ready to be scaled and processed.

Processing methods

CHELSEA BUNS

1 Mould the dough piece round and rest for 8–10 minutes to allow the dough to recover.
2 Pin the dough piece to a large rectangle, measuring 30 cm × 70 cm (12" × 28").
3 Brush the surface with melted butter, leaving 2.5 cm (1") at the bottom edge for sealing purposes.
4 Mix together 60 g (2.25 oz) of brown sugar, and 5 g of mixed spice, then sprinkle evenly over the dough piece.
5 Sprinkle 300 g (10.75 oz) of currants evenly over the dough piece.
6 Moisten the bottom edge with water.
7 Roll up the dough pieces, Swiss Roll fashion. During the rolling process, ensure the roll is kept tight.

8 Brush the roll with melted butter.
9 Cut the dough piece into 36 equal portions. Place them into a warm, greased Chelsea Bun tray, flat side down.
10 Prove at 38–40°C (100–104°F) in humid conditions.
11 Bake at 232°C (450°F) for 15 minutes.
12 After baking, remove from the tray immediately and place on a cooling wire. Dredge with sugar whilst the buns are still hot.

CURRANT BUNS

1 Mix 200 g (7 oz) of currants through the dough.
2 Scale 41 at 50 g (1.75 oz) and mould round.
3 Rest for 8–10 minutes to allow the dough pieces to recover.
4 Re-mould the dough pieces into a ball shape.
5 Place the dough pieces onto a warm, greased tray.
6 Brush the tops of the dough pieces with eggwash.
7 Prove at 38–40°C (100–104°F) in humid conditions.
8 Bake at 232°C (450°F) for 10–15 minutes.
9 After baking, remove the buns from the tray immediately and place onto a cooling wire.

BUTTER BUNS

1 Scale 37 at 50 g (1.75 oz) and mould round.
2 Rest for 8–10 minutes to allow the dough pieces to recover.
3 Pin out the dough pieces very thinly into a flat round shape.
4 Brush the dough pieces with melted butter and fold in half.
5 Again, brush the surface with melted butter and fold into a quarter.
6 Place onto a warm, well greased tray and brush with eggwash.
7 Prove at 38–40°C (100–104°F) in humid conditions.
8 Bake at 232°C (450°F) for 10–15 minutes.
9 After baking, remove the buns from the tray immediately and place onto a cooling wire.

DOUGHNUTS

Ingredients

Kilo	Gram	%	Ingredients	lb	oz
1	000	100.00	bread flour	2	3.50
	15	1.50	salt		0.50
	10	1.00	dough conditioner		0.50
	100	10.00	shortening		3.50
	50	5.00	yeast		1.75
	550	55.00	water	1	3.75
	30	3.00	sugar		1.00
1	755		Gross weight	3	14.50
1	711		Net weight	3	13.00

Production Points

Dough temperature	**27°C (81°F)**
Bulk Fermentation Time	**Nil**
Knock back	**N/A**
Scaling weight	**50 g (1.75 oz)**
Yield	**34**
Frying temperature	**190°C (374°F)**
Frying time	**2–4 mins**

Mixing method

1. Sieve together the flour, salt and dough conditioner.
2. Using a spiral or conventional mixer, add the shortening and rub through the dry ingredients on slow speed.
3. Disperse the yeast into tempered water, dissolve the sugar, then add to the above ingredients.
4. Using a spiral or conventional mixer, mix on slow speed for 2 minutes.
5. Check for extremes in consistency and adjust as necessary.
6. To complete the mixing method follow the appropriate mixing process.
   - spiral mixer – mix on fast speed for 6–8 minutes
   - conventional mixer – mix on speed 1 for 20 minutes or speed 2 for 10 minutes.
7. After the completion of the mixing method, the dough is ready to be scaled and processed.

Round Doughnuts

Processing methods

1 Scale 34 at 50 g (1.75 oz) and mould round.
2 Rest for 8–10 minutes to allow the dough pieces to recover.
3 Now form one of the following shapes:
Ring Doughnut
i Pin out the dough piece to a flat round shape, 1.25 cm (0.5") deep.
ii Cut and remove the centre using a 2 cm (0.75") diameter plain cutter.
Round Doughnut
Re-mould the dough piece into a ball shape.
Finger Doughnut
Roll the dough piece to a finger shape 10 cm (4") long.
4 Place the dough pieces onto a warm, lightly-oiled perforated tray.
5 Prove at 38–40°C (100–104°F) in humid conditions.
6 Fry the doughnuts at 190°C (347°F) for 2–4 minutes.
7 After frying, roll the doughnuts into caster sugar immediately.

Note: Ring doughnuts can be served plain. It is common practice for round and finger doughnuts to be finished and decorated with jam, curds, cream, custard, fruit and chocolate.

Croissants (see p. 140)

CROISSANTS

Ingredients

Kilo	Gram	%	Ingredients	lb	oz
1	000	100.00	strong bread flour	2	3.50
	20	2.00	salt		0.75
	10	1.00	dough conditioner		0.50
	45	4.50	yeast		1.50
	660	66.00	milk	1	7.50
	80	8.00	sugar		3.00
	450	45.00	butter or pastry margarine	1	0.00
2	265		Gross weight	5	00.75
2	208		Net weight	4	14.75

Production Points

Dough temperature	**21°C (70°F)**
Bulk Fermentation Time	**Nil**
Knock back	**N/A**
Scaling weight	**60–70 g (2–2.5 oz)**
Yield	**31–36**
Baking temperature	**238°C (460°F)**
Baking time	**12–15 mins**

Note: Croissant butter is able to withstand the rolling and folding during the lamination process.

Mixing method

1. Sieve together the flour, salt and dough conditioner.
2. Disperse the yeast into tempered milk, add and dissolve the sugar and add to the above ingredients.
3. Using a spiral or conventional mixer, mix on slow speed for 2 minutes.
4. Check for extremes in consistency and adjust as necessary.
5. To complete the mixing method, follow the appropriate mixing process.
   - spiral mixer – mix on fast speed for 2 minutes
   - conventional mixer – mix on speed 1 for 6 minutes.
6. After the completion of the mixing method, mould the dough piece round and rest for 8–10 minutes to allow it to recover. The dough is now ready for lamination.

Processing method

1. Pin the dough to a rectangle 2 cm (0.75") deep.
2. Cover two-thirds of the dough with butter or pastry margarine.
3. Bring the uncovered dough into the centre, fold again to create two layers of butter or pastry margarine sandwiched between three layers of dough.
4. As for the lamination of puff pastry, proceed to give the dough three half turns.

   Note: Do not allow any rest periods between the half turns.

5. Pin the dough to 4–5 mm (0.25") thick.
6. Cut triangles from the dough as in Figure 10(a).
7. Holding the pointed end, firmly roll up dough piece from the wide end. Keep the dough piece tight during the rolling process to ensure that a good shape is obtained.
8. Now form the shape of a crescent.
9. Place the shaped dough pieces onto a warm, greased tray.
10. Brush the dough pieces with eggwash.
11. Prove at 32–34°C (89–93°F) in slightly humid conditions.
12. Bake at 238°C (460°F) for 12–15 minutes.
13. After baking, remove the croissants from the tray immediately and place onto a cooling wire.

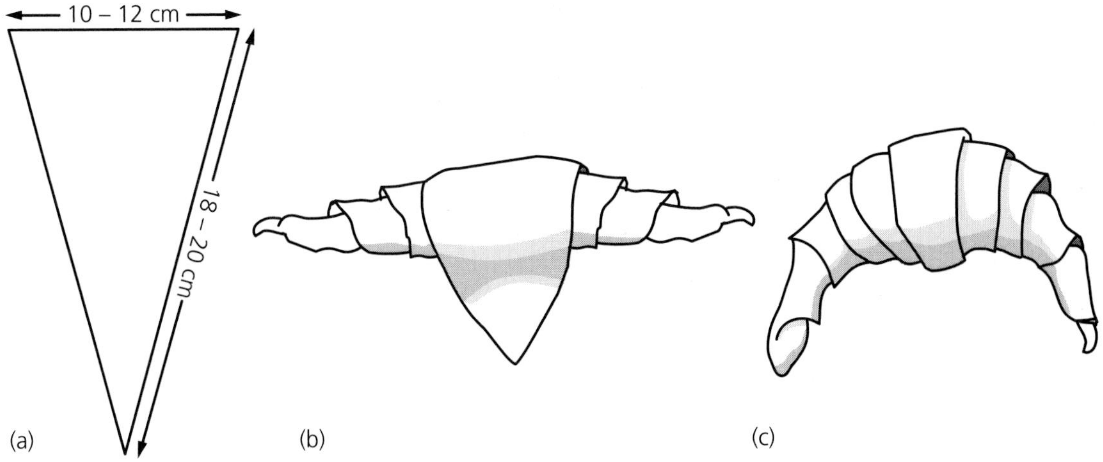

Figure 10 Croissants: (a) pin the dough out (b) roll up the dough piece (c) form the shape of a crescent

DANISH PASTRIES

(See colour plate 9.)

Ingredients

Kilo	Gram	%	Ingredients	lb	oz
1	000	100.00	bread flour	2	3.50
	10	1.00	salt		0.25
	10	1.00	dough conditioner		0.25
	220	22.00	egg		8.00
	555	55.50	cold milk	1	3.75
	50	5.00	sugar		1.75
	110	11.00	yeast		4.00
	660	66.00	cold butter or pastry margarine	1	7.50
2	615		Gross weight	5	13.00
2	549		Net weight	5	10.75

Mixing method

1 Sieve together the flour, salt and dough conditioner.
2 Mix the egg and milk together, add and dissolve the sugar, then disperse the yeast through the solution and add to the above ingredients.
3 Using a spiral or conventional mixer, mix on slow speed for 2 minutes.
4 Check for extremes in consistency and adjust as necessary.
5 To complete the mixing method follow the appropriate mixing process.
   - spiral mixer – mix on fast speed for 2 minutes
   - conventional mixer – mix on speed 1 for 6 minutes.
6 After the completion of the mixing method, mould the dough piece round and rest for 8–10 minutes to allow it to recover. The dough is now ready for lamination.

Processing method

1 Follow the lamination process as described in stages 1–5 for Croissants.
2 Cut the dough into 10 cm (4") squares and form one of the following shapes.

Production Points

Dough temperature	**21°C (70°F)**
Bulk Fermentation Time	**Nil**
Knock back	**N/A**
Scaling weight	**60–70 g (2–2.5 oz)**
Yield	**36–42**
Baking temperature	**238°C (460°F)**
Baking time	**10–15 mins**

Note: Croissant butter may also be used for the production of Danish Pastries.

Imperial Star

i Using a knife or scotch scraper, make a cut from each corner towards the centre as in Figure 11(a).

ii Fold each numbered point into the centre until they overlap, then secure with the thumb.

Bears Paws

i Pipe softened macaroon paste across the centre of the dough piece in Figure 11(b).

ii Moisten the bottom edge with water, fold over and secure.

iii Using a knife or scotch scraper, make four cuts as illustrated.

iv Bend the dough piece until an arc shape is formed.

Boats

i Moisten two opposite corners of the square.

ii Fold the corners into the centre until they overlap. Secure with the thumb.

Duchess

i Fold over to form a triangle. Using a knife or scotch scraper, make two cuts as illustrated.

ii Unfold the dough piece and moisten the edges.

iii Take the cut sides to the opposite end. They will overlap, now secure in position.

3 Place the shaped dough pieces onto a warm, greased tray.
4 Brush the dough pieces with eggwash.
5 Prove at 32–34°C (89–93°F) in slightly humid conditions.
6 Bake at 238°C (460°F) for 12–15 minutes.
7 After baking, whilst the pastries are hot brush with boiled apricot puree and water icing.
8 After baking remove the pastries from the tray and place onto a cooling wire.

Note: It is common practice to finish Danish Pastries with roasted nuts, custard, glazed and fresh fruits.

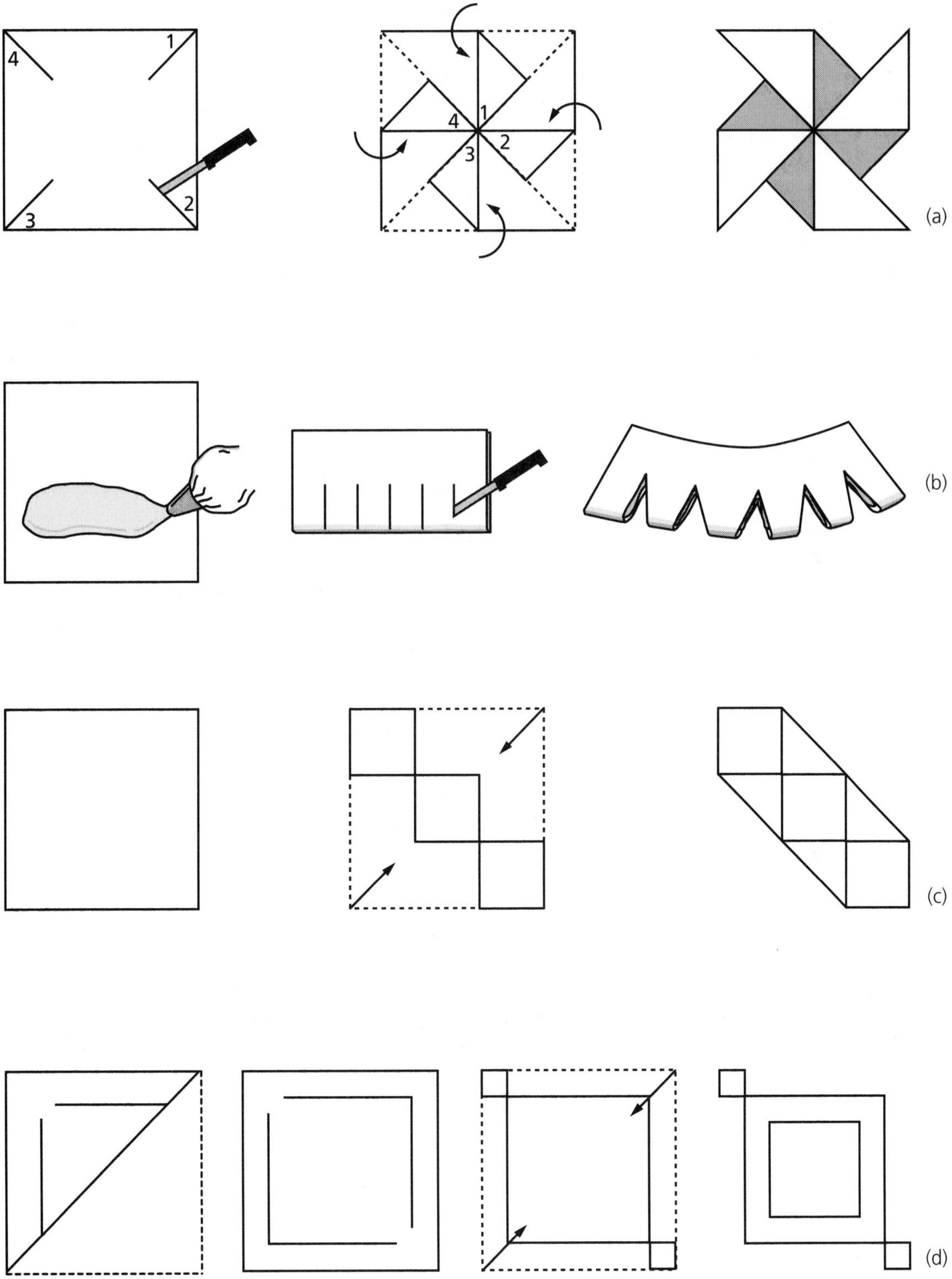

Figure 11 Danish pastries: (a) Imperial star (b) Bears paws (c) Boats (d) Duchess

FARLS

Ingredients

Kilo	Gram	%	Ingredients	lb	oz
	550	50.00	medium flour	1	3.50
	550	50.00	brown flour	1	3.50
	20	1.80	salt		0.75
	30	2.70	skimmed milk powder		1.00
	45	4.00	baking powder		1.50
	5	0.45	dough conditioner		0.25
	30	2.70	shortening		1.00
	20	1.80	yeast		0.75
	670	61.00	water	1	8.00
1	920		Gross weight	4	4.25
1	872		Net weight	4	2.50

Production Points

Dough temperature	**21°C (70°F)**
Bulk Fermentation Time	**Nil**
Knock back	**N/A**
Scaling weight	**450 g (1 lb)**
Yield	**4**
Baking temperature	**226°C (440°F)**
Baking time	**20–25 mins**

Mixing method

1. Using a coarse sieve, sieve together the flour, salt, skimmed milk powder, baking powder and dough conditioner.
2. Using a spiral or conventional mixer, add the shortening and rub through on slow speed.
3. Disperse the yeast into tempered water and add to the above ingredients.
4. Using a spiral or conventional mixer, mix on slow speed until a dough is formed.

   Note: Do not attempt to develop the dough as for standard doughs.

5. After the completion of the mixing method, the dough is ready to be scaled and processed.

Processing method

1. Scale 4 at 450 g (1 lb) and mould round.
2. Using a rolling pin, flatten the dough pieces to 3 cm (1.25") deep.
3. Place the dough pieces onto a warm, greased tray.
4. Cut the dough pieces into four equal quarters.
5. Brush the tops with eggwash and sprinkle with bran flakes.
6. Bake at 226°C (440°F) for 20–25 minutes.
7. After baking, remove the farls from the tray and place onto a cooling wire.

CHAPTER

seven

The Sponge and Dough Process

This is a two-stage process which has been used for many years to produce bread and fermented products.

Some bakers prefer this breadmaking process because of the improved flavour produced during the fermentation period of the sponge, which is evident in the final product. There is also a superior crumb quality, and an extended shelf life; this breadmaking process is therefore favoured for the production of competition and exhibition items.

This breadmaking process also offers the baker with an opportunity to reduce the cost of raw materials during daily production, as it eliminates the need for dough conditioners.

THE SPONGE

A sponge is a basic dough made from the four main ingredients, flour, salt, yeast and water. The sponge is then allowed to ferment for 12–16 hours in bulk, and the rate of fermentation is controlled by:

- the level of yeast
- the level of salt
- the water temperature and final dough temperature
- the use of strong bread flour to provide the tolerance required for the long fermentation period.

MIXING METHOD

This is an outline of the mixing method, but each recipe contains a more detailed description of the method.

Stage one – the sponge

1 Sieve together the dry ingredients.
2 Disperse the yeast into tempered water and add to the dry ingredients.
3 Form a dough.
4 Check consistency.
5 Mix until a smooth, clear dough is obtained and gluten forming proteins are fully developed.
6 Cover the dough and maintain the dough temperature.
7 After completion of the fermentation time, the sponge is ready to be added to the freshly made dough.

Stage two – the dough

1 Mix all of the ingredients together for 2 minutes, and form a dough.
2 Break the sponge into pieces and add them to the dough.
3 Mix until a smooth and clear dough is obtained and the gluten forming proteins are fully developed.
4 Cover the dough and keep warm during the Bulk Fermentation Time.
5 The dough is now ready to be scaled and processed.

The effect of sponge on dough

When sponge is added to dough at the rate of 25% of the flour weight, the fresh flour is ripened very quickly. Therefore a standard bread flour can be used for the dough stage and a Bulk Fermentation Time of only 30 minutes is sufficient prior to processing.

Versatility of sponge

As a sponge can be made from white or brown flour, it is possible to add sponge to many bread and fermented products. Another feature of sponge is that it can also be added to dough which is made from the Mechanical Dough Development process, or from the Activated Dough Development process.

ADVANTAGES AND DISADVANTAGES

Advantages

1 There is no need for a special mixing machine.
2 There is no need to use a dough conditioner at the dough stage.
3 The Bulk Fermentation Time is significantly reduced after the dough stage.
4 The addition of sponge confers the following improvements to the final product:
   - a better flavour
   - an improved crumb structure.

Disadvantages

1 Extra time and planning of production is required, as the sponge must be made the day before.
2 The sponge requires more attention by staff, for example, temperature control.
3 The fermenting sponge requires space.

Oven Chart

Product	Baking temperature in °C (°F)	Baking time in minutes	Additional control procedures
Long Cut Tin Bread	232 (450)	30–35	Open damper for final 10 mins
Batch Bread	232 (450)	30	" " " "
Lge Sandwich Baps	245 (470)	12–15	" " " " 5 mins
Fruit Bread	210 (410)	20	" " " "
Ciabatta	240 (464)	20	" " " "

RECIPES USING THE SPONGE AND DOUGH PROCESS

WHITE OVERNIGHT SPONGE (12–16 HOURS)

Ingredients

Kilo	Gram	%	Ingredients	lb	oz
1	000	100.00	bread flour	2	3.50
	20	2.00	salt		0.75
	10	1.00	yeast		0.50
	500	50.00	water	1	1.00
1	530		Gross weight	3	5.75
1	335		Net weight	3	2.25

Production Points

Dough temperature	**21°C (70°F)**
Bulk Fermentation Time	**12–16 hours**
Knock back	**N/A**

Note: This recipe is suitable for adding to all white doughs made by the sponge and dough process. Add sponge at the rate of 25% of the flour weight.

Mixing method

1. Sieve together the flour and salt.
2. Disperse the yeast into tempered water and add to the above ingredients.
3. Using a spiral or conventional mixer, mix on slow speed for 2 minutes.
4. Check for extremes in consistency and adjust as necessary.
5. To complete the mixing method follow the appropriate mixing process.
   - spiral mixer – mix on fast speed for 4–6 minutes
   - conventional mixer – mix on speed 1 for 10 minutes.
6. Place the dough in a polythene bag or plastic container, and maintain a room temperature of a maximum of 21°C (70°F).
7. After the completion of the BFT, the dough is ready for use.

BROWN OVERNIGHT SPONGE

Ingredients

Kilo	Gram	%	Ingredients	lb	oz
1	000	100.00	brown flour	2	3.50
	20.0	2.00	salt		0.75
	7.5	0.75	yeast		0.25
	530.0	53.00	water	1	3.00
1	557		Gross weight	3	7.50
1	463		Net weight	3	4.00

Production Points

Dough temperature	**21°C (70°F)**
Bulk Fermentation Time	**12–16 hours**
Knock back	**N/A**

Note: This sponge is suitable for adding to all brown doughs made by the sponge and dough process. Add sponge at the rate of 25% of the flour weight.

Mixing method

1. Using a coarse sieve, sieve together the flour and salt.
2. Disperse the yeast into tempered water and add to the above ingredients.
3. Using a spiral or conventional mixer, mix on slow speed for 2 minutes.
4. Check for extremes in consistency and adjust as necessary.
5. To complete the mixing method follow the appropriate mixing process.
   - spiral mixer – mix on fast speed for 4–6 minutes
   - conventional mixer – mix on speed 1 for 10 minutes.
6. Place the dough in a polythene bag or plastic container and maintain a room temperature of a maximum of 21°C (70°F).
7. After the completion of the BFT, the dough is ready for use.

LONG CUT TIN BREAD

Ingredients

Kilo	Gram	%	Ingredients	lb	oz
1	000	100.00	bread flour	2	3.50
	25	2.50	salt		1.00
	20	2.00	skimmed milk powder		0.75
	25	2.50	shortening		1.00
	30	3.00	yeast		1.00
	570	57.00	water	1	4.50
	250	25.00	sponge		9.00
1	920		Gross weight	4	4.75
1	872		Net weight	4	3.00

Production Points

Dough temperature	**27°C (81°F)**
Bulk Fermentation Time	**30 mins**
Knock back	**N/A**
Scaling weight	**900 g (2 lb)**
Yield	**2**
Baking temperature	**232°C (450°F)**
Baking time	**30–35 mins**

Note: This recipe is also suitable for the production of Small White Tin Bread, Farmhouse, Large White, Multi-Piece Bread, Sandwich Bread and Tinned Coburg.

Mixing method

1 Sieve together the flour, salt and skimmed milk powder.
2 Using a spiral or conventional mixer, add the shortening and rub through the dry ingredients on slow speed.
3 Disperse the yeast into the tempered water and add to the above ingredients.
4 Using a spiral or conventional mixer, mix on slow speed for 2 minutes.
5 Break the sponge into pieces, add them to the dough and mix through.
6 Check for extremes in consistency and adjust as necessary.
7 Now follow the appropriate mixing process.
   - spiral mixer – mix on fast speed for 6–8 minutes
   - conventional mixer – mix on speed 1 for 15 minutes or speed 2 for 10 minutes.
8 Cover the dough and keep it warm during the Bulk Fermentation Time.
9 After the completion of the BFT, the dough is ready to be scaled and processed.

Processing method

1 Scale 2 at 900 g (2 lb) and mould round.
2 Rest for 8–10 minutes to allow the dough pieces to recover.
3 Re-mould the dough pieces and form them into a long cylinder shape to fit the tin.
4 Place the dough pieces into warm, greased long bread tins.
5 Prove at 38–40°C (100–104°F) in humid conditions.
6 After three-quarters of the final proof, dust with flour and cut down the centre of the dough piece.

   Note: This cut should be approximately 1 cm (0.5") deep.

7 Return the dough pieces to the final prover for the remaining proving time.
8 Bake at 232°C (450°F) for 30–35 minutes.
9 After baking, remove the bread from the tins immediately and place onto a cooling wire.

Plate 1 Small White TIn Bread, Farmhouse (see p. 76)

Plate 2 Plaited Milk Bread (see p. 79)

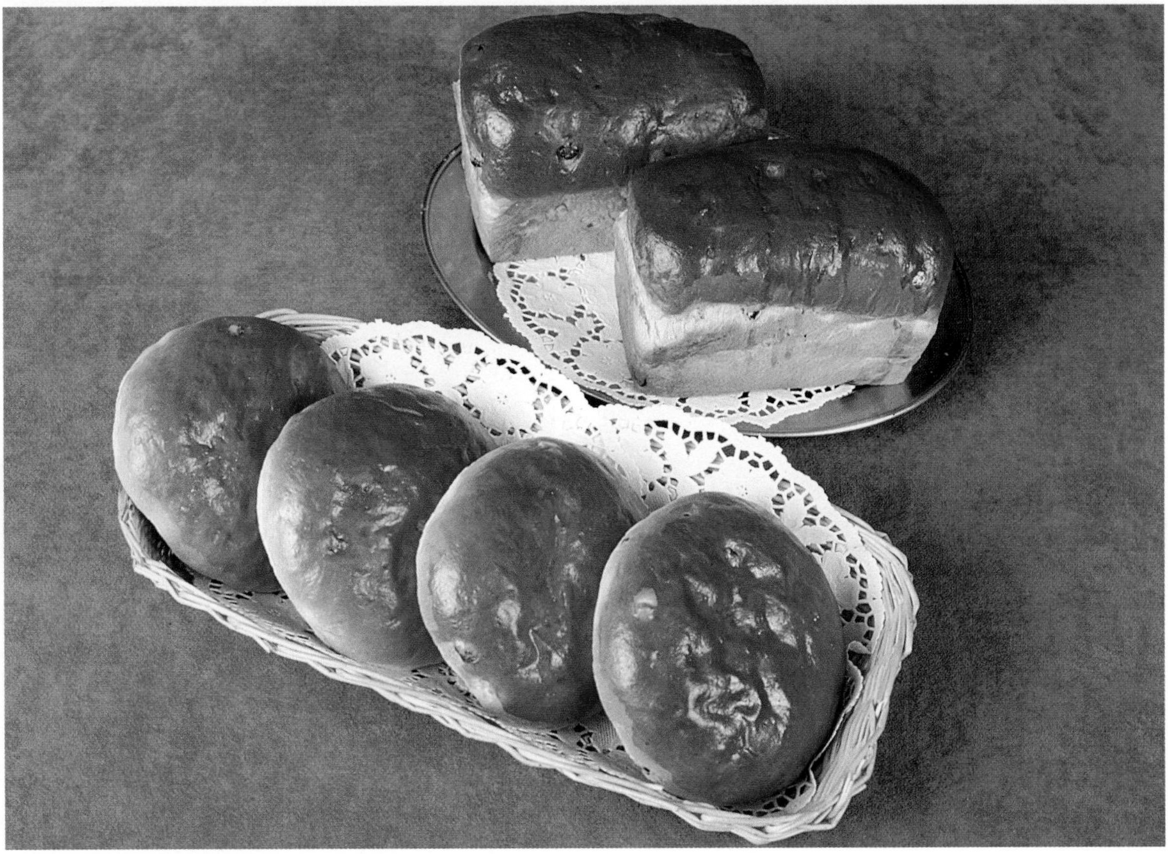

Plate 3 Teacakes (see p. 96), Fruit Bread (see p. 153)

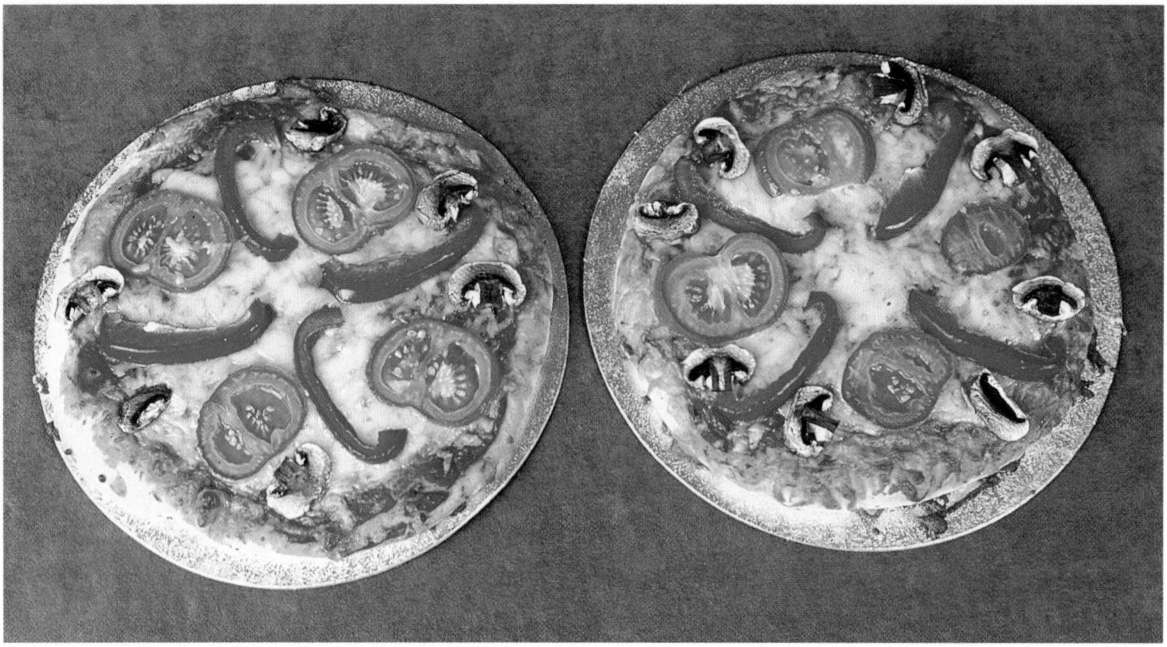

Plate 4 Pizzas (see p. 102)

Plate 5 Vegetable Pasty (see p. 235)

Plate 6 Small Brown Tin Bread, Farmhouse (see p. 77)

Plate 7 Loaf Cake selection (see p. 269)

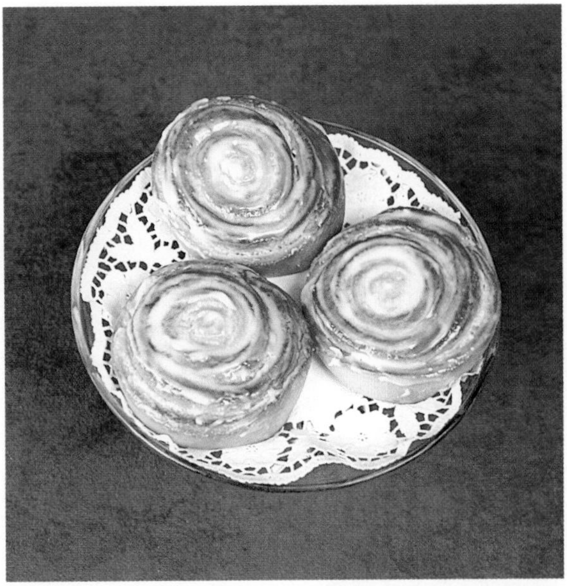

Plate 8 Belgian Buns (see p. 163)

Plate 9 Danish Pastries (see p. 141)

Plate 10 Savoury Flan (see p. 209)

Plate 11 Pork Pie/Pork and Egg Pie (see p. 214)

Plate 12 Pizza Pie (see p. 211)

Plate 13 Cream Slices (see p. 237)

Plate 14 Apple Charlottes (see p. 183)

Plate 15 Summer Fruit Tart (see p. 184)

Plate 16 Fruit Flan (see p. 181)

Plate 17 Sponge Curls, Drops, Fingers (see pp. 291–293)

Plate 18 Peach Melba (see p. 182)

Plate 19 Fruit Torte (see p. 303)

Plate 20 Meringue Shells, Nests and Fingers (see p. 322)

Plate 21 Scone Rounds, Fruit Scones (see p. 251)

Plate 22 Choux Buns and Chocolate Eclairs (see p. 320)

Plate 23 Plain and Chocolate Swiss Rolls (see p. 295)

Plate 24 Carrot Cake squares (see p. 288)

Plate 25 Range of sandwiches (see Chapter 14)

BATCH BREAD

Ingredients

Kilo	Gram	%	Ingredients	lb	oz
4	500	100.00	strong bread flour	10	000
	90	2.00	salt		3.25
	90	2.00	skimmed milk powder		3.25
	60	1.30	shortening		2.25
	90	2.00	yeast		3.25
2	430	54.00	water	5	6.75
1	120	25.00	sponge	2	8.00
8	380		Gross weight	18	10.75
8	170		Net weight	18	3.25

Production Points

Dough temperature	**27°C (81°F)**
Bulk Fermentation Time	**30 mins**
Knock back	**N/A**
Scaling weight	**450 g (1 lb)**
Yield	**18**
Baking temperature	**232°C (450°F)**
Baking time	**30 mins**

Note: This recipe is also suitable for the production of Cottage Bread, Danish Bread, Bloomers, Tiger Bread and Coburgs.

Mixing method

1 Sieve together the flour, salt and skimmed milk powder.
2 Using a spiral or conventional mixer, add the shortening and rub through the dry ingredients on slow speed.
3 Disperse the yeast into the tempered water and add to the above ingredients.
4 Using a spiral or conventional mixer, mix on slow speed for 2 minutes.
5 Break the sponge into pieces, add them to the dough and mix through.
6 Check for extremes in consistency and adjust as necessary.
7 Now follow the appropriate mixing process.
- spiral mixer – mix on fast speed for 6–8 minutes
- conventional mixer – mix on speed 1 for 15 minutes or speed 2 for 10 minutes.

8 Cover the dough and keep it warm during the Bulk Fermentation Time.
9 After the completion of the BFT, the dough is ready to be scaled and processed.

Processing method

1 Scale 18 at 450 g (1 lb) and mould round.
2 Rest for 8–10 minutes to allow the dough pieces to recover.
3 Re-mould the dough pieces and form them into a long baton shape.
4 Brush the sides of each dough piece with vegetable oil or melted butter.

Note: This ensures that the bread will separate easily after baking.

5 Place the dough pieces close together in a 2 × 9 formation on a warm, greased tray fitted with a metal frame.
6 Prove at 38–40°C (100–104°F) in humid conditions.
7 Bake at 232°C (450°F) for 30 minutes.
8 After baking remove the bread from the tray immediately and place onto a cooling wire. Allow the bread to cool, prior to separation.

LARGE SANDWICH BAPS AND SCOTCH BAPS

Ingredients

Kilo	Gram	%	Ingredients	lb	oz
1	000	100.00	bread flour	2	3.50
	20	2.00	salt		0.75
	20	2.00	skimmed milk powder		0.75
	50	5.00	shortening		1.75
	30	3.00	yeast		1.00
	580	58.00	water	1	4.75
	250	25.00	sponge		9.00
1	950		Gross weight	4	5.50
1	901		Net weight	4	3.75

Production Points

Dough temperature	**27°C (81°F)**
Bulk Fermentation Time	**30 mins**
Knock back	**N/A**
Scaling weight	
Large	**100 g (3.5 oz)**
Scotch	**80 g (2.75 oz)**
Yield	
Large	**19**
Scotch	**23**
Baking temperature	**245°C (470°F)**
Baking time	
Large	**12–15 mins**
Scotch	**10–12 mins**

Note: This recipe is suitable for the production of Bread Rolls, Divider Buns, Bridge Rolls, Finger Rolls and Burger Buns.

Mixing method

1 Sieve together the flour, salt and skimmed milk powder.
2 Using a spiral or conventional mixer, add the shortening and rub through the dry ingredients on slow speed.
3 Disperse the yeast into the tempered water and add to the above ingredients.
4 Using a spiral or conventional mixer, mix on slow speed for 2 minutes.
5 Break the sponge into pieces, add them to the dough and mix through.
6 Check for extremes in consistency and adjust as necessary.
7 Now follow the appropriate mixing process.
- spiral mixer – mix on fast speed for 6–8 minutes
- conventional mixer – mix on speed 1 for 15 minutes or speed 2 for 10 minutes.

8 Cover the dough and keep it warm during the Bulk Fermentation Time.
9 After the completion of the BFT, the dough is ready to be scaled and processed.

Processing method

Large Sandwich Baps

1 Scale 19 at 100 g (3.5 oz) and mould round.
2 Rest for 8–10 minutes to allow the dough pieces to recover.
3 Pin out the dough pieces to a flat, round shape.
4 Place the dough pieces onto a warm, greased tray.
5 Prove at 38–40°C (100–104°F) in humid conditions.
6 Bake at 245°C (470°F) for 12–15 minutes.
7 After baking, remove the baps from the tray immediately and place onto a cooling wire.

Scotch Baps

1 Scale 23 at 80 g (2.75 oz) and mould round.
2 Rest for 8–10 minutes to allow the dough pieces to recover.
3 Pin out the pieces to an oval shape.
4 Place the dough pieces onto a warm, greased tray.
5 Prove at 38–40°C (100–104°F) in humid conditions.
6 Prior to baking, dust the dough pieces with bread flour.

Scotch Baps

7 Bake at 245°C (470°F) for 10–12 minutes.
8 After baking, remove the baps from the tray immediately and place onto a cooling wire.

FRUIT BREAD

(See colour plate 3.)

Ingredients

Kilo	Gram	%	Ingredients	lb	oz
1	000	100.00	bread flour	2	3.50
	10	1.00	salt		0.25
	40	4.00	skimmed milk powder		1.50
	100	10.00	shortening		3.50
	60	6.00	yeast		2.25
	700	70.00	water	1	9.00
	100	10.00	sugar		3.50
	250	25.00	sponge		9.00
	300	30.00	currants		10.75
	150	15.00	sultanas		5.25
	50	5.00	mixed peel		1.75
2	760		Gross weight	6	2.25
2	691		Net weight	5	15.75

Production Points

Dough temperature	**27°C (81°F)**
Bulk Fermentation Time	**Nil**
Knock back	**N/A**
Scaling weight	**330 g (11.75 oz)**
Yield	**8**
Baking temperature	**210°C (410°F)**
Baking time	**20 mins**

Mixing method

1 Sieve together the flour, salt and skimmed milk powder.
2 Using a spiral or conventional mixer, add the shortening and rub through the dry ingredients.
3 Disperse the yeast into tempered water, add and dissolve the sugar then add to the above ingredients.
4 Using a spiral or conventional mixer, mix on slow speed for 2 minutes.
5 Break the sponge into pieces, add them to the dough and mix through.
6 Check for extremes in consistency and adjust as necessary.
7 Now follow the appropriate mixing process.
- spiral mixer – mix on fast speed for 6–8 minutes
- conventional mixer – mix on speed 1 for 15 minutes or speed 2 for 10 minutes.

8 After completion of the mixing time, mix the currants, sultanas and mixed peel together. Add to the dough and mix through on slow speed until thoroughly dispersed.

Processing method

1 Scale 8 at 330 g (11.75 oz) and mould round.
2 Rest for 8–10 minutes to allow the dough pieces to recover.
3 Re-mould the dough pieces and form them into a cylinder shape.
4 Place the dough pieces into warm, greased, short small bread tins.

5 Prove at 38–40°C (100–104°F) in humid conditions.
6 Bake at 210°C (410°F) for 20 minutes.
7 After baking, remove the bread from the tins immediately and place onto a cooling wire.

CIABATTA

Ingredients

Kilo	Gram	%	Ingredients	lb	oz
2	000	100.00	flour	4	7.50
	40	2.00	salt		1.50
	20	1.00	diastatic malt flour		0.50
	30	1.50	yeast		1.00
1	300	65.00	water	2	14.00
	60	3.00	extra virgin olive oil		2.00
1		50.00	sponge	2	4.00
4	450		Gross weight	9	14.50
4	338		Net weight	9	10.00

Production Points

Dough temperature	**27°C (81°F)**
Bulk Fermentation Time	**30 mins**
Knock back	**N/A**
Scaling weight	**350 g (12.5 oz)**
Yield	**approx 12**
Baking temperature	**240°C (464°F)**
Baking time	**20 mins**

Mixing method

1 Sieve together the flour, salt and diastatic malt flour.
2 Disperse the yeast into tempered water.
3 Add the olive oil to the yeast and water solution, and add to the above ingredients.
4 Using a spiral or conventional mixer, mix on slow speed for 2 minutes.
5 Break the sponge into pieces, add them to the dough and mix through.
6 Check for extremes in consistency and adjust as necessary.
7 Now follow the appropriate mixing process.
   - spiral mixer – mix on fast speed for 6–8 minutes
   - conventional mixer – mix on speed 1 for 15 minutes or speed 2 for 10 minutes.
8 Cover the dough and keep warm during the BFT.

Ciabatta

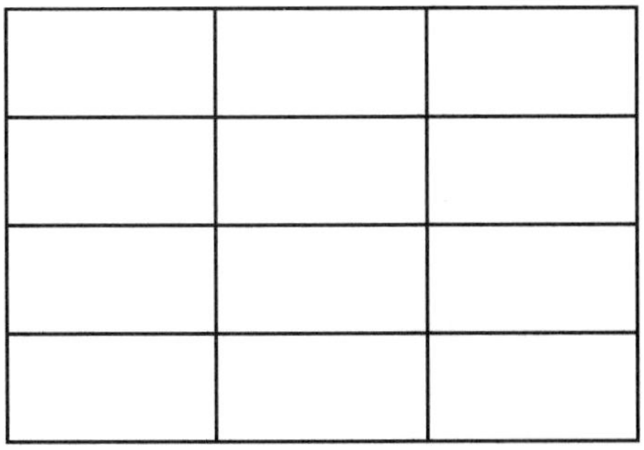

Figure 12 Divide the Ciabatta dough on the flour board

Processing method

1 Pin out the dough to approximately 2–3 cm thick.
2 Place onto a floured board measuring 75 × 45 cm (30 × 18"). The base of the board should be fully covered.
3 Cover and leave to rest in a warm place for 30 minutes. The proving temperature should be no higher than 28°C (82°F).
4 Using a scotch scraper, cut out 12 rectangular shaped dough pieces to weigh approximately 350 g (12.5 oz). Divide the ciabatta dough on the floured board as illustrated.
5 Stretch the dough pieces lengthwise and place onto a warm tray lined with silicone paper. Care must be taken not to de-gas the dough pieces.
6 Dust the dough pieces with flour.
7 Bake immediately at 240°C (464°F) for 20 minutes.
8 After baking, remove the ciabatta from the tray immediately and place onto a cooling wire.

Note:

- The dough must be handled carefully to ensure that the gas and shape are retained during the processing, in order to obtain the dark open crumb that is characteristic of ciabatta.
- Ciabatta does not require a period of final proof.

CHAPTER

eight

The Ferment and Dough Process

The ferment and dough process has been used for many years to produce rich fermented products.

This is a two stage process which is necessary for some fermented products which contain very high levels of enriching ingredients.

For example, high levels of fat and sugar would retard the activity of yeast, but the initial stage known as the ferment provides the yeast with the ideal conditions for fermentation activity: food, moisture, warmth and time.

The ferment prepares the yeast for the second stage of the mixing process where it will come into contact with the high levels of enriching ingredients.

THE FERMENT

A ferment is made from 10–20% of the total flour weight, all of the water content, all of the yeast and part of the sugar content. The ferment should contain sugar at a level of 10% to ensure the yeast performs to its maximum capability. The remaining ingredients are added during the second stage. The ferment is then allowed to stand for 30 minutes at a temperature of 32–37°C (89–99°F) to ensure that rapid fermentation takes place.

MIXING METHOD

This is an outline of the mixing method. Each recipe contains a more detailed description of the method.

Stage one – the ferment

1 Using a suitable container, disperse the yeast into tempered water.
2 Add and dissolve the sugar.
3 Sieve the flour and whisk through.
4 Place the solution in a warm place and allow it to ferment for 30 minutes.

Stage two – the dough

1 Sieve the dry ingredients together.
2 Add the fat content and rub through the dry ingredients.
3 Mix the egg and sugar together and add this at the same time as the ferment.
4 Form a dough.
5 Check consistency.
6 Mix until a smooth and clear dough is obtained and the gluten forming proteins are fully developed.
7 Cover the dough and keep warm during the BFT.
8 After 30–40 minutes of the BFT, knock back the dough. At this stage, mix the fruit content through the dough.
9 After the remaining BFT, the dough is ready to be scaled and processed.

Activity in the ferment

A ferment offers yeast the ideal conditions for fermentation:

- moisture
- warmth
- food
- time.

These conditions ensure that the yeast can multiply rapidly and therefore obtain an ideal start to the fermentation of rich doughs.

Reasons for a ferment

Rich dough contains high levels of ingredients which have a retarding effect upon the fermentation activity of yeast. Some doughs contain such a high level of sugar, fat, egg, fruit and spices that it is possible for the yeast to be killed.

ADVANTAGES AND DISADVANTAGES

Advantages

1 The ferment ensures that the yeast is thoroughly dispersed and multiplies rapidly.
2 The yeast is given a good start in rich doughs.
3 There is no need for a special mixing machine.
4 There is no need to use a dough conditioner at the dough stage.
5 An improved volume, colour, flavour and texture is obtained.

Disadvantages

1 Extra timing and planning of production is required.
2 The process involves two mixing operations.
3 The process requires more attention by staff, for example, temperature control.
4 Extra space is required for the ferment.

OVEN CHART

Product	Baking temperature in °C (°F)	Baking time in minutes	Additional control procedures
Spiced Buns	232 (450)	12–15	Open damper for final 5 mins
Stollen	218 (424)	20–25	" " " 10 mins
Bath Buns	215 (440)	15	" " " 5 mins
Bara Brith	205 (400)	35–40	" " " 10 mins
Belgian Buns	232 (450)	10–15	" " " 5 mins

RECIPES USING THE FERMENT AND DOUGH PROCESS

SPICED BUNS

Ingredients

Kilo	Gram	%	Ingredients	lb	oz
Ferment					
	80	8.00	yeast		2.75
	460	46.00	water at 35–40°C (95–104°F)	1	0.25
	50	5.00	sugar		1.75
	200	20.00	strong bread flour		7.00
Dough					
	800	80.00	strong bread flour	1	12.50
	10	1.00	salt		0.50
	30	3.00	skimmed milk powder		1.00
	150	15.00	shortening		5.25
	75	7.50	egg		2.75
	100	10.00	sugar		3.50
	200	20.00	currants		7.00
	100	10.00	sultanas		3.50
	50	5.00	mixed peel		1.75
	15	1.50	bun spice		0.50
2	320		Gross weight	5	2.00
2	262		Net weight	5	0.00

Production Points

Ferment time	**30 mins**
Dough temperature	**27°C (81°F)**
Bulk Fermentation Time	**30 mins**
Knock back	**N/A**
Scaling weight	**60 g (2 oz)**
Yield	**37**
Baking temperature	**232°C (450°F)**
Baking time	**12–15 mins**

Note: This recipe is also suitable for the production of Hot Cross Buns.

Mixing method

FERMENT STAGE

1 Using a suitable container, disperse the yeast into tempered water.
2 Add and dissolve the sugar.
3 Sieve the flour, add and whisk through until a smooth solution is obtained.
4 Place the solution in a warm place and allow it to ferment for 30 minutes.

DOUGH STAGE

1 Sieve together the flour, salt and skimmed milk powder.
2 Using a spiral or conventional mixer, add the shortening and rub through the dry ingredients on slow speed.
3 Mix the egg, sugar and bun spice together. Now add this solution and the ferment to the above ingredients.
4 Using a spiral or conventional mixer, mix on slow speed for 2 minutes.
5 Check for extremes in consistency and adjust as necessary.
6 To complete the mixing method follow the appropriate mixing process.
   - spiral mixer – mix on fast speed for 6–8 minutes
   - conventional mixer – mix on speed 1 for 15 minutes or speed 2 for 10 minutes.
7 Cover the dough and keep warm during the BFT.
8 After 30–40 minutes of the BFT, knock back the dough. At this stage, bring the fruit together and mix it through the dough.
9 After the remaining BFT, the dough is ready to be scaled and processed.

Processing method

1 Scale 37 at 60 g (2 oz) and mould round.
2 Rest for 8–10 minutes to allow the dough pieces to recover.
3 Re-mould the dough pieces and place them onto a warm, greased tray.
4 Prove at 38–40°C (100–104°F) in humid conditions.

5 Bake at 232°C (450°F) for 12–15 minutes.
6 On withdrawal from the oven, brush with after-bake glaze.
7 Now place the buns onto a cooling wire.

Note: These buns may be finished by dipping the tops into a plain or flavoured icing.

STOLLEN

Ingredients

Kilo	Gram	%	Ingredients	lb	oz
Ferment					
	80	8.00	yeast		2.75
	460	46.00	water at 35–40°C (95–104°F)	1	0.50
	50	5.00	sugar		1.75
	200	20.00	strong bread flour		7.00
Dough					
	800	80.00	strong bread flour	1	12.50
	10	1.00	salt		0.50
	30	3.00	skimmed milk powder		1.00
	200	20.00	butter		7.00
	100	10.00	egg		3.50
	100	10.00	sugar		3.50
	10	1.00	lemon paste		0.50
	800	80.00	sultanas	1	12.50
	100	10.00	mixed peel		3.50
2	940		Gross weight	6	8.50
2	866		Net weight	6	6.00

Mixing method

FERMENT STAGE

1 Using a suitable container, disperse the yeast into tempered water.
2 Add and dissolve the sugar.
3 Sieve the flour, add and whisk through until a smooth solution is obtained.
4 Place the solution in a warm place and allow it to ferment for 30 minutes.

DOUGH STAGE

1 Sieve together the flour, salt and skimmed milk powder.
2 Using a spiral or conventional mixer, add the butter and rub through the dry ingredients on slow speed.
3 Mix the egg, sugar and lemon paste together. Now add this solution and the ferment to the above ingredients.
4 Using a spiral or conventional mixer, mix on slow speed for 2 minutes.
5 Check for extremes in consistency and adjust as necessary.
6 To complete the mixing method follow the appropriate mixing process.
- spiral mixer – mix on fast speed for 6–8 minutes
- conventional mixer – mix on speed 1 for 15 minutes or speed 2 for 10 minutes.

7 Cover the dough and keep warm during the BFT.
8 After 30–40 minutes of the BFT, knock back the dough. At this stage, bring the fruit together and mix it through the dough.
9 After the remaining BFT, the dough is ready to be scaled and processed.

Processing method

1 Scale 7 at 400 g (14.25 oz) and mould into a baton shape.

Production Points

Ferment time	30 mins
Dough temperature	27°C (81°F)
Bulk Fermentation Time	1 hour
Knock back	30–40 mins
Scaling weight:	
Dough	400 g (14.25 oz)
Marzipan	50 g (1.75 oz)
Yield	7
Baking temperature	218°C (424°F)
Baking time	20–25 mins

2 Rest for 8–10 minutes to allow the dough pieces to recover.
3 Using a rolling pin, slightly flatten the dough piece.
4 Roll out the 50 g (1.75 oz) piece of marzipan to a finger shape. Place it onto the dough piece, slightly off centre.
5 Using water, moisten one edge of the dough piece. Fold over to cover the marzipan and seal the edge.
6 Place the dough pieces onto a warm, greased tray.
7 Prove at 38–40°C (100–104°F) in humid conditions.
8 Bake at 218°C (424°F) for 20–25 minutes.
9 On withdrawal from the oven, brush with melted butter and dredge heavily with icing sugar.
10 Now place the Stollen onto a cooling wire.

BATH BUNS

Ingredients

Kilo	Gram	%	Ingredients	lb	oz
Ferment					
	55	5.50	yeast		2.00
	290	29.00	water at 35–40°C (95–104°F)		10.25
	30	3.00	sugar		1.00
	200	20.00	strong bread flour		7.00
Dough					
	800	80.00	strong bread flour	1	12.50
	10	1.00	salt		0.50
	450	45.00	butter	1	0.00
	290	29.00	egg		10.25
	290	29.00	sultanas		10.25
	50	5.00	mixed peel		1.75
	450	45.00	nib sugar	1	0.00
2	915		Gross weight	6	7.50
2	842		Net weight	6	5.00

Mixing method

FERMENT STAGE

1 Using a suitable container, disperse the yeast into tempered water.
2 Add and dissolve the sugar.
3 Sieve the flour, add and whisk through until a smooth solution is obtained.
4 Place the solution in a warm place and allow it to ferment for 30 minutes.

DOUGH STAGE

1 Sieve together the flour and salt.
2 Using a spiral or conventional mixer, add the butter and rub through the dry ingredients on slow speed.
3 Add the egg and the ferment.
4 Using a spiral or conventional mixer, mix on slow speed for 2 minutes.
5 Check for extremes in consistency and adjust as necessary.
6 To complete the mixing method follow the appropriate mixing process.
- spiral mixer – mix on fast speed for 6–8 minutes
- conventional mixer – mix on speed 1 for 15 minutes or speed 2 for 10 minutes.

7 Cover the dough and keep warm during the BFT.
8 After 30–40 minutes of the BFT, knock back the dough. At this stage, bring the fruit together and mix it through the dough.

Production Points

Ferment time	**30 mins**
Dough temperature	**27°C (81°F)**
Bulk Fermentation Time	**1 hour**
Knock back	**30–40 mins**
Scaling weight	**70 g (2.5 oz)**
Yield	**40**
Baking temperature	**215–220°C (420–428°F)**
Baking time	**15 mins**

9 After the remaining BFT, add the nib sugar and mix through. The dough is now ready to be scaled and processed.

Processing method

1 Scale 40 at 70 g (2.5 oz) and place onto a warm, greased tray.

Note: The dough pieces must not be moulded, as they should have a rocky appearance.

2 Brush the dough pieces with eggwash.
3 Prove at 32°C (90°F) in humid conditions.
4 After proving, sprinkle the dough pieces with nib sugar.
5 Bake at 215–220°C (420–428°F) for 15 minutes.
6 After baking, remove the buns from the tray immediately and place onto a cooling wire.

BELGIAN BUNS

(See colour plate 8.)

Ingredients

Kilo	Gram	%	Ingredients	lb	oz
Ferment					
	70	7.00	yeast		2.50
	480	48.00	water at 35–40°C (95–104°F)	1	1.25
	50	5.00	sugar		1.75
	200	20.00	bread flour		7.00
Dough					
	800	80.00	bread flour	1	12.50
	10	1.00	salt		0.50
	40	4.00	skimmed milk powder		1.50
	100	10.00	shortening		3.50
	100	10.00	egg		3.50
	50	5.00	sugar		1.75
1	900		Gross weight	4	3.75
1	852		Net weight	4	2.00

Mixing method

FERMENT STAGE

1 Using a suitable container, disperse the yeast into tempered water.
2 Add and dissolve the sugar.
3 Sieve the flour, add and whisk through until a smooth solution is obtained.
4 Place the solution in a warm place and allow it to ferment for 30 minutes.

DOUGH STAGE

1 Sieve together the flour, salt and skimmed milk powder.
2 Using a spiral or conventional mixer, add the shortening and rub through the dry ingredients on slow speed.
3 Mix the egg and sugar together. Now add this solution and the ferment to the above ingredients.
4 Using a spiral or conventional mixer, mix on slow speed for 2 minutes.
5 Check for extremes in consistency and adjust as necessary.
6 To complete the mixing method follow the appropriate mixing process.
- spiral mixer – mix on fast speed for 6–8 minutes

Production Points	
Ferment time	**30 mins**
Dough temperature	**27°C (81°F)**
Bulk Fermentation Time	**1 hour**
Knock back	**30–40 mins**
Scaling weight	**approx 50 g (1.75 oz)**
Yield	**approx 40**
Baking temperature	**232°C (450°F)**
Baking time	**10–15 mins**

This recipe is also suitable for the production of Teacakes, Iced Fingers, Cream Buns (Cookies), Chelsea Buns, Currant Buns and Butter Buns, with the necessary additions.

- conventional mixer – mix on speed 1 for 15 minutes or speed 2 for 10 minutes.

7 Cover the dough and keep warm during the BFT.
8 After 30–40 minutes of the BFT, knock back the dough.
9 After the remaining BFT, the dough is ready to be scaled and processed.

Processing method

1 Mould the dough piece round and rest for 8–10 minutes to allow the dough piece to recover.
2 Pin the dough piece to a large rectangle, measuring 30 cm × 80 cm (12 × 32").
3 Soften 500 g (1 lb 3.50 oz) of macaroon paste with water and spread it over the dough piece. Leave 2.5 cm (1") at the bottom for sealing purposes.
4 Moisten the bottom edge with water.
5 Roll the dough piece, Swiss Roll fashion. During the rolling process, ensure the roll is kept tight.
6 Cut the dough piece into 40 equal portions and place them onto a warm, greased tray, flat side down.
7 Prove at 38–40°C (100–104°F) in humid conditions.
8 Bake at 232°C (450°F) for 10–15 minutes.
9 After baking, remove the buns from the tray and place onto a cooling wire.
10 Apply a thin coating of water icing or fondant to the tops of the buns.

BARA BRITH

Mixing method

FERMENT STAGE

1 Using a suitable container, disperse the yeast into tempered water.
2 Add and dissolve the sugar.
3 Sieve the flour, add and whisk through until a smooth solution is obtained.
4 Place the solution in a warm place and allow it to ferment for 30 minutes.

DOUGH STAGE

1 Sieve together the flour, salt, skimmed milk powder and mixed spice.

Ingredients

Kilo	Gram	%	Ingredients	lb	oz
Ferment					
	50	6.00	yeast		1.75
	360	45.00	water at 35–40°C (95–104°F)		12.75
	40	5.00	sugar		1.50
	160	20.00	bread flour		5.75
Dough					
	640	80.00	bread flour	1	7.00
	10	1.25	salt		0.25
	25	3.00	skimmed milk powder		1.00
	10	1.25	mixed spice		0.25
	80	10.00	butter or margarine		2.75
	120	15.00	egg		4.25
	80	10.00	sugar		2.75
	600	75.00	currants	1	5.50
	240	30.00	sultanas		8.50
	240	30.00	raisins		8.50
	120	15.00	mixed peel		4.25
2	775		Gross weight	6	2.75
2	705		Net weight	6	0.00

Production Points

Ferment time	**30 mins**
Dough temperature	**27°C (81°F)**
Bulk Fermentation Time	**1 hour**
Knock back	**30–40 mins**
Scaling weight	**450 g (1 lb)**
Yield	**6**
Baking temperature	**205°C (400°F)**
Baking time	**35–40 mins**

2 Using a spiral or conventional mixer, add the butter and rub through the dry ingredients on slow speed.
3 Mix the egg and sugar together. Now add this solution and the ferment to the above ingredients.
4 Using a spiral or conventional mixer, mix on slow speed for 2 minutes.
5 Check for extremes in consistency and adjust as necessary.
6 To complete the mixing method, follow the appropriate mixing process.
   - spiral mixer – mix on fast speed for 6–8 minutes
   - conventional mixer – mix on speed 1 for 15 minutes or speed 2 for 10 minutes.
7 Cover the dough and keep warm during the BFT.
8 After 30–40 minutes of the BFT, knock back the dough. At this stage, bring the fruit together and mix it through the dough.
9 After the remaining BFT, the dough is ready to be scaled and processed.

Processing method

1 Scale 6 at 450 g (1 lb) and mould round.
2 Rest for 8–10 minutes to allow the dough pieces to recover.
3 Re-mould the dough pieces and form them into a cylinder shape.
4 Place the dough pieces into warm, greased, small bread tins and brush the tops with eggwash.
5 Prove at 38–40°C (100–104°F) in humid conditions.
6 Bake at 205°C (400°F) for 35–40 minutes.
7 After baking, remove the bread from the tins immediately and place onto a cooling wire.

C H A P T E R

nine

Short pastry processes

For many years, the baker has enjoyed producing and developing a wide range of products made from short pastry. A number of factors have influenced the development of this product group; the most significant factor has been the introduction of a bake-off facility within the retail outlet which provides customers with hot, freshly-baked savouries.

The development has coincided with the demand from the public at large for quick, tasty, wholesome and filling hot food from take-away operations. The take-away concept has spread to sweet items, notably the increased popularity of American Cookie Biscuits. However, traditional products such as the custard tart and the pork pie are still in great demand.

SHORTPASTE – CATEGORIES AND CHARACTERISTICS

Short pastry can be divided into three categories:

1 Sweet pastries – apple pies, jam tarts etc.
2 Enriched pastries – shortbread, flap jacks etc.
3 Savouries – minced beef pie, chicken and mushroom pie etc.

Short pastry can vary from being crisp, firm or soft and crumbly in character. It should have shortness to the eating quality and break down easily during consumption.

The aim of mixing

There are three aims in mixing ingredients for short pastry:

1 To disperse and dissolve ingredients.
2 To prevent the complete formation of gluten forming proteins.
3 To form a clear paste.

Basic ingredients

The basic ingredients required to make short pastry are medium flour, sugar or salt, soft fat and liquids.

Temperature of ingredients

Prior to mixing short pastry, the raw materials should be held at 16–21°C (61–70°F). This will assist in the mixing process and consistency of the short pastry.

Creating shortness in pastry

The mixing methods for sweet pastry, cold savoury paste, hot savoury paste and enriched paste involves the insulation of flour particles from moisture. This is achieved by surrounding flour particles with fat, thus creating a barrier to the moisture content, which prevents the complete formation of gluten forming proteins. Mixing short pastry in this way ensures that a short, tender pastry is obtained. The fats used to make short pastry are as follows:

- sweet paste – butter, cake margarine and shortening

- enriched paste – butter, cake margarine and shortening.
- savoury paste – shortening and lard

MIXING METHODS

This is an outline for each of the mixing methods used to make short pastry. A more detailed description of each method can be found in the recipe for sweet paste, savoury paste and enriched paste.

RUB-IN METHOD

1 Sieve together the dry ingredients.
2 Rub the fat through the dry ingredients to a crumble.
3 Mix together the sugar or salt with the liquid and add to the above.
4 Mix to a smooth paste.

HOT-PASTE METHOD

As for rub-in method, but using hot water.

BOILED PASTE

1 Sieve the flour and place into a bowl.
2 Bring the water, salt and fat to the boil, then pour onto the flour.
3 Mix to a smooth paste.
4 Allow to cool.

HIGH SPEED METHOD

Using a high speed mixing machine, place all of the ingredients into the mixing chamber and mix them for 15–20 seconds.

Points to consider when processing shortpaste

- do not over mix
- keep the addition of scraps to a minimum; add at a rate of 10% to freshly made shortpaste
- do not over-handle short pastry
- avoid excessive dusting
- use pinning guides to obtain a consistent thickness
- use a mechanical blocking machine to process large amounts of pastry.

Storage

Unbaked short pastry products can be stored under refrigerated and frozen conditions. This offers the baker the following advantages:

1 The opportunity to build up stock level and even out production levels.
2 Fresh products at the point of sale.
3 Reduced level of waste.
4 The opportunity to maximise sales.

Baking

A general guide to the baking temperature of short pastry products is:

- sweet pastries – 204°C (400°F).
- enriched pastries – 177–190°C (350–374°F).
- savouries – 225°C (440°F).

The baking temperature will depend upon the following considerations:

- shape, size and depth
- density
- sugar content
- product characteristics.

Cooling

SWEET PASTRY PRODUCTS

Sweet pastry bases which are finished and decorated must be thoroughly cooled prior to processing. Sweet pastry products such as apple pies can be baked to meet customer demands throughout the day. However, some products (fruit slices) must be cool to facilitate clean cutting of the shapes.

ENRICHED PASTRY PRODUCTS

Enriched pastry products which are to be finished and decorated or wrapped must be thoroughly cooled prior to processing. Products such as American Cookie Biscuits are baked freshly throughout the day to meet the demands of the customers.

SAVOURY PRODUCTS

It is common practice for savoury products to be sold hot, straight from the oven. This is achieved by baking savouries to the demands from the customer throughout the day. The reheating of savoury product must be thorough and is subject to VAT. Wrapped savouries must be cooled quickly, and stored or displayed in refrigerated conditions as stated in the Food Safety (General Food Hygiene) Regulations 1995.

OVEN CHARTS

Sweet pastries

Product	Baking temperature in °C (°F)	Baking time in minutes	Additional control procedure
Jam & Lemon Tarts	204 (400)	20	Open damper for final 5 mins
Custard Tarts	204 (400)	20	" " " 10 mins
Sm Apple Pies	204 (400)	25	" " " 5 mins
Lge Apple Pies	204 (400)	25	" " " "
Sm & Lge Fruit Pies	204 (400)	25	" " " "
Sweetmince Pies	204 (400)	20	" " " "
Sm Fruit Tart Bases	204 (400)	20	" " " "
Fruit Flan Bases	204 (400)	25	" " " "
Peach Melba Bases	204 (400)	20	" " " "
Apple Charlotte Bases	204 (400)	20	" " " "
Summer Fruit Tart Bases	190 (374)	20	" " " "
Apple Slice	204 (400)	30	" " " "
Fruit Slice	204 (400)	30	" " " "

Enriched pastries

Product	Baking temperature in °C (°F)	Baking time in minutes	Additional control procedures
Shrewsbury Biscuits	200 (392)	15–20	Open damper for final 5 mins
Shortbread	182 (360)	20	" " " "
Viennese Biscuits	190 (374)	15–20	" " " "
Gingerbread Biscuits	180 (356)	15	" " " "
Gingerbread People	180 (356)	20	" " " "
Flapjacks	177 (350)	25	" " " "
American Cookie Biscuits	170 (338)	20	" " " "

Savouries

Product	Baking temperature in °C (°F)	Baking time in minutes	Additional control procedures
Sm/Lge Minced Beef Pie	225 (440)	25	Open damper for final 5 mins
Sm/Lge Minced Beef & Onion Pie	225 (440)	25	" " " "
Sm/Lge Minced Beef & Potato Pie	225 (440)	25	" " " "
Sm/Lge Minced Beef & Vegetable Pie	225 (440)	25	" " " "
Sm/Lge Steak & Kidney Pie	225 (440)	25	" " " "
Sm/Lge Chicken & Mushroom Pie	225 (440)	25	" " " "
Sm/Lge Corned Beef Pie	225 (440)	25	" " " "
Sm/Lge Vegetable Pie	225 (440)	25	" " " "
Sm/Lge Vegetarian Mince & Vegetable Pie	225 (440)	25	" " " "
Sm/Lge Bacon & Egg Pie	225 (440)	25	" " " "
Sm/Lge Minced Beef & Bacon Pie	225 (440)	25	" " " "
Sm/Lge Curried Chicken Pie	225 (440)	25	" " " "
Sm/Lge Mexican Minced Beef Pie	225 (440)	25	" " " "
Savoury Flans	204 (400)	25	" " " " 10 mins
Corned Beef Slice	225 (440)	30	" " " " 5 mins
Pizza Pie	210 (410)	25	" " " "
Sm Pork Pie	225 (440)	40	" " " " 10mins
Sm Pork & Egg Pie	225 (440)	40	" " " "
Lge Pork Pie	225 (440)	60	" " " "
Lge Pork & Egg Pie	225 (440)	60	" " " "
Sm Mutton Pie	225 (440)	25	" " " " 5 mins

RECIPES FOR MAKING SWEET PASTES

A QUALITY SWEET PASTE, RUB-IN METHOD

Ingredients

Kilo	Gram	%	Ingredients	lb	oz
1	000	100.00	medium flour	2	3.50
	550	55.00	butter	1	3.50
	250	25.00	sugar		8.50
	125	12.50	egg		4.25
1	925		Gross weight	4	3.75
1	848		Net weight	4	1.00

1 Sieve the flour.
2 Rub the butter through the flour to a crumble by hand or machine.
3 Mix the sugar and egg together and add to the above.
4 Mix until a smooth paste is obtained.

Note: Do not toughen the paste by over-mixing.

B SWEET PASTE, RUB-IN METHOD

Ingredients

Kilo	Gram	%	Ingredients	lb	oz
1	000	100.00	medium flour	2	3.50
	550	55.00	cake margarine	1	3.50
	250	25.00	sugar		8.50
	125	12.50	egg		4.25
1	925		Gross weight	4	3.75
1	848		Net weight	4	1.00

1 Sieve the flour.
2 Rub the cake margarine through the flour to a crumble by hand or machine.
3 Mix the sugar and egg together and add to the above.
4 Mix until a smooth paste is obtained.

Note: Do not toughen the paste by over-mixing.

C COMMERCIAL SWEET PASTE, RUB-IN METHOD

Ingredients

Kilo	Gram	%	Ingredients	lb	oz
1	000	100.00	medium flour	2	3.50
	60	6.00	skimmed milk powder		2.00
	500	50.00	cake margarine	1	1.50
	170	17.00	sugar		6.00
	140	14.00	water		5.00
1	870		Gross weight	4	2.00
1	795		Net weight	3	15.25

1 Sieve the flour and skimmed milk powder together.
2 Rub the cake margarine through the dry ingredients to a crumble by hand or machine.
3 Mix the sugar and water together and add to the above.
4 Mix until a smooth paste is obtained.

Note: Do not toughen the paste by over-mixing.

RECIPES USING SWEET PASTES

JAM AND LEMON TARTS

Use recipe A, B or C for sweet pastry; all are suitable for this product.

Processing method

Yield approx 50

Note: The appropriate mechanical blocking machine may be used for stages 1, 2 and 3.

1 Pin out the sweet paste to approximately 4 mm ($\frac{3}{16}$") thick.
2 Using a fluted cutter which is slightly larger than the shallow foil or tin, cut out the bases.
3 Place the sweet paste base into the foil or tin and carefully thumb it into position.
4 Prepare the jam or curd for depositing, by mixing until a smooth consistency is obtained.
5 Using a piping bag or depositor, fill each base sufficiently with jam or lemon curd.
6 Bake at 204°C (400°F) for approximately 20 minutes until the sweet paste is golden brown in colour.

Note:

- To prevent the filling from boiling over the edge of the base:
  - **i** Use a jam or curd which contains a high level of fruit.
  - **ii** Do not overfill the base.
- On withdrawal from the oven, take extra care when handling tarts containing boiling jam or curd. Burns from these materials can be severe.

CUSTARD TARTS

Ingredients

Kilo	Gram	%	Ingredients	lb	oz
1	500	100.00	fresh milk	3	5.50
	370	24.60	shell egg		13.25
	245	16.30	sugar		8.75
2	115		Gross weight	4	11.50

Use recipe A, B or C for sweet pastry; all are suitable for this product.

Processing method

Yield approx 40

Note: The appropriate mechanical blocking machine may be used for stages 1, 2 and 3.

1 Pin out the sweet paste to approximately 5 mm (0.25") thick.
2 Using a fluted cutter which is slightly larger than the deep foil or tin, cut out the bases.
3 Place the sweet paste base into the foil or tin and carefully thumb into position.
4 Prepare the custard filling as follows:

Mixing method

- whisk all of the ingredients together
- use immediately.

5 Using a funnel depositor or jug, fill each base sufficiently with the custard filling.
6 Sprinkle a pinch of nutmeg in the centre of each tart.
7 Bake at 204°C (400°F) for approximately 20 minutes until the filling is set.

SMALL APPLE PIES

Ingredients

Kilo	Gram	%	Ingredients	lb	oz
1	500	100.00	unsweetened tinned apple	3	5.50
	225	15	sugar		8.00
1	725		Gross weight	3	13.50

Use recipe A, B or C for sweet pastry; all are suitable for this product.

Processing method

Yield approx 30

Note: The appropriate mechanical blocking machine may be used for stages 1, 2, 3 and 7.

1 Pin out the sweet paste to approximately 5 mm (0.25") thick.
2 Using a fluted cutter which is slightly larger than the deep foil or tin, cut out the 30 bases required.
3 Place the sweet paste base into the foil or tin and carefully thumb into position.
4 Using the remaining sweet paste, pin out to approximately 3 mm (0.125") thick and cut out 30 lids to fit on top of the pastry cases.
5 Prepare the apple filling as follows:

Mixing method

- chop the apple into small pieces
- add the sugar and mix through thoroughly.

Note: The level of sugar may need to be adjusted. This will depend upon the bitterness of the apples.

6 Fill each base sufficiently with the apple filling.
7 Place the sweet paste lid over the filling.
8 Bake at 204°C (400°F) for approximately 25 minutes.
9 On withdrawal from the oven, dredge the pies with caster sugar.

LARGE APPLE PIES

Ingredients

Kilo	Gram	%	Ingredients	lb	oz
1	100	100.00	unsweetened tinned apple	2	7.00
	165	15	sugar		6.00
1	265		Gross weight	2	13.00

Use recipe A, B or C for sweet pastry; all are suitable for this product.

Processing method

Yield approx 6

Note: The appropriate mechanical blocking machine may be used for stages 1, 2, 3, 7, 8 and 9.

1 Scale 6 bases at 175 g (6.25 oz) and mould round.
2 Scale 6 lids at 125 g (4.5 oz) and mould round.
3 Pin out the bases to cover a 15 cm (6") diameter shallow foil or tin. Place the base into the foil or tin and thumb into position.
4 Pin out the lids to cover a 15 cm (6") diameter shallow foil or tin.
5 Prepare the apple filling as follows:

Small and large apple pies

Mixing method

- chop the apple into small pieces
- add the sugar and mix through thoroughly.

Note: The level of sugar may need to be adjusted. This will depend upon the bitterness of the apple.

6 Fill each base with 200 g (7.25 oz) of apple filling.
7 Moisten the edge of the base with water. Place the lid over the filling and secure in position.
8 Using a knife, trim the excess pastry from the edge.
9 Between thumb and forefinger, crimp the edge of the pie.
10 Using a pointed knife, make two vents in the top to allow steam to escape.
11 Bake at 204°C (400°F) for 25 minutes.
12 On withdrawal from the oven, dredge the pies with caster sugar.

LARGE AND SMALL FRUIT PIES

There are many varieties of filling which can be used to make a range of fruit pies; below is a selection of the most popular fillings. To produce any of these varieties, follow the processing methods for Small and Large Apple Pies. Simply replace the apple filling with the filling of your choice.

Fillings for fruit pies

APPLE AND RASPBERRY

Filling for 30 Small Pies:

Ingredients

Kilo	Gram	%	Ingredients	lb	oz
	900	100.00	unsweetened tinned apple	2	0.00
	225	25.00	sugar		8.00
	30	3.30	pre-gelatinised starch		1.00
	600	66.60	raspberries	1	5.50
1	755		Gross weight	3	14.50

Filling for 6 Large Pies:

Ingredients

Kilo	Gram	%	Ingredients	lb	oz
	660	100.00	unsweetened tinned apple	1	7.00
	165	25.00	sugar		6.00
	20	3.00	pre-gelatinised starch		0.75
	440	66.60	raspberries	1	0.00
1	285		Gross weight	2	13.75

Mixing method

1 Chop the apple into small pieces.
2 Mix the sugar and pre-gelatinised starch together. Add to the above and mix through.
3 Add the prepared raspberries and blend through carefully.

APPLE AND BLACKBERRY

Filling for 30 Small Pies:

Ingredients

Kilo	Gram	%	Ingredients	lb	oz
	900	100.00	unsweetened tinned apple	2	0.00
	225	25.00	sugar		8.00
	30	3.30	pre-gelatinised starch		1.00
	600	66.60	blackberries	1	5.50
1	755		Gross weight	3	14.50

Filling for 6 Large Pies:

Ingredients

Kilo	Gram	%	Ingredients	lb	oz
	660	100.00	unsweetened tinned apple	1	7.00
	165	25.00	sugar		6.00
	20	3.00	pre-gelatinised starch		0.75
	440	66.60	blackberries	1	0.00
1	285		Gross weight	2	13.75

Mixing method

1 Chop the apple into small pieces.
2 Mix the sugar and pre-gelatinised starch together. Add to the above and mix through.
3 Add the prepared blackberries and blend through carefully.

RHUBARB

Filling for 30 Small Pies:

Ingredients

Kilo	Gram	%	Ingredients	lb	oz
1	500	100.00	rhubarb	3	5.50
	30	2.00	pre-gelatinised starch		1.00
	225	15.00	sugar		8.00
1	755		Gross weight	3	14.50

Filling for 6 Large Pies:

Ingredients

Kilo	Gram	%	Ingredients	lb	oz
1	100	100.00	rhubarb	2	7.00
	20	1.80	pre-gelatinised starch		0.75
	165	15.00	sugar		6.00
1	285		Gross weight	2	13.75

Mixing method

1 Peel and chop the rhubarb into chunks.
2 Rinse the rhubarb in cold water.
3 Mix the sugar and pre-gelatinised starch together. Add to the above and mix through throughly.

DUTCH APPLE

Filling for 30 Small Pies:

Ingredients

Kilo	Gram	%	Ingredients	lb	oz
1	400	100.00	unsweetened tinned apple	3	2.00
	140	10.00	sugar		5.00
	25	1.80	pre-gelatinised starch		1.00
	5	0.35	cinnamon		0.25
	140	10.00	sultanas		5.00
1	710		Gross weight	3	13.25

Filling for 6 Large Pies:

Ingredients

Kilo	Gram	%	Ingredients	lb	oz
1	050	100.00	unsweetened tinned apple	2	5.50
	105	10.00	sugar		3.75
	20	1.90	pre-gelatinised starch		0.75
	3.50	0.35	cinnamon		0.125
	105	10.00	sultanas		3.75
1	283		Gross weight	3	14.00

Mixing method

1 Chop the apple into small pieces.
2 Mix the sugar, pre-gelatinised starch and cinnamon together. Add to the above and mix thoroughly.
3 Add the sultanas and mix through thoroughly.

CONVENIENCE FILLINGS

There are many convenience fillings available to the baker. These fillings are popular because they are:

- easy to store
- available all year round
- ready to use
- consistent in quality.

Available fillings include blackcurrant, cherry, and blackcurrant and apple.

SWEETMINCE PIES

Sweet mince pies

Use recipe A, B or C for sweet pastry; all are suitable for this product.

Ingredients

Kilo	Gram	%	Ingredients	lb	oz
	220	100.00	currants		8.00
	120	54.00	sultanas		4.25
	120	54.00	raisins		4.25
	145	65.00	Barbados sugar		5.00
	5	2.20	mixed spice		0.25
	145	65.00	suet		5.00
	130	59.00	mixed peel		4.50
	155	70.00	unsweetened tinned apple		5.50
	60	27.00	lemon zest & juice		2.00
	60	27.00	orange zest & juice		2.00
	160	72.00	brandy		5.75
1	320		Gross weight	2	14.50

Processing method

Yield approx 32

Note: The appropriate mechanical blocking machine may be used for stages 1, 2, 3 and 7.

1 Pin out the sweet paste to approximately 4 mm ($\frac{3}{16}$")
thick.
2 Using a fluted cutter which is slightly larger than the medium deep foil or tin, cut out 32 bases.
3 Place the sweet paste base into the foil or tin and carefully thumb into position.
4 Using the remaining sweet paste, pin out to approximately 3 mm (0.125") thick and cut out 32 lids to fit on top of the pastry case.
5 Prepare the sweetmince filling as follows:

Mixing method

- mix together the currants, sultanas and raisins
- mix the Barbados sugar with the mixed spice and add to the above
- add the suet, mixed peel and chopped apple to above
- mix together the lemon zest and juice, orange zest and juice and brandy. Add to above and mix all of the ingredients together
- place into a suitable container until required.

6 Fill each base sufficiently with the sweetmince filling.
7 Place the sweet paste lid over the filling.
8 Bake at 204°C (400°F) for approximately 20 minutes.
9 On withdrawal from the oven, dredge the pies with icing or caster sugar.

SMALL FRUIT TARTS

Ingredients

Kilo	Gram	Ingredients	lb	oz
	800	fresh or tinned fruit	1	12.25
	700	quick-setting jelly	1	8.75
	650	fresh cream	1	7.00

Use recipe A, B or C for sweet pastry; all are suitable for this product.

Processing method

Yield approx 50

Note: The appropriate mechanical blocking machine may be used for stages 1, 2 and 3.

1 Pin out the sweet paste to approximately 4 mm ($\frac{3}{16}$") thick.
2 Using a fluted cutter which is slightly larger than the shallow foil or tin, cut out the bases.
3 Place the sweet paste base into the foil or tin and carefully thumb into position.
4 Bake at 204°C (400°F) for approximately 20 minutes until the sweet paste is golden brown in colour.
5 On withdrawal from the oven, allow the baked cases to cool.
6 When cool, prepare one of the following fruits and place into the pastry case:
   - fresh strawberries – remove the calyx and leaves, wash quickly in cold water and allow to dry. Depending upon the size, use whole or in halves.
   - tinned mandarins, peaches and cherries – drain and allow to dry.
7 Cover the fruit with appropriately coloured and flavoured quick-setting jelly. Allow the jelly to set.
8 Using a star tube, pipe a ring or rosette of fresh cream onto the tart.

Note: These tarts are a perishable product and must be stored or displayed in a refrigerated area.

FRUIT FLANS

Ingredients

Kilo	Gram	Ingredients	lb	oz
1	200	fresh or tinned fruit	2	10.50
1	350	quick-setting jelly	2	15.50
1	300	fresh cream	2	14.00

Fruit flans

(See colour plate 16.)

Use recipe A, B or C for sweet pastry; all are suitable for this product.

Processing method

Yield approx 9

Note: The appropriate mechanical blocking machine may be used for stages 1, 2, 3 and 4.

1 Scale 9 at 195 g (7 oz) and mould round.
2 Pin out the bases to cover a 15 cm (6") diameter flan foil, tin or ring. Place the base into the foil, tin or ring and thumb into position.
3 Using a knife, trim the excess pastry from the edge.
4 The edge of the flan may be left plain or crimped with the thumb and forefinger.
5 Bake at 204°C (400°F) for approximately 25 minutes until the sweet paste is golden brown in colour.
6 On withdrawal from the oven, allow the baked cases to cool.
7 When cool, prepare and arrange fresh or tinned fruit in an attractive design within the pastry case.

Note: The fruits stated for Small Fruit Tarts are also suitable for Fruit Flans. Other fruits suitable for flans are:

- pineapple rings – drain and allow to dry
- tinned pears – drain and allow to dry
- bananas – peel, slice and use immediately
- kiwi fruit – peel and slice for use.

8 Cover the fruit with appropriately coloured and flavoured quick-setting jelly. Allow the jelly to set.
9 Using a star tube, pipe:
   - a rope of fresh cream around the edge of the flan; or
   - six rosettes of fresh cream evenly spaced on the top of the flan.

Note: These flans are a perishable product and must be stored or displayed in a refrigerated area.

PEACH MELBAS

Ingredients

Kilo	Gram	Ingredients	lb	oz
	800	chopped peaches	1	12.25
1	200	fresh cream	2	10.50
1	300	peach coloured fondant	2	14.00

(See colour plate 18.)

Use recipe A, B or C for sweet pastry; all are suitable for this product.

Processing method

Yield   approx 60

Note: The appropriate mechanical blocking machine may be used for stages 1, 2 and 3.

1 Pin out the sweet paste to approximately 3 mm (0.125") thick.
2 Using a fluted cutter which is slightly larger than the medium deep foil or tin, cut out the bases.
3 Place the sweet paste base into the foil or tin and carefully thumb it into position.
4 Bake at 204°C (400°F) for approximately 20 minutes until the sweet paste is golden brown in colour.
5 On withdrawal from the oven, allow the baked cases to cool.
6 When cool, place a small quantity of peach into the baked case. Prior to use the peaches should be drained, dried and chopped.
7 Using a plain tube, pipe a large bulb of fresh cream over the peach. It is important for the cream bulb to be a smooth, round shape.
8 Warm some fondant to 37°C (99°F) and colour it peach. Adjust the consistency using stock syrup.
9 Beginning at the top of the fresh cream bulb and working downwards, pipe the fondant in a spiral manner until the cream bulb is fully covered. Allow the fondant to set.
10 Using deep coloured peach fondant, begin at the top and pipe a thin spiral over the covered bulb.

Note:

- prior to covering the fresh cream bulb with fondant, it may be necessary to chill the melba.
- peach melbas are a perishable product and must be stored or displayed in a refrigerated area.

APPLE CHARLOTTES

Ingredients

Kilo	Gram	Ingredients	lb	oz
	800	chopped sweetened apple	1	12.25
	500	fresh cream	1	1.75
	200	roasted nibbed almonds		700

(See colour plate 14.)

Use recipe A, B or C for sweet pastry; all are suitable for this product.

Processing method

Yield approx 40

Note: The appropriate mechanical blocking machine may be used for stages 1, 2 and 3.

1 Pin out the sweet paste to approximately 5 mm (0.25") thick.
2 Using a fluted cutter which is slightly larger than the deep foil or tin, cut out the bases.
3 Place the sweet paste base into the foil or tin and carefully thumb it into position.
4 Fill one-third of the pastry base with chopped, sweetened apple.
5 Bake at 204°C (400°F) for approximately 20 minutes until the sweet paste is golden brown in colour.
6 On withdrawal from the oven, allow the baked cases to cool.
7 Prepare the custard as follows:

Ingredients for custard

Kilo	Gram	%	Ingredients	lb	oz
1	000	100.00	fresh milk	2	3.50
	100	10.00	cornflour		3.50
	150	15.00	sugar		5.75
	200	20.00	egg		7.00
	5	0.50	vanilla flavour		0.25
	3	0.30	egg colour		0.125
	100	10.00	whipped cream		3.50
1	558		Gross weight	3	7.50

Mixing method

- add the cornflour to a small amount of the milk, all of the egg, the vanilla flavour and egg colour; mix through thoroughly
- add the sugar to the remaining milk and bring to the boil
- remix the cornflour solution and pour into the boiling milk and sugar, stirring continuously until the custard thickens
- allow to stand for 10 minutes, then blend the whipped cream through.

8 Pour sufficient custard into the baked case. Allow to cool and set.
9 Pipe a rosette of fresh cream on top of the custard.
10 Sprinkle roasted nib almonds onto the cream rosette.

SUMMER FRUIT TARTS

(See colour plate 15.)

Use recipe A, B or C for sweet pastry; all are suitable for this product.

Materials required to make 44 Summer Fruit Tarts

Kilo	Gram	Ingredients	lb	oz
1	000	frangipane filling (p. 316)	2	3.50
1	200	rich custard filling	2	10.50
	550	apple	1	3.50
		44 small strawberries		
		44 slices of kiwi fruit		
		44 blackberries		
		44 raspberries		
		44 seedless grapes		
		44 pitted cherries		
1	000	clear jelly	2	3.50

Processing method

Yield approx 44

Note:

- this product requires a 10 cm (4") diameter shallow foil or tin to accommodate the filling and decoration.
- the appropriate mechanical blocking machine may be used for stages 1, 2, 3 and 4.

1 Pin out the sweet paste to approximately 4 mm ($\frac{3}{16}$") thick.
2 Using a fluted cutter which is slightly larger than the shallow foil or tin, cut out the bases.
3 Place the sweet paste base into the foil or tin and carefully thumb it into position.
4 Pipe a spiral of frangipane filling into each sweet paste base.
5 Bake at 190°C (374°F) for approximately 20 minutes.
6 On withdrawal from the oven, allow the baked cases to cool.
7 Prepare a rich custard filling by blending together equal quantities of whipped fresh cream and cold custard. Using a plain tube, pipe the filling over the frangipane within the pastry case. Keep the filling flat and level.
8 Clean and prepare, sliced apple, strawberries, sliced kiwi, blackberries, grapes, cherries and raspberries. Neatly arrange fruit on top of the rich custard filling.
9 Glaze all of the fruit with a clear jelly.

APPLE SLICE

Use recipe A, B or C for sweet pastry; all are suitable for this product.

Ingredients

Kilo	Gram	%	Ingredients	lb	oz
2	200	100.00	unsweetened tinned apple	4	14.00
	330	15.00	sugar		12.00
	100	4.50	pre-gelatinised starch		3.50
2	630		Gross weight	5	13.50

Processing method

Yield 30

1 Pin out 850 g (1lb 14 oz) of sweet pastry and line a small baking tray measuring 37.5 × 45 cm (15 × 18").
2 Prepare the apple filling as follows:

Mixing method

- chop the apple into small pieces
- mix the sugar and pre-gelatinised starch together. Add to the above and mix through thoroughly.

Note: The level of sugar may need to be adjusted. This will depend upon the bitterness of the apple.

3 Place the apple filling onto the sweet paste base and spread evenly.
4 Pin out 930 g (2 lb 1.25 oz) of sweet pastry and cover the filling.
5 Trim off the excess pastry from the top edge.
6 Using pastry wheels 6 × 5, mark the pastry into 30 squares.
7 Bake at 204°C (400°F) for approximately 30 minutes.
8 On withdrawal from the oven, dredge the slice with caster sugar.
9 Allow the slice to cool thoroughly, then cut into squares.

FRUIT SLICES

There are many varieties of filling that can be used to make a range of fruit slices. Below you will find a selection of the most popular fillings. To produce any of these varieties, follow the processing methods for Apple Slice; simply replace the apple filling with the filling of your choice.

Fillings for Fruit Slice

CURRANT

Ingredients

Kilo	Gram	%	Ingredients	lb	oz
1	600	100.00	currants	3	9.00
	240	15.00	cake crumbs		8.50
	240	15.00	sugar		8.50
	25	1.50	mixed spice		1.00
	400	25.00	unsweetened tinned apple		14.50
2	505		Gross weight	5	9.50

Mixing method

- mix together the currants, cake crumbs, sugar and mixed spice
- chop the apple, add to above and mix thoroughly.

APPLE AND RASPBERRY

Ingredients

Kilo	Gram	%	Ingredients	lb	oz
1	320	100.00	unsweetened tinned apple	2	14.00
	330	25.00	sugar		12.00
	150	11.36	pre-gelatinised starch		5.25
	880	66.60	raspberries	1	15.50
2	680		Gross weight	5	14.75

Mixing method

- chop the apple into small pieces
- mix the sugar and pre-gelatinised starch together, add to above and mix through thoroughly
- add the raspberries and blend through carefully.

APPLE AND RASPBERRY

Ingredients

Kilo	Gram	%	Ingredients	lb	oz
1	320	100.00	unsweetened tinned apple	2	14.00
	330	25.00	sugar		12.00
	150	11.36	pre-gelatinised starch		5.25
	880	66.60	blackberries	1	15.50
2	680		Gross weight	5	14.75

Mixing method

- chop the apple into small pieces
- mix the sugar and pre-gelatinised starch together, add to above and mix through thoroughly
- add the blackberries and blend through carefully.

DUTCH APPLE

Ingredients

Kilo	Gram	%	Ingredients	lb	oz
2	100	100.00	unsweetened tinned apple	4	11.00
	210	10.00	sultanas		7.50
	210	10.00	sugar		7.50
	7.00	0.33	cinnamon		0.25
	125	5.90	pre-gelatinised starch	4.50	
2	652		Gross weight	5	14.75

Mixing method

- chop the apple and mix with the sultanas
- mix the sugar, cinnamon and pre-gelatinised starch together, add to above and mix through thoroughly.

(See overleaf for recipes using enriched pastes.)

RECIPES USING ENRICHED PASTES

SHREWSBURY BISCUITS

Ingredients

Kilo	Gram	%	Ingredients	lb	oz
	600	100.00	medium flour	1	5.50
	5	0.83	nutmeg		0.25
	360	60.00	butter or cake margarine		13.00
	100	16.60	sugar		3.50
	100	16.60	egg		3.50
	5	0.83	lemon essence		0.25
	100	16.60	currants		3.50
1	270		Gross weight	2	13.50
1	219		Net weight	2	11.50

Production Points

Biscuit weight	**approx 60 g (2 oz)**
Yield	**20**
Baking temperature	**200°C (392°F)**
Baking time	**15–20 mins**

Mixing method

1 Sieve together the flour and nutmeg.
2 Add the butter or cake margarine and rub through to a crumble.
3 Mix the sugar and egg together, add the lemon essence, then add to the dry ingredients.
4 Mix to a half clear paste. Add the currants and mix to a smooth clear paste. Do not over mix the paste.

Processing method

1 Pin out the paste to approximately 5 mm (0.25") thick.
2 Using an 11 cm (4.5") fluted cutter, cut out the biscuits.
3 Carefully place the biscuits onto a greased tray.
4 Bake at 200°C (392°F) for 15–20 minutes.
5 On withdrawal from the oven, dredge the biscuits with caster sugar.

Shortbread .

SHORTBREAD

Ingredients

Kilo	Gram	%	Ingredients	lb	oz
1	000	100.00	medium flour	2	3.50
	620	62.00	butter	1	6.25
	400	40.00	sugar		14.25
2	020		Gross weight	4	8.00
1	939		Net weight	4	5.00

Production Points

Biscuit weight:	
fingers	**approx 25 g (1 oz)**
rounds	**120 g (4.25 oz)**
Yield:	
fingers	**approx 75**
rounds	**16**
Baking temperature	**182°C (360°F)**
Baking time	**approx 20 mins**

Mixing method

1 Sieve the flour and sugar together.
2 Add the butter and mix through until a smooth paste is obtained.

Processing methods

FINGERS

1 Pin out the paste to approximately 1.5 cm (0.5") thick.
2 Dock the surface of the paste lightly.
3 Mark and cut into fingers 2.5 × 7.5 cm (1 × 3").
4 Place the biscuits onto a greased tray.
5 Bake at 182°C (360°F) for approximately 20 minutes.
6 On withdrawal from the oven, dredge the shortbread fingers with caster sugar and allow to cool.

ROUNDS

1 Scale 16 at 120 g (4.25 oz) and mould round.
2 Dust the round shallow mould with ground rice.
3 Place the paste into the mould, press and flatten until the paste completely fills the mould.
4 Reverse the mould and tap lightly until the round is released.
5 Place the rounds onto a greased tray.
6 Using a scotch scraper, mark the rounds into four equal segments.
7 Bake at 182°C (360°F) for approximately 20 minutes.
8 On withdrawal from the oven, dredge the shortbread rounds with caster sugar and allow to cool.

Note: There are many decorative moulds which can be used to produce specialist shortbread.

VIENNESE BISCUITS

Ingredients

Kilo	Gram	%	Ingredients	lb	oz
1	000	100.00	butter or margarine	2	3.50
1	000	100.00	medium flour	2	3.50
	140	14.00	egg		5.00
	130	13.00	cornflour		4.50
	320	32.00	icing sugar		11.50
2	590		Gross weight	5	12.00
2	525		Net weight	5	9.50

Production Points

Yield	**approx 124**
Baking temperature	**190°C (374°F)**
Baking time	**15–20 mins**

Mixing method

1 Sieve the flour, add to the butter or margarine. Blend together then beat on fast speed for 10 minutes until light.
2 Add the egg in a steady stream on slow speed and scrape down.
3 Beat on fast speed for 1 minute.
4 Sieve together the cornflour and icing sugar, add to above and mix on slow speed until half clear.
5 Scrape down, then mix on slow speed until clear.

Processing method

1 Using a savoy bag and star tube, pipe fingers or rosettes onto a greased tray.
2 Bake at 190°C (374°F) for 15–20 minutes.
3 On withdrawal from the oven, allow the biscuits to cool on the tray.
4 Sandwich the fingers or rosettes together with jam.
5 The fingers or rosettes can now be dipped into chocolate flavoured coating as follows:
- Fingers – dip the ends into chocolate flavoured coating and allow to set.
- Rosettes – half dip the rosette into chocolate flavoured coating and allow to set.

GINGER BISCUITS AND PEOPLE

Ingredients

Kilo	Gram	%	Ingredients	lb	oz
	720	100.00	bread flour	1	9.75
	20	2.77	bicarbonate of soda		0.75
	10	1.38	ground ginger		0.50
	10	1.38	mixed spice		0.50
	180	25.00	cake margarine		6.50
	420	58.00	golden syrup		15.00
	90	12.50	egg		3.25
	240	35.00	sugar		8.50
	240	35.00	brown sugar		8.50
1	930		Gross weight	4	5.25
1	852		Net weight	4	2.50

Mixing method

1 Sieve together the bread flour, bicarbonate of soda, ground ginger and mixed spice.
2 Add the cake margarine and rub through until a crumble is obtained.
3 Break the golden syrup down with egg, add the sugars and mix through. Add to above.
4 Mix until a smooth paste is obtained.

Processing methods

BISCUITS

1 Pin out the paste to approximately 4 mm ($\frac{3}{16}$") thick.
2 Using an 8 cm (3.5") plain cutter, cut out the biscuits.

Production Points

Yield:	
biscuits	**approx 60**
people	**approx 30**
Baking temperature	**180°C (356°F)**
Baking time:	
biscuits	**approx 15 mins**
people	**approx 20 mins**

3 Carefully place the biscuits onto a greased tray.
4 Bake at 180°C (356°F) for approximately 15 minutes.
5 On withdrawal from the oven, allow the biscuits to cool on the tray.

GINGERBREAD PEOPLE

1 Pin out the paste to approximately 5 mm (0.25") thick.
2 Using a gingerbread people cutter, cut out the people.
3 Carefully place the people onto a greased tray.
4 Bake at 180°C (356°F) for 20 minutes.
5 On withdrawal from the oven, allow the people to cool on the tray.
6 When cool, use royal icing and chocolate flavoured coating to pipe eyes and other features.

FLAPJACKS

Ingredients

Kilo	Gram	%	Ingredients	lb	oz
1	000	100.00	rolled oats	2	3.50
	140	14.00	ground hazelnuts		5.00
	500	50.00	cake margarine	1	1.75
	250	25.00	shortening		9.00
	500	50.00	brown sugar	1	1.75
	190	19.00	treacle		6.75
2	580		Gross weight	5	11.75
2	475		Net weight	5	8.00

Production Points

Yield:	
squares	**30**
fingers	**60**
Baking temperature	**177°C (350°F)**
Baking time	**approx 25 mins**

Mixing method

1 Place the rolled oats and ground hazelnuts in a bowl.
2 Melt the cake margarine and shortening, add the brown sugar and treacle, and mix together. Add to the above.
3 Mix all of the ingredients together until they are thoroughly dispersed.

Flapjacks

Processing method

1 Pour the mixture into a small baking tray measuring 37 × 45 cm (15 × 18") which has been lined with silicone paper.
2 Spread the mixture evenly over the tray.
3 Bake at 177°C (350°F) for approximately 25 minutes.
4 On withdrawal from the oven, allow the flapjack to cool in the tray.
5 Remove the flapjack from the tray.
6 Using pastry wheels or cutting guide, mark the flapjack into fingers or squares.

Note:
- Additions – a variety of flapjacks can be produced by adding one of the following ingredients at a rate of 10–15% of the gross weight: currants, sultanas, raisins, apple, dried apricots and glazed cherries.
- Finishes – flapjacks can be finished by dipping parts of the finger and squares into chocolate flavoured coating.

AMERICAN COOKIE BISCUITS

Ingredients

Kilo	Gram	%	Ingredients	lb	oz
	530	88.00	light brown sugar	1	3.00
	565	94.50	butter or margarine	1	4.00
	15	2.50	egg		0.50
	45	7.30	apple syrup		1.50
	45	7.30	plain yoghurt		1.50
	245	41.00	rolled oats		8.75
	600	100.00	medium flour	1	5.50
	35	6.00	baking powder		1.25
	140	23.50	chocolate chips		5.00
2	220		Gross weight	4	15.00
2	131		Net weight	4	12.00

Mixing method

1 Beat the light brown sugar with the butter or margarine on fast speed for 10 minutes.
2 Add the egg on slow speed, scrape down, then beat on fast speed for 15 seconds.
3 Mix together the apple syrup and plain yoghurt, add to above and mix on slow speed until clear.
4 Sieve together the flour and baking powder and then mix the rolled oats through the flour.
5 Add the dry ingredients to above and mix on slow speed until half clear.
6 Add the chocolate chips and mix on slow speed until a clear dough is obtained. Do not over mix the dough.

Processing method

1 Pin out the dough to approximately 5 mm (0.25") thick.
2 Using a 7.5 cm (3") plain cutter, cut out the biscuits.
3 Carefully place the biscuits onto a tray lined with silicone.
4 Bake at 170°C (338°F) for approximately 20 minutes.

Production Points

Biscuit weight	**approx 55 g (2 oz)**
Yield	**36**
Baking temperature	**170°C (338°F)**
Baking time	**approx 20 mins**

5 On withdrawal from the oven, allow the biscuits to cool on the tray.

Note:

- Additions – a variety of American Cookie Biscuits can be produced by replacing the chocolate chips with one of the following ingredients: white chocolate chips, raisins, desiccated coconut, nib almonds, peanuts, or diced apple.
- Novelties – these cookies can be made slightly larger to produce a range of novelty faces using popular children's sweets.

American cookies

RECIPES FOR MAKING SAVOURY PASTES

A COLD PASTE – RUB-IN METHOD

Ingredients

Kilo	Gram	%	Ingredients	lb	oz
1	000	100.00	medium flour	2	3.50
	15	1.50	salt		0.50
	450	45.00	shortening or lard	1	0.00
	440	44.00	cold water		15.75
1	905		Gross weight	4	3.75
1	828		Net weight	4	1.00

Mixing method

1 Sieve the flour and salt together.
2 Rub the shortening or lard through the flour to a crumble by hand or machine.
3 Add the water, mix until a smooth paste is obtained.

Note: Do not toughen the paste by over-mixing.

B HOT PASTE – RUB-IN METHOD

Ingredients

Kilo	Gram	%	Ingredients	lb	oz
1	000	100.00	medium flour	2	3.50
	15	1.50	salt		0.50
	450	45.00	shortening or lard	1	0.00
	450	45.00	hot water at approx 60°C (140°F)	1	0.00
1	905		Gross weight	4	4.00
1	838		Net weight	4	1.50

Mixing method

1 Sieve the flour and salt together.
2 Rub the shortening or lard through the flour to a crumble by hand or machine.
3 Add the hot water, mix until a smooth paste is obtained.

Note:

- do not toughen the paste by over-mixing
- allow the paste to cool before processing begins.

RECIPES USING SAVOURY PASTES

SMALL MINCED BEEF PIE

Use recipe A or B for savoury paste; both are suitable for this product.

Processing method

Yield 18

Note: The appropriate mechanical blocking machine may be used for stages 1, 2, 3 of the processing method, and stages 8 and 9 of the cooking method.

1 Pin out the savoury paste to approximately 4 mm ($\frac{3}{16}$") thick.
2 Using a plain cutter that is slightly larger than the shallow foil or tin, cut out the 18 bases at approximately 55 g (2 oz) in weight.
3 Place the savoury paste base into the foil or tin and carefully thumb it into position.
4 Using the remaining savoury paste pin out to approximately 4 mm ($\frac{3}{16}$") thick and cut out 18 lids at approximately 45 g (1.5 oz) in weight to fit the pastry case.
5 Prepare the minced beef filling as follows.

Ingredients

Kilo	Gram	%	Ingredients	lb	oz
1	000	100.00	minced beef	2	3.50
	500	50.00	water	1	1.00
	15	1.50	salt		0.50
	5	0.50	pepper		0.25
	10	1.00	meat extract flavour		0.50
	30	3.00	cornflour		1.00
	50	5.00	water		1.75
1	610		Gross weight	3	8.50

Cooking method

1 Place the minced beef, water, salt, pepper and meat extract flavour into a pan and bring to the boil.
2 Reduce the heat and allow to simmer for 10 minutes.
3 Mix the cornflour and water together, add to the above while stirring continuously.
4 When the filling has thickened, remove from the heat.
5 Allow the filling to cool to 21°C (70°F) before processing begins.
6 Moisten the top edge of the savoury paste base.
7 Fill each base with approximately 80 g (2.75 oz) of minced beef filling.
8 Place the savoury paste lid over the filling and secure to the base.
9 Between thumb and forefinger crimp the edge of the pie.
10 Brush the top of the pie with eggwash.

11 Using a pointed knife make two vents in the top to allow steam to escape.
12 Bake at 225°C (440°F) for 25 minutes.

LARGE MINCED BEEF PIE

Use recipe A or B for savoury paste; both are suitable for this product.

Processing method

Yield 5

Note: The appropriate mechanical blocking machine may be used for stages 1, 2, 3 of the processing method and stages 8 and 9 of the cooking method.

1 Scale 5 bases at 200 g (7.25 oz) and mould round.
2 Scale 5 lids at 160 g (5.75 oz) and mould round.
3 Pin out the bases to cover a 15 cm (6") diameter shallow foil or tin. Place base into the foil or tin and carefully thumb into position.
4 Pin out the lids to cover a 15 cm (6") diameter shallow foil or tin.
5 Prepare the minced beef filling as follows.

Ingredients

Kilo	Gram	%	Ingredients	lb	oz
	850	100.00	minced beef	1	14.50
	425	50.00	water		15.25
	15	1.75	salt		0.50
	4	0.47	pepper		0.25
	10	1.17	meat extract flavour		0.50
	25	2.90	cornflour		1.00
	40	4.70	water		1.50
1	369		Gross weight	3	1.50

Cooking method

1 Place the minced beef, water, salt, pepper and meat extract flavour into a pan and bring to the boil.
2 Reduce the heat and allow to simmer for 10 minutes.
3 Mix the water and cornflour together. Add to the above while stirring continuously.
4 When the filling has thickened, remove from the heat.
5 Allow the filling to cool to 21°C (70°F) before processing begins.
6 Fill each base with 250 g (9 oz) of minced beef filling.
7 Moisten the edge of the base with water, place the lid over the filling and secure in position.
8 Using a knife trim the excess pastry from the edge.
9 Between thumb and forefinger, crimp the edge of the pie.
10 Brush the top of the pie with eggwash.
11 Using a pointed knife, make two vents in the top to allow steam to escape.
12 Bake at 225°C (440°F) for 25 minutes.

Small minced beef pies

LARGE AND SMALL SAVOURY PIES

There are many varieties of fillings which can be used to make a range of savoury pies. Below you will find a selection of the most popular fillings – traditional and innovative reflecting the direction of the consumer's taste. To produce any of these varieties, follow the processing method for Small and Large Minced Beef Pies. Simply replace the minced beef filling with the filling of your choice.

Minced beef and onion filling

Filling for 18 Small Pies:

Ingredients

Kilo	Gram	%	Ingredients	lb	oz
	800	100.00	minced beef	1	12.50
	200	25.00	chopped onions		7.25
	500	62.50	water	1	1.50
	15	1.90	salt		0.50
	5	0.60	pepper		0.25
	10	1.25	meat extract flavour		0.50
	30	3.75	cornflour		1.00
	50	6.25	water		1.75
1	610		Gross weight	3	9.25

Filling for 5 Large Pies:

Ingredients

Kilo	Gram	%	Ingredients	lb	oz
	680	100.00	minced beef	1	8.75
	270	25.00	chopped onions		6.00
	425	62.50	water		15.75
	15	2.20	salt		0.50
	4	0.60	pepper		0.25
	10	1.50	meat extract flavour		0.50
	25	3.70	cornflour		1.00
	40	5.90	water		1.50
1	369		Gross weight	3	1.25

COOKING METHOD

1 Place the minced beef, chopped onions, water, salt, pepper and meat extract flavour into a pan and bring to the boil.
2 Reduce the heat and allow to simmer for 10 minutes.
3 Mix the water and cornflour together. Add to the above while stirring continuously.
4 When the filling has thickened, remove from the heat.
5 Allow the filling to cool to 21°C (70°F) before processing begins.

Minced beef and potato filling

Filling for 18 Small Pies:

Ingredients

Kilo	Gram	%	Ingredients	lb	oz
	600	100.00	minced beef	1	5.50
	500	83.30	water	1	1.50
	15	2.50	salt		0.50
	5	0.83	pepper		0.25
	10	1.66	meat extract flavour		0.50
	30	5.00	cornflour		1.00
	50	8.33	water		1.75
	400	66.60	uncooked diced potato		14.25
1	610		Gross weight	3	9.25

Filling for 5 Large Pies:

Ingredients

Kilo	Gram	%	Ingredients	lb	oz
	510	100.00	minced beef	1	2.25
	425	83.30	water		15.25
	15	2.90	salt		0.50
	4	0.78	pepper		0.25
	10	1.96	meat extract flavour		0.50
	2.5	4.90	cornflour		1.00
	40	7.84	water		1.50
	340	66.60	uncooked diced potato		12.25
1	369		Gross weight	3	1.50

COOKING METHOD

1 Place the minced beef, water, salt, pepper and meat extract flavour into a pan and bring to the boil.
2 Reduce the heat and allow to simmer for 10 minutes.
3 Mix the water and cornflour together. Add to the above while stirring continuously.
4 When the filling has thickened, remove from the heat, add the uncooked diced potato and stir through.
5 Allow the filling to cool to 21°C (70°F) before processing begins.

Minced beef and vegetable filling

Filling for 18 Small Pies:

Ingredients

Kilo	Gram	%	Ingredients	lb	oz
	500	100.00	minced beef	1	1.00
	140	28.00	chopped onions		5.00
	500	100.00	water	1	1.00
	15	3.00	salt		0.50
	5	1.00	pepper		0.25
	10	2.00	meat extract flavour		0.50
	140	28.00	diced potato		5.00
	140	28.00	diced carrot		5.00
	80	16.00	peas		3.00
	30	6.00	cornflour		1.00
	50	10.00	water		1.75
1	610		Gross weight	3	8.00

Filling for 5 Large Pies:

Ingredients

Kilo	Gram	%	Ingredients	lb	oz
	425	100.00	minced beef		15.25
	120	28.00	chopped onions		4.25
	425	100.00	water		15.25
	15	3.50	salt		0.50
	4	0.94	pepper		0.25
	10	2.35	meat extract flavour		0.50
	120	28.00	diced potato		4.25
	120	28.00	diced carrot		4.25
	65	15.30	peas		2.25
	25	5.90	cornflour		1.00
	40	9.40	water		1.50
1	369		Gross weight	3	1.25

COOKING METHOD

1. Place the minced beef, chopped onions, water, salt, pepper and meat extract flavour into a pan and bring to the boil.
2. Reduce the heat and allow to simmer for 10 minutes.
3. Add the diced potato, diced carrots and peas and stir through.
4. Mix the water and cornflour together, add to the above while stirring continuously.
5. When the filling has thickened, remove from the heat.
6. Allow the filling to cool to 21°C (70°F) before processing begins.

Steak and kidney filling

Filling for 18 Small Pies:

Ingredients

Kilo	Gram	%	Ingredients	lb	oz
	850	100.00	lean diced beef	1	14.25
	150	17.50	diced kidney		5.25
	500	100.00	water	1	1.50
	15	1.76	salt		0.50
	5	0.58	pepper		0.25
	10	1.17	meat extract flavour		0.50
	30	3.52	cornflour		1.00
	50	5.88	water		1.75
1	610		Gross weight	3	9.00

Filling for 5 Large Pies:

Ingredients

Kilo	Gram	%	Ingredients	lb	oz
	725	100.00	lean diced beef	1	10.00
	125	17.25	diced kidney		4.50
	425	59.85	water		15.25
	15	2.00	salt		0.50
	4	0.55	pepper		0.25
	10	1.40	meat extract flavour		0.50
	25	3.45	cornflour		1.00
	40	5.63	water		1.50
1	369		Gross weight	3	1.50

COOKING METHOD

1 Place the lean diced beef, diced kidney, water, salt, pepper and meat extract flavour into a pan and bring to the boil.
2 Reduce the heat and allow to simmer for 40 minutes.
3 Mix the water and cornflour together. Add to the above while stirring continuously.
4 When the filling has thickened remove from the heat.
5 Allow the filling to cool to 21°C (70°F) before processing begins.

Note: For Steak Pies, replace the diced kidney with lean diced beef.

Chicken and mushroom filling

Filling for 18 Small Pies:

Ingredients

Kilo	Gram	%	Ingredients	lb	oz
	80	16.00	margarine		3.00
	80	16.00	medium flour		3.00
	520	104.00	milk	1	2.50
	165	33.00	water		6.00
	15	3.00	salt		0.50
	2	0.40	pepper		pinch
	500	100.00	diced cooked chicken	1	1.00
	285	57.00	sliced mushrooms		10.00
1	647		Gross weight	3	10.00

Filling for 5 Large Pies:

Ingredients

Kilo	Gram	%	Ingredients	lb	oz
	65	15.47	margarine		2.25
	65	15.47	medium flour		2.25
	435	103.00	milk		15.50
	140	33.30	water		5.00
	15	3.57	salt		0.50
	1	0.23	pepper		pinch
	420	100.00	diced cooked chicken		15.00
	240	57.00	sliced mushrooms		8.50
1	381		Gross weight	3	1.00

COOKING METHOD

1 Place the margarine into a pan and melt down slowly.
2 Add the flour and cook until a roux is obtained. Remove from heat.
3 Mix the milk and water together. Add to the above slowly while stirring continuously. Return to the heat, continue to stir until a thick smooth sauce is obtained.
4 Add the salt, pepper and sliced mushrooms and stir through.
5 Allow to cool to 21°C (70°F), then add and stir through the diced cooked chicken.
6 The filling is now ready for processing.

Corned beef and potato filling

Filling for 18 Small Pies:

Ingredients

Kilo	Gram	%	Ingredients	lb	oz
	800	100.00	corned beef	1	12.50
	650	81.00	mashed potato	1	7.25
	200	25.00	chopped onion		7.25
1	650		Gross weight	3	11.00

Filling for 5 Large Pies:

Ingredients

Kilo	Gram	%	Ingredients	lb	oz
	670	100.00	corned beef	1	8.00
	545	81.00	mashed potato	1	3.50
	170	25.00	chopped onion		6.00
1	385		Gross weight	3	1.50

MIXING METHOD

1 Mix all the ingredients together until a smooth consistency is obtained.

Note: Mashed potato must be cold.

Vegetable filling

Filling for 18 Small Pies:

Ingredients

Kilo	Gram	%	Ingredients	lb	oz
	300	60.00	diced carrot		10.75
	300	60.00	diced swede		10.75
	200	40.00	chopped onions		7.25
	200	40.00	sliced mushrooms		7.25
	150	30.00	peas		5.50
	500	100.00	mashed potato	1	1.00
	15	3.00	salt		0.50
	5	1.00	pepper		0.25
1	670		Gross weight	3	11.25

Filling for 5 Large Pies:

Ingredients

Kilo	Gram	%	Ingredients	lb	oz
	250	60.00	diced carrot		9.00
	250	60.00	diced swede		9.00
	165	40.00	chopped onions		6.00
	165	40.00	sliced mushrooms		6.00
	125	30.00	peas		4.50
	415	100.00	mashed potato		15.00
	15	3.00	salt		0.50
	4	1.00	pepper		0.25
1	389		Gross weight	3	2.25

COOKING METHOD

1 Place the diced carrot, diced swede, chopped onions and sliced mushrooms into a pan with sufficient water and bring to the boil.
2 Reduce the heat and allow to simmer for 10 minutes.

3 Remove from the heat and drain the water from the vegetables.
4 Add the peas, mashed potato, salt and pepper and mix together thoroughly.
5 The filling is now ready for processing.

Note: To make a curried vegetable pie, simply add curry powder to the filling at a rate of 2% of the total weight of ingredients. This equals 30 g (1 oz) curry powder for the small pie filling and 25 g (0.75 oz) curry powder for the large pie filling.

Vegetarian mince and vegetable filling

Filling for 18 Small Pies:

Ingredients

Kilo	Gram	%	Ingredients	lb	oz
	500	100.00	hydrated soya mince	1	1.00
	140	28.00	chopped onions		5.00
	500	100.00	water	1	1.00
	15	3.00	salt		0.50
	5	1.00	pepper		0.25
	10	2.00	yeast extract		0.50
	140	28.00	diced potato		5.00
	140	28.00	diced carrot		5.00
	80	15.00	peas		3.00
	20	4.00	cornflour		0.75
	50	10.00	water		1.75
1	600		Gross weight	3	7.75

Filling for 5 Large Pies:

Ingredients

Kilo	Gram	%	Ingredients	lb	oz
	425	100.00	hydrated soya mince		15.25
	120	28.00	chopped onions		4.25
	425	100.00	water		15.25
	15	3.50	salt		0.50
	4	0.94	pepper		0.25
	10	2.35	yeast extract		0.50
	120	28.00	diced potato		4.25
	120	28.00	diced carrot		4.25
	65	15.30	peas		2.25
	15	3.50	cornflour		0.50
	40	9.40	water		1.50
1	359		Gross weight	3	0.75

COOKING METHOD

1 Place the hydrated soya mince, chopped onions, water, salt, pepper and yeast extract into a pan and bring to the boil.
2 Reduce the heat and allow to simmer for 5 minutes.
3 Add the diced potato, diced carrot and peas and stir through.
4 Mix the water and cornflour together. Add to the above while stirring continuously.

5 When the filling has thickened, remove from the heat.
6 Allow the filling to cool to 21°C (70°F) before processing begins.

Bacon and egg filling

Filling for 18 Small Pies:

Ingredients

Kilo	Gram	%	Ingredients	lb	oz
	800	100.00	lean bacon	1	12.50
	800	100.00	fresh egg	1	12.50
	10	1.25	salt		0.50
	5	0.60	pepper		0.25
1	615		Gross weight	3	9.75

Filling for 5 Large Pies:

Ingredients

Kilo	Gram	%	Ingredients	lb	oz
	690	100.00	lean bacon	1	8.50
	690	100.00	fresh egg	1	8.50
	10	1.40	salt		0.50
	4	0.57	pepper		0.25
1	394		Gross weight	3	1.75

MIXING METHOD

1 Remove the rind and cut the bacon into small pieces.
2 Add the salt and pepper to the egg and beat lightly.
3 Use equal quantities of bacon and egg for each pie.

Note: To make a Bacon, Cheese and Egg Pie, simply replace 50% of the bacon with grated cheese.

Minced beef and smoked bacon filling

Filling for 18 Small Pies:

Ingredients

Kilo	Gram	%	Ingredients	lb	oz
	300	43.00	chopped smoked bacon		10.75
	700	100.00	minced beef	1	9.00
	500	71.00	water	1	1.00
	10	1.40	salt		0.50
	5	0.70	pepper		0.25
	10	1.40	meat extract flavour		0.50
	30	4.30	cornflour		1.00
	50	7.10	water		1.75
1	605		Gross weight	3	18.75

Filling for 5 Large Pies:

Ingredients

Kilo	Gram	%	Ingredients	lb	oz
	225	43.00	chopped smoked bacon		9.00
	595	100.00	minced beef	1	5.25
	425	71.00	water		15.25
	10	1.70	salt		0.50
	4	0.67	pepper		0.25
	10	1.70	meat extract flavour		0.50
	25	4.20	cornflour		1.00
	40	6.70	water		1.50
1	364		Gross weight	3	1.25

COOKING METHOD

1 Remove the rind and chop the bacon into small pieces.
2 Place the minced beef, chopped smoked bacon, water, salt, pepper and meat extract flavour into a pan and bring to the boil.
3 Reduce the heat and allow to simmer for 10 minutes.
4 Mix the water and cornflour together. Add to the above while stirring continuously.
5 When the filling has thickened, remove from the heat.
6 Allow the filling to cool to 21°C (70°F) before processing begins.

Curried chicken filling

Filling for 18 Small Pies:

Ingredients

Kilo	Gram	%	Ingredients	lb	oz
	75	10.00	margarine		2.50
	15	2.00	crushed fresh garlic		0.50
	75	10.00	medium flour		2.50
	30	4.00	curry powder		1.00
	475	62.00	milk	1	1.00
	140	18.00	water		5.00
	15	2.00	salt		0.50
	760	100.00	cooked diced chicken	1	11.50
	95	12.50	mango chutney		3.50
1	680		Gross weight	3	12.00

Filling for 5 Large Pies:

Ingredients

Kilo	Gram	%	Ingredients	lb	oz
	60	10.00	margarine		2.25
	10	1.60	crushed fresh garlic		0.50
	60	10.00	medium flour		2.25
	25	4.00	curry powder		1.00
	390	62.00	milk		14.00
	115	18.00	water		4.00
	10	1.60	salt		0.50
	625	100.00	cooked diced chicken	1	7.00
	80	12.50	mango chutney		3.00
1	375		Gross weight	3	2.00

COOKING METHOD

1 Place the margarine and crushed fresh garlic into a pan and melt down slowly.
2 Blend together the flour and curry powder. Add to the above and cook until a roux is obtained. Remove from the heat.
3 Mix the milk and water together. Add to the above slowly while stirring continuously. Return to the heat. Continue to stir until a smooth thick sauce is obtained.
4 Add the salt and stir through.
5 Allow to cool to 21°C (70°F), then add and stir through the diced cooked chicken and mango chutney.
6 The filling is now ready for processing.

Curried chicken pie

Mexican minced beef filling

Filling for 18 Small Pies:

Ingredients

Kilo	Gram	%	Ingredients	lb	oz
	40	5.70	vegetable oil		1.50
	105	15.00	chopped onions		3.75
	5	0.70	crushed garlic		0.25
	700	100.00	minced beef	1	9.00
	55	7.80	chopped green peppers		2.00
	7	1.00	chilli sauce		0.25
	3	0.40	cumin		0.12
	15	2.10	tomato puree		0.50
	15	2.10	medium flour		0.50
	5	0.70	salt		0.25
	560	80.00	drained tinned tomatoes	1	4.00
	160	23.00	drained tinned red kidney beans		5.75
1	670		Gross weight	3	11.50

Filling for 5 Large Pies:

Ingredients

Kilo	Gram	%	Ingredients	lb	oz
	30	5.30	vegetable oil		1.00
	85	15.10	chopped onions		3.00
	5	0.90	crushed garlic		0.25
	560	100.00	minced beef	1	4.00
	45	8.00	chopped green peppers		1.50
	5	0.90	chilli sauce		0.25
	2	0.30	cumin		0.12
	15	2.70	tomato puree		0.50
	15	2.70	medium flour		0.50
	5	0.90	salt		0.25
	450	80.00	drained tinned tomatoes	1	0.00
	130	23.00	drained tinned red kidney beans		4.50
1	347		Gross weight	3	0.00

COOKING METHOD

1. Fry the chopped onions, crushed garlic, minced beef and chopped green peppers in vegetable oil for approximately 3 minutes.
2. Add the chilli powder, cumin, tomato puree, medium flour and salt to the above and cook for 1 minute.
3. Add the tinned tomatoes and red kidney beans and mix through until thoroughly dispersed.
4. Simmer for 15 minutes.
5. Allow to cool to 21°C (70°F). The filling is now ready for processing.

SHEPHERDS PIE

Use recipe A or B for savoury paste; both are suitable for this product.

Processing method

Yield 30

Note: The appropriate mechanical blocking machine may be used for stages 1, 2, and 3.

1 Pin out the savoury paste to approximately 5 mm (0.25") thick.
2 Using a fluted cutter which is slightly larger than the deep foil or tin, cut out 30 bases at approximately 60 g (2 oz) in weight.
3 Place the savoury paste base into the foil or tin and carefully thumb into position.
4 Prepare the minced beef filling as below:

Ingredients

Kilo	Gram	%	Ingredients	lb	oz
1	400	100.00	minced beef	3	2.00
	700	50.00	water	1	9.00
	20	1.50	salt		0.75
	5	0.35	pepper		0.25
	15	1.00	meat extract flavour		0.50
	40	2.85	cornflour		1.50
	70	5.00	water		2.50
2	250		Gross weight	4	0.50

Cooking method

- place the minced beef, water, salt, pepper and meat extract flavour into a pan and bring to the boil
- reduce the heat and allow to simmer for 10 minutes
- mix the cornflour and water together. Add to the above while stirring continuously
- when the filling has thickened, remove from the heat
- allow the filling to cool to 21°C (70°F) before processing begins.

5 Fill each base with approximately 70 g (2.5 oz) of minced beef filling.
6 Prepare mash potato and using a savoy bag and star tube, pipe in a spiral or zig-zag motion to cover the filling.
7 Bake at 225°C (440°F) for 25 minutes.

Note: The appearance and flavour can be enhanced by sprinkling grated cheese over the piped potato.

SAVOURY FLANS

(See colour plate 10.)

Use recipe A or B for savoury paste; both are suitable for this product.

Ingredients

Kilo	Gram	%	Ingredients	lb	oz
	640	50.00	fresh eggs	1	7.00
	130	10.00	soft flour		4.50
	320	25.00	cream		11.50
1	280	100.00	milk	2	14.00
	10	0.78	salt		0.50
	4	0.30	pepper		0.25
2	384		Gross weight	5	5.75

Processing method

Yield 9

Note: The appropriate mechanical blocking machine may be used for stages 1, 2, 3 and 4.

1 Scale 9 bases at 200 g (7.25 oz) and mould round.
2 Pin out the bases to cover a 15 cm (6") diameter flan foil or tin.
3 Place the base into the foil or tin and thumb into position.
4 Trim the excess paste from the top edge of the foil.

Note: The pastry edge may be crimped or left plain.

5 Use one of the following fillings to cover the base of the flan case:
- 50 g (1.75 oz) grated cheese and 50 g (1.75 oz) chopped onions
- 60 g (2 oz) diced ham and 50 g (1.75 oz) grated cheese
- 100 g (4 oz) chopped bacon
- 40 g (1.5 oz) leek and 85 g (3 oz) chopped bacon
- 110 g (4 oz) tuna fish
- 70 g (2.5 oz) prawn and 30 g (1 oz) flaked crab
- 50 g (1.75 oz) salami and 50 g (1.75 oz) pepperami
- 30 g (1 oz) mushrooms, 30 g (1 oz) carrots, 20 g (0.75 oz) onions or leek, 20 g (0.75 oz) peas and 20 g (0.75 g) sweetcorn
- 35 g (1.25 oz) green peppers, 35 g (1.25 oz) yellow peppers and 35 g (1.25 oz) red peppers.

6 Prepare the savoury custard filling as below:

Mixing method

- place the egg into a bowl and beat lightly
- sieve the flour and whisk into the egg
- mix the cream and milk together. Add to the above slowly, whisking continuously
- add and whisk the salt and pepper through.

7 Cover and fill the pastry case with savoury custard.

8 Bake at 204°C (400°F) for approximately 25 minutes.
9 On withdrawal from the oven, allow the flans to cool on the tray.

CORNED BEEF AND POTATO SLICE

Use recipe A or B for savoury paste; both are suitable for this product.

Ingredients

Kilo	Gram	%	Ingredients	lb	oz
1	000	111.00	cold mashed potato	2	3.50
	900	100.00	corned beef	2	0.00
	400	44.4	chopped onion		14.50
	10	1.10	salt		0.50
	5	0.50	pepper		0.25
2	315		Gross weight	5	2.75

Processing method

Yield 30

1 Pin out 900 g (2 lb) savoury paste and cover the base of a 37.5 × 45 cm (15 × 18") baking tray.
2 Prepare the corned beef and potato filling as follows:

Corned beef potato slice

Mixing method

- place all the ingredients into a bowl and mix to a smooth consistency.

3 Place the filling onto the pastry base and spread it evenly within the tray.
4 Pin out 900 g (2 lb) of savoury paste and cover the filling.
5 Trim the excess paste from the top edge of the tray.
6 Using pastry wheels, 6 × 5, mark the pastry into 30 squares.

7 Brush the top of the pastry with eggwash.
8 Bake at 225°C (440°F) for approximately 30 minutes.
9 On withdrawal from the oven, allow the slice to cool thoroughly then cut into squares.

PIZZA PIE

(See colour plate 12.)

Use recipe A or B for savoury paste; both are suitable for this product.

Ingredients

Kilo	Gram	%	Ingredients	lb	oz
	600	100.00	drained tinned tomatoes	1	5.50
	30	5.00	tomato puree		1.00
	5	1.00	salt		0.25
	1	0.20	pepper		pinch
	1	0.10	sweet basil		pinch
	2	0.30	oregano		0.12
	60	10.00	pre-gelatinised starch		2.25
	480	80.00	chopped ham	1	1.25
	420	70.00	chopped onions		15.00
	240	40.00	sliced mushrooms		8.50
	75	12.50	chopped red pepper		2.50
	75	12.50	chopped green pepper		2.50
	360	60.00	sweetcorn		13.00
2	349		Gross weight	5	4.00

Processing method

Yield 30

Note: The appropriate mechanical blocking machine may be used for stages 1, 2 and 3.

1 Pin out the savoury paste to approximately 5 mm (0.25") thick.
2 Using a fluted cutter which is slightly larger than the deep foil or tin, cut out the savoury bases at approximately 55 g (2 oz) in weight.
3 Place the savoury paste base into the foil or tin and carefully thumb into position.
4 Prepare the pizza filling as below:

Mixing method

- crush the tinned tomatoes and mix together with the tomato puree
- add the salt, pepper, sweet basil and oregano and stir through
- sprinkle the pre-gelatinised starch in whilst stirring continuously
- add the chopped ham, chopped onions, sliced mushrooms, chopped red and green pepper and sweetcorn, and mix until thoroughly dispersed.

5 Fill each base with approximately 70 g (2.5 oz) of pizza filling.
6 Sprinkle grated mozzarella cheese over the filling.
7 Bake at 210°C (410°F) for approximately 25 minutes.

Note: For a softer texture to the mozzarella cheese topping, add midway through the baking process.

BOILED PASTE

Ingredients

Kilo	Gram	%	Ingredients	lb	oz
1	000	100.00	medium flour	2	3.50
	500	50.00	boiling water	1	1.00
	15	1.50	salt		0.50
	450	45.00	shortening or lard	1	0.00
1	965		Gross weight	4	5.00
1	847		Net weight	4	1.00

Mixing method

1 Sieve the flour and place it into a mixing bowl.
2 Boil together the water, salt and shortening or lard.
3 Pour the boiling liquid into the flour and mix through until a smooth paste is obtained.

Note:
- do not over mix
- allow the paste to cool before processing begins.

SMALL PORK PIE

Use the recipe for boiled paste.

Ingredients

Kilo	Gram	%	Ingredients	lb	oz
1	250	100.00	minced pork	2	12.50
	125	10.00	minced bacon		4.50
	25	2.00	salt		1.00
	10	0.70	pepper		0.50
	125	10.00	breadcrumbs		4.50
	75	6.00	water		2.75
1	610		Gross weight	3	9.75

Processing method

Yield 18

Note: The appropriate mechanical blocking machine may be used for stages 1, 2, 3, 9 and 10.

1 Pin out the savoury paste to approximately 5 mm (0.25") thick.
2 Using a plain cutter which is slightly larger than the deep foil or tin, cut out 18 bases at approximately 60 g (2 oz) in weight.
3 Place the savoury paste base into the foil or tin and carefully thumb into position.
4 Using the remaining savoury paste, pin out to approximately 4 mm ($\frac{3}{16}$") thick and cut out 18 lids to approximately 40 g (1.5 oz) in weight to fit the pastry case.
5 Cut out a small hole of 5 mm (0.25") diameter from the centre of the lid.
6 Prepare the pork filling as follows:

Mixing method

- place all ingredients into a bowl and mix together thoroughly.

7 Fill each base with approximately 85 g (3 oz) of pork filling.

8 Moisten the top edge of the savoury paste base.
9 Place the savoury paste lid over the filling and secure to the base.
10 Between thumb and forefinger, crimp the top edge of the pie.
11 Brush the top of the pie with eggwash.
12 Bake at 225°C (440°F) for approximately 40 minutes.
13 On withdrawal from the oven, allow the pies to cool.
14 Prepare some aspic jelly and fill each pie with jelly through the hole in the pastry lid. Allow the jelly to set.

SMALL PORK AND EGG PIE

Use the recipe for Boiled Paste (increased by 50%).

Processing method

Yield 26

Note: The appropriate mechanical blocking machine may be used for stages 1, 2, 3, 9 and 10.

1 Follow stages 1–6 for Small Pork Pies.
2 Place and level 30 g (1 oz) of pork filling into the pastry base.
3 Place half a boiled egg onto the pork filling in the centre of the pie.
4 Place 25 g (1 oz) of pork filling over the egg and level.
5 Follow stages 8–14 for Pork Pie.

LARGE PORK PIE

Use the recipe for Boiled Paste.

Processing method

Yield 5

Note: The appropriate mechanical blocking machine may be used for stages 1, 2, 3, 9 and 10.

1 Scale 5 bases at 200 g (7.25 oz) and mould round.
2 Scale 5 lids at 160 g (5.75 oz) and mould round.
3 Pin out the bases to cover a 15 cm (6") diameter flan foil or tin.

4 Place base into the foil or tin and carefully thumb into position.
5 Pin out the lids to cover a 15 cm (6") diameter shallow foil or tin.
6 Cut out a small hole 5 mm (0.25") diameter from the centre of the lid.
7 Prepare the pork filling as for Small Pork Pies.
8 Fill each base with approximately 310 g (11 oz) of pork filling.
9 Moisten the top edge of the savoury paste base.
10 Place the savoury paste lid over the filling and secure to the base.
11 Between thumb and forefinger, crimp the top edge of the pie.
12 Brush the top of the pie with eggwash.
13 Bake at 225°C (440°F) for approximately 60 minutes.
14 On withdrawal from the oven, allow the pies to cool.
15 Prepare some aspic jelly and fill each pie with jelly through the hole in the pastry lid. Allow the jelly to set.

LARGE PORK AND EGG PIE

(See colour plate 11.)

Use the recipe for Boiled Paste (increased by 50%).

Processing method

Yield 7

Note: The appropriate mechanical blocking machine may be used for stages 1, 2, 3, 9 and 10.

1 Follow stages 1–7 for Large Pork Pies.
2 Place and level 110 g (4 oz) of pork filling into the pastry base.
3 Place 4 halves of boiled egg onto the pork filling to make four quarters within the pie.
4 Place 100 g (3.5 oz) of pork filling over the eggs and level.
5 Follow stages 9–15 for Large Pork Pie.

SMALL MUTTON PIE

Use recipe for Boiled Paste.

Ingredients

Kilo	Gram	%	Ingredients	lb	oz
	700	100.00	minced mutton	1	9.00
	100	14.30	chopped onions		3.50
1	000	143.00	water	2	3.75
	10	1.40	salt		0.50
	5	0.70	pepper		0.25
	5	0.70	mace		0.25
	60	8.60	cornflour		2.00
	100	14.30	water		3.50
1	980		Gross weight	4	5.75

Processing method

Yield 24

Note: The appropriate mechanical blocking machine may be used for stages 1, 2, 3, 9 and 10.

1 Pin out the savoury paste to approximately 3 mm (0.125") thick.
2 Using a plain cutter which is slightly larger than the deep foil or tin, cut out 24 bases at approximately 45 g (1.5 oz) in weight.
3 Place the savoury paste base into the foil or tin and carefully thumb into position.
4 Using the remaining savoury paste, pin out to approximately 3 mm (0.125") thick and cut out 24 lids to approximately 30 g (1 oz) in weight to fit the pastry case.
5 Cut out a small hole of 5 mm (0.25") diameter from the centre of the lid.
6 Prepare the mutton filling as follows:

Cooking method

- place the minced mutton, chopped onions, water, salt, pepper and mace into a pan and bring to the boil
- reduce the heat and allow to simmer for 10 minutes
- mix the cornflour and water together. Add to the above while stirring continuously
- when the filling has thickened, remove from the heat
- allow the filling to cool to 21°C (70°F) before processing begins.

7 Fill each base with approximately 80 g (2.75 oz) of mutton filling.
8 Moisten the top edge of the savoury paste base.
9 Place the savoury paste lid over the filling and secure to the base.
10 Brush the top of the pie with eggwash.
11 Bake at 225°C (440°F) for approximately 25 minutes.

C H A P T E R

ten

Puff pastry processes

Puff pastry has been produced for many centuries, and has gradually become more sophisticated over that time. The advances made in the development of fats, flour and machinery have aided a complex manufacturing process, while production has become faster and more consistent. However, despite technical improvements, it remains essential for the baker to observe key stages which are central to the successful production of puff pastry products.

Increasing public demand for products based upon puff pastry has forced technical progress within this category of pastries. This increase in popularity has resulted in puff pastries becoming a major part of the baker's production.

CHARACTERISTICS OF PUFF PASTRY

Puff pastries should have the following characteristics:

- a good volume of even expansion
- a crisp surface
- a light and flaky internal structure.

The aim of mixing and lamination

- to disperse and dissolve ingredients to form a dough
- to hydrate and develop the gluten forming proteins within the dough, which give it a degree of elasticity
- to incorporate fat and create alternate layers of very thin dough and fat. This process is known as lamination.

TYPES OF PUFF PASTRY

There are three types of puff pastry:

1 Half puff.
2 Three quarter puff.
3 Full puff.

These terms refer to the level of fat in relation to the level of flour within the recipe. Therefore, the amount of fat in each type of puff pastry is as follows:

- half puff pastry contains fat at the rate of 50% of the flour weight.
- three quarter puff pastry contains fat at the rate of 75% of the flour weight.
- full puff pastry contains fat at the rate of 100% of the flour weight.

Basic ingredients

The basic ingredients required to make puff pastry are: strong flour, salt, cake margarine, water and pastry margarine.

FATS ESSENTIAL FOR PUFF PASTRY

To produce successful puff pastry products, it is essential to use a hard fat which can withstand the lamination process. The fat needs to be plastic in nature, to tolerate the rolling and folding involved during small scale production, or rigorous mechanised methods.

Types of fat

PASTRY MARGARINES AND FATS

Pastry margarines and fats are formulated to give them:

- a high melting point of between 35–44°C (95–111°F)
- a plastic nature
- the ability to be pinned out very thinly.

BUTTER

Butter is used to make high quality puff pastry for its fine flavour. The inclusion of butter requires the use of refrigeration to keep the paste cool and prevent the butter from softening.

CAKE MARGARINE AND SHORTENING

It is normal to include some soft fat in the dough stage of three quarter and full puff pastry. The soft fat improves the handling performance during the rolling process and confers shortness to the eating quality of puff pastries. Soft fat should be used at a rate of 10% of the flour weight, and should be counted as part of the total fat content.

PENCIL FAT

A recent development in the technology of pastry fat has seen the introduction of pencil fat. Pencil fat is in the form of a pellet and is added at the dough stage to form a rough puff pastry. The formulation and nature of pencil fat reduces the number of half turns required. Puff pastry made with pencil fat is suitable for products that do not require a high volume, such as pies, pasties and slices.

Temperature of fat

Pastry margarine and fat should be used at 16–18°C (61–65°F) to ensure that layers of dough and fat are created satisfactorily. If the margarine and fat are too cold, they can rupture the structure of the layers and have an adverse effect upon the volume. Margarine and fat which is too soft will be squeezed out and prevent the formation of layers.

Temperature and consistency of dough

The dough must be cool to prevent the fat from softening, in order to ensure the formation of layers of dough and fat. Cold water must therefore be used at the dough stage. The dough must be of a consistency to assist the lamination process. If the dough is used too tight, it will squeeze out the fat and prevent the formation of layers; but if it is too soft, it will again have an adverse effect upon the lamination process and volume.

MIXING METHODS AND INCORPORATING FAT

The methods used to produce puff pastry are:

- Scotch
- English
- French
- High Speed.

Scotch method

This is an outline of the Scotch method of making puff pastry. A more detailed description can be found in the recipes for puff pastry.

1 The pastry margarine is cut into small cubes and incorporated during the formation of a dough made from bread flour, salt, cake margarine and cold water.
2 It is essential that the dough is not overmixed and the cubes of pastry margarine remain intact.
3 The paste is now ready for the lamination process.

English method

This is an outline of the English method of making puff pastry. A more detailed description can be found in the recipes for puff pastry.

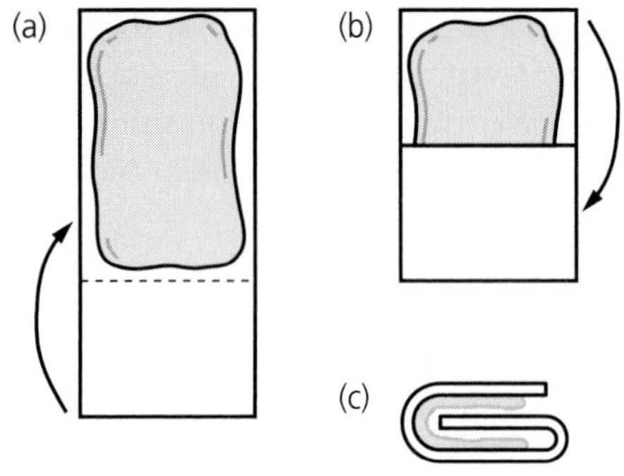

Figure 13 English method

1 A dough is made from bread flour, salt, cake margarine and cold water.
2 The dough is then allowed to rest until it has become relaxed.
3 Pin the dough to a large rectangle, 1.25 cm (0.5") thick.
4 Prepare the pastry margarine by cutting it into small, even pieces.
5 Place the pieces of pastry margarine over two-thirds of the rectangle of dough.
6 Fold the uncovered third of dough over the pastry margarine (Figure 13a).
7 Fold again (Figure 13b), to obtain three layers of dough and two layers of pastry margarine (Figure 13c).
8 The paste is now ready for the lamination process.

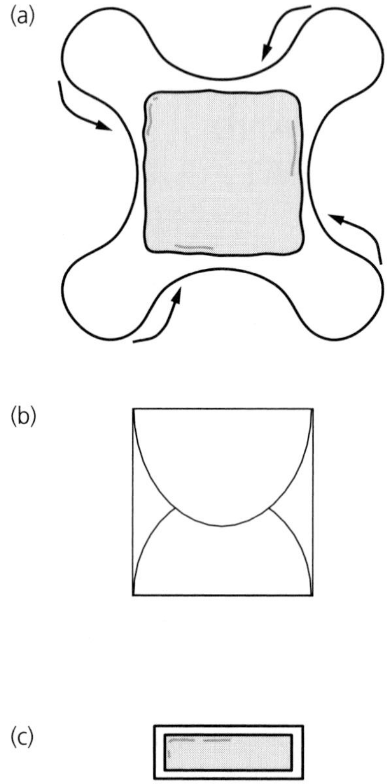

Figure 14 French method

French method

This is an outline of the French method of making puff pastry. A more detailed description can be found in the recipes for puff pastry.

1 A dough is made from bread flour, salt, cake margarine and cold water.
2 The dough is then allowed to rest until it has become relaxed.
3 Pin the dough to a square, 2.5 cm (1") thick.
4 Pin out each corner of the square to create an open envelope shape which has a thick square in the centre.
5 Prepare the pastry margarine by flattening and shaping it into a square which fits within the centre of the dough piece (Figure 14a).
6 Fold in each corner of the dough piece to encase the pastry margarine (Figure 14b), to obtain two layers of dough and one layer of pastry margarine (Figure 14c).
7 The paste is now ready for the lamination process.

High speed mixing method

The use of high speed mixing machines for making puff paste is well established within the baking and food industry. This is because they enable large batches to be mixed in a very short time. The mixing method and incorporation of the pastry margarine is based upon the Scotch method:

1 Dissolve the salt in cold water and place the solution into the mixing chamber.
2 Place the bread flour into the mixing chamber.
3 Cut the pastry margarine into cubes and place them on top of the flour within the mixing chamber.
4 Mix for 10–40 seconds until a rough paste containing cubes of pastry margarine is obtained.
5 Allow the dough to rest for 10 minutes until it has become relaxed.
6 The paste is now ready for the lamination process.

Note: During the high speed mixing of puff pastry, the gluten is modified and the need for rest periods during the lamination process can be eliminated.

THE LAMINATION PROCESS

The method used to incorporate the pastry margarine into the dough is irrelevant to the lamination process. Once the pastry margarine has been incorporated into the dough, the paste is ready for the lamination process. There are two methods of lamination for puff pastry:

1 Half turn.
2 Book fold.

Half turn

The pastry must be given six half turns to create the required number of layers of dough and fat.

1 Pin out the paste to a large rectangle, 1.25 cm (0.5") thick.
2 Fold the paste into three as follows:
   i Fold the bottom third up over the middle third (Figure 15a and b).
   ii Fold the top third down to complete a half turn (Figure 15c).
3 Repeat stages 1 and 2, cover with polythene to prevent the paste from skinning, then allow it to rest for 20 minutes until the paste has become relaxed.
4 Repeat stages 1, 2 and 3.
5 Repeat stages 1, 2 and 3 again.
6 The puff pastry is now ready for processing to begin.

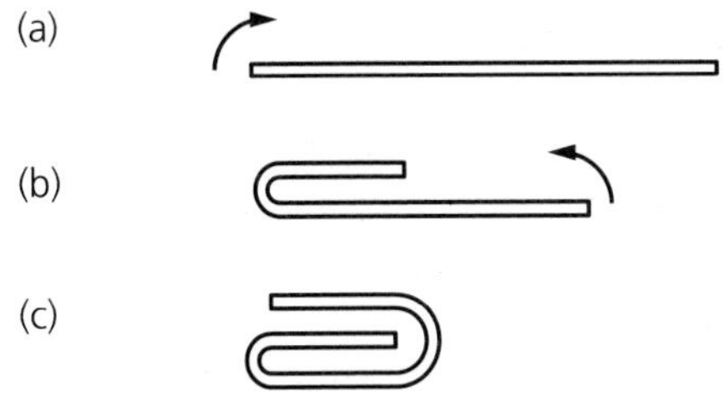

Figure 15 Half turn

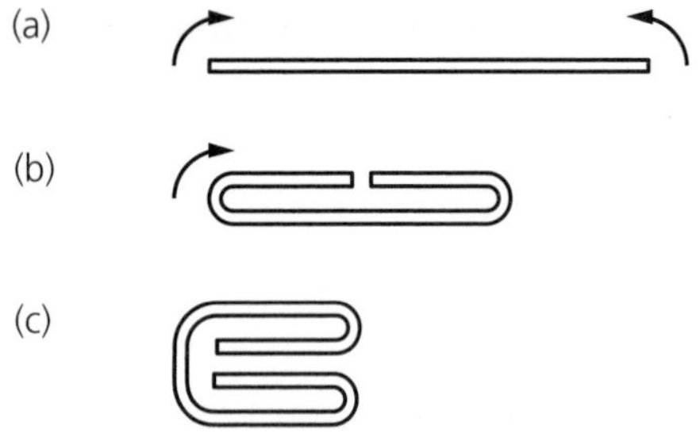

Figure 16 Book Fold

Book Fold

The pastry must be given three bookfolds to create the required number of layers of dough and fat.

1 Pin out the paste to a large rectangle, 1.25 cm (0.5") thick.
2 Fold both ends until they meet in the centre of the paste (Figure 16a and b).
3 Now fold the whole paste in half again to complete the bookfold (Figure 16c).
4 Cover with polythene to prevent the paste from skinning, and allow it to rest for 20 minutes until the paste has become relaxed.
5 Repeat stages 1, 2, 3 and 4.
6 Repeat stages 1, 2, 3 and 4 again.
7 The puff pastry is now ready for processing to begin.

Laminators for large scale production

Large scale production of puff pastry involves the use of machines known as laminators, in conjunction with the high speed mixing method. The rough pastry produced by the high speed mixer is fed into the laminator via a hopper. The paste is extruded by rollers in a continuous sheet onto a reciprocating conveyor belt, concertina fashion, until six to nine layers are built up. This block of paste has the equivalent to four half turns. This large piece of paste is then cut into a block and requires two further half turns prior to processing.

POINTS TO CONSIDER WHEN PROCESSING PUFF PASTRY

1 All rest periods must be strictly observed.
2 Use medium strength flour for dusting purposes.
3 During the lamination process, always brush off excess dusting flour prior to folding.
4 Use pinning guides when appropriate to obtain a consistent thickness.
5 Keep the addition of trimmings to a minimum. Add at the rate of 10% to freshly made puff pastry.
6 Trimming must be in a relaxed condition prior to adding to freshly made puff pastry.

7 Maintain layers of puff pastry when adding trimmings to freshly made puff pastry.

Storage of puff pastry

Puff pastry can be stored under refrigerated and frozen conditions, in a block prior to processing or as unbaked products. This offers the baker the following advantages:

1 The opportunity to build up stock levels and even out production schedules.
2 Fresh products at the point of sale.
3 Reduced levels of waste.

Conditioning and baking puff pastry products

PRIOR TO BAKING

It is essential to allow puff pastry products to rest for a minimum of 30 minutes prior to baking. This rest period is necessary in order to prevent shrinkage and ensure that maximum expansion occurs during the baking process.

BAKING TEMPERATURE

A general guide to the baking temperature for puff pastry products is:

1 Filled and sugar finished products: 215–220°C (420–430°F).
2 Savoury and eggwashed products: 225–230°C (440–446°F).
3 Unfilled products: 230–235°C (446–456°F).

The baking temperature will depend upon the following;

- shape, size and depth
- density
- sugar content
- product characteristics.

DURING BAKING

During the initial stages of the baking process, the layers of pastry margarine melt and the gluten in the layers of the dough begins to expand. Pressure from steam generated from the water in the dough assists the expansion process. Once the product has achieved maximum volume, the humidity within the oven chamber must be released. The final stages of the baking process must take place in a dry atmosphere to assist in the coagulation of the gluten forming proteins and setting of the structure. Removing puff pastry products from the oven before baking is complete, will result in the structure collapsing.

Cooling

SAVOURY PRODUCTS

It is common practice for savoury products to be sold hot straight from the oven. This is achieved by baking savouries to the demands from customers throughout the day. The reheating of savoury products must be thorough and is subject to VAT. Savouries that are wrapped must be cooled quickly, and stored or displayed in refrigerated conditions as stated in the Food Safety (Temperature Control) Regulations 1995.

CONFECTIONERY PRODUCTS

Puff pastry bases that are to be finished and decorated with perishable materials, must be thoroughly cooled prior to processing.

All puff pastry products are best if baked and sold the same day.

OVEN CHART

Product	Baking temperature in °C (°F)	Baking time in minutes	Additional control procedure
Cornish Pasties	204 (400)	30	Open damper for final 10 mins
Sausage Rolls	225 (440)	25	" " " " 5 mins
Cheese & Onion Pasties	225 (440)	25	" " " "
Corned Beef & Onion Pasties	225 (440)	25	" " " "
Leek & Bacon Pasties	225 (440)	25	" " " "
Chicken & Mushroom Pasties	225 (440)	25	" " " "
Curried Chicken Pasties	225 (440)	25	" " " "
Mexican Minced Beef Pasties	225 (440)	25	" " " "
Vegetable Pasties	225 (440)	25	" " " "
Savoury Slice	225 (440)	35	" " " " 10 mins
Apple Turnovers	215 (420)	25	" " " " 5 mins
Cream Slice Bases	230 (446)	15–20	" " " "
Palmiers	215 (420)	20	" " " "
Cream Coronet	215 (420)	25	" " " "
Mille-Feuille Bases	230 (446)	20	" " " "
Vol-au-vents	230 (446)	25	" " " "
Cream Horns	215 (420)	25	" " " "
Eccles Cakes	215 (420)	20	" " " "

RECIPES FOR MAKING PUFF PASTRY

SCOTCH METHOD

Half puff

Ingredients

Kilo	Gram	%	Ingredients	lb	oz
1	000	100.00	bread flour	2	3.50
	15	1.50	salt		0.50
	560	56.00	cold water	1	4.00
	500	50.00	pastry margarine	1	1.00
2	075		Gross weight	4	9.00
1	992		Net weight	4	6.00

Three quarter puff

Ingredients

Kilo	Gram	%	Ingredients	lb	oz
1	000	100.00	bread flour	2	3.50
	15	1.50	salt		0.50
	100	10.00	cake margarine		3.50
	560	56.00	cold water	1	4.00
	650	65.00	pastry margarine	1	7.25
2	325		Gross weight	5	2.75
2	232		Net weight	4	15.50

Method of mixing

1 Sieve together the flour and salt.
2 For three quarter puff pastry only – add the cake margarine and rub through by hand or machine.
3 Add the cold water to above and mix until half clear.
4 Cut the pastry margarine into small cubes, add to above and mix until a rough puff paste is obtained.

Note: Do not overmix, as cubes of pastry margarine must remain intact.

Lamination

1 Proceed to give the paste a total of six half turns. Allow the paste to rest for 20 minutes after the second and fourth half turns.
2 After the sixth and final half turn, and before processing begins, allow the puff paste to rest for a further 20 minutes to recover from the lamination process.

Three quarter puff pastry

Ingredients

Kilo	Gram	%	Ingredients	lb	oz
1	000	100.00	bread flour	2	3.50
	10	1.00	salt		0.50
	100	10.00	cake margarine		3.50
	560	56.00	cold water	1	4.00
	650	65.00	pastry margarine	1	7.25
2	320		Gross weight	5	2.75
2	227		Net weight	4	15.50

Full puff pastry

Ingredients

Kilo	Gram	%	Ingredients	lb	oz
1	000	100.00	bread flour	2	3.50
	10	1.00	salt		0.50
	120	12.00	cake margarine		3.50
	560	56.00	cold water	1	4.00
	880	88.00	pastry margarine	1	15.50
2	570		Gross weight	5	11.00
2	467		Net weight	5	7.50

ENGLISH METHOD

Mixing method

1 Sieve together the flour and salt.
2 Add the cake margarine and rub through by hand or machine.
3 Add the cold water, and mix for 3–4 minutes until a smooth, clear dough is obtained.
4 Rest for 5 minutes to allow the dough to recover.

Incorporation of pastry margarine

1 Pin the dough to a large rectangle 1.25 cm (0.5") thick.
2 Prepare the pastry margarine by cutting it into small even pieces.
3 Place the pieces of pastry margarine over two-thirds of the rectangle of dough.
4 Fold the uncovered third of dough over the pastry margarine.
5 Fold again to obtain three layers of dough and two layers of pastry margarine.
6 The paste is now ready for the lamination process.

Lamination

1 Proceed to give the paste a total of six half turns. Allow the paste to rest for 20 minutes after the second and fourth half turns.
2 After the sixth and final half turn, and before processing begins, allow the puff paste to rest for a further 20 minutes to recover from the lamination process.

FRENCH METHOD

Ingredients

Use the same ingredients as for the English Method.

Mixing method

Follow stages 1, 2, 3 and 4 of the mixing method for the English Method.

Incorporation of pastry margarine

1 Pin the dough to a square 2.5 cm (1") thick.
2 Pin out each corner of the square to create an open envelope shape that has a thick square in the centre.
3 Prepare the pastry margarine by flattening and shaping it into a square that fits squarely within the centre of the dough piece.
4 Fold each corner of the dough piece to encase the pastry margarine to obtain two layers of dough and one layer of pastry margarine.

Lamination

1 Proceed to give the paste a total of six half turns. Allow the paste to rest for 20 minutes after the second and fourth half turns.
2 After the sixth and final half turn, and before processing begins, allow the puff paste to rest for a further 20 minutes to recover from the lamination process.

RECIPES USING PUFF PASTRY

CORNISH PASTIES

Using the recipe for half puff pastry, make puff pastry by the Scotch method.

Ingredients for filling

Kilo	Gram	%	Ingredients	lb	oz
	800	100.00	minced beef	1	12.50
	650	81.00	diced potato	1	7.25
	300	37.50	diced swede		10.75
	250	31.00	chopped onions		9.00
	15	1.90	salt		0.75
	5	0.60	pepper		0.25
2	020		Gross weight	4	8.50

Processing method

Yield approx 24

1 Pin out the puff pastry to approximately 4 mm ($\frac{3}{16}$") thick.
2 Using a 15 cm (6") diameter plain cutter, cut out the bases.
3 Prepare the Cornish Pasty filling as follows:

Mixing method

- place all ingredients in a bowl and mix together thoroughly.

4 Lay out the puff pastry bases in rows, then place 80 g (3 oz) of filling into the centre of each puff pastry base.

5 Dampen the edge of half of each puff pastry base with water.
6 Fold the base up to enclose the filling and seal well.
7 Using the thumb and forefinger, fold and secure the seam of the base into a twist. The twist may be positioned at the top or side of the pasty.
8 Place the pasties onto a tray lined with silicone paper and allow a rest period of 30 minutes before baking.
9 Brush the pasties with eggwash. Using a pointed knife, make two vents in the top.
10 Bake at 204°C (400°F) for approximately 30 minutes.

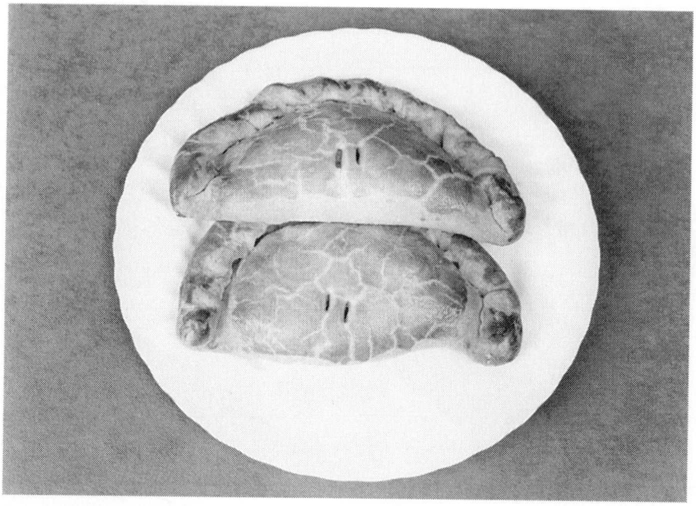

Cornish pasties

SAUSAGE ROLLS

Make the puff pastry using the recipe for half or three quarter puff pastry.

Ingredients for filling

Kilo	Gram	%	Ingredients	lb	oz
	700	100.00	minced beef or pork	1	9.00
	365	52.00	rusks or breadcrumbs		13.00
1	000	143.00	cold water	2	2.00
	20	2.80	salt		0.75
	5	0.70	pepper		0.25
2	090		Gross weight	4	9.00

Processing method

Yield approx 40

1 Pin out the puff pastry to a large rectangle 45 cm (18") wide and 4 mm ($\frac{3}{16}$") thick. The length of the rectangle is determined by the thickness.
2 Using pastry wheels or a measuring guide, cut the puff pastry into four strips, 11 cm (4.5") wide.
3 Prepare the sausage roll filling as follows:

Mixing method

- place all ingredients in a bowl and mix together thoroughly
- should it be necessary, add cold water to obtain a piping consistency.

4 Using a savoy bag and plain tube, pipe the filling onto the strip and slightly off centre.
5 Dampen the narrow edge of the puff pastry with water.
6 Fold the wide edge of the puff pastry over until the filling is completely enclosed and sealed in.
7 Mark and cut the strips into 10 cm (4") long rolls.
8 Place the sausage rolls onto a tray lined with silicone paper and allow a rest period of 30 minutes before baking.
9 Brush the sausage rolls with eggwash. Use a sharp knife to make a series of angled vents in the top.
10 Bake at 225°C (440°F) for approximately 25 minutes.

Sausage rolls

CHEESE AND ONION PASTIES

Make the puff pastry using the recipe for half or three quarter puff pastry.

Ingredients for filling

Kilo	Gram	%	Ingredients	lb	oz
	280	40.00	potato powder		10.00
	800	114.00	boiling water	1	12.50
	700	100.00	grated cheese	1	9.00
	200	28.50	chopped onions		7.00
	200	28.50	egg		7.00
2	180		Gross weight	4	13.50

Processing method

Yield approx 26

1 Pin out the puff pastry to approximately 4 mm ($\frac{3}{16}$") thick.
2 Using a 15 cm (6") diameter plain cutter, cut out the bases.
3 Prepare the cheese and onion filling as follows:

Mixing method

- add the boiling water to the potato powder and mix to a smooth consistency
- allow to cool
- add the grated cheese, chopped onions and egg. Mix through until thoroughly dispersed.

4 Lay out the puff pastry bases in rows, then place approximately 70 g (2.5 oz) of filling into the centre of each base.
5 Dampen the edge of half of each puff pastry base with water.
6 Fold one side of the puff pastry over to enclose the filling and seal the join firmly.
7 Place the pasties onto a tray lined with silicone paper and allow a rest period of 30 minutes before baking.
8 Brush the pasties with eggwash. Use a sharp knife to make two vents in the top.
9 Bake at 225°C (440°F) for approximately 25 minutes.

SAVOURY PASTIES

A variety of fillings can be used to make a range of savoury pasties. Below you will find a selection of the most popular fillings. To produce any of these varieties, follow the processing method for cheese and onion pasties. Simply replace the cheese and onion filling with the filling of your choice.

Cheese and onion pasty/Corned beef and onion pasty

Corned beef and onion

Filling for 26 pasties:

Ingredients for filling

Kilo	Gram	%	Ingredients	lb	oz
1	000	100.00	corned beef	2	3.50
	650	65.00	mashed potato	1	7.50
	450	45.00	chopped onions	1	00.0
2	100		Gross weight	4	11.00

MIXING METHOD

- mix all the ingredients together until a smooth consistency is obtained.

Note: The mashed potato must be cold. The filling is now ready for processing.

Leek and bacon

Filling for 26 Pasties:

Ingredients for filling

Kilo	Gram	%	Ingredients	lb	oz
	850	142.00	mashed potato	1	14.50
	75	12.50	margarine		2.50
	600	100.00	bacon pieces	1	5.50
	600	100.00	chopped leek	1	5.50
	10	1.70	pepper		0.50
2	135		Gross weight	4	12.50

MIXING METHOD

- mix all the ingredients together until thoroughly dispersed

Note: The mashed potato must be cold. The filling is now ready for processing.

Filling for 26 Pasties:

Ingredients for filling

Kilo	Gram	%	Ingredients	lb	oz
	100	15.60	margarine		3.50
	100	15.60	medium flour		3.50
	600	94.00	milk	1	5.50
	210	33.00	water		7.50
	20	3.00	salt		0.75
	3	0.40	pepper		0.12
	640	100.00	diced cooked chicken	1	7.00
	365	57.00	sliced mushroom		13.00
2	038		Gross weight	4	9.12

Chicken and mushroom

COOKING METHOD

1 Place the margarine into a pan and melt down slowly.
2 Add the flour and cook until a roux is obtained. Remove from the heat.
3 Mix the milk and water together. Add to the above slowly, stirring continuously until a smooth sauce is obtained.
4 Return to the heat and stir continuously until the sauce thickens.
5 Add the salt, pepper and sliced mushrooms and stir through.
6 Allow to cool to 21°C (70°F) then add and stir through the diced cooked chicken.
7 The filling is now ready for processing.

Filling for 26 Pasties:

Ingredients for filling

Kilo	Gram	%	Ingredients	lb	oz
	95	9.80	margarine		3.50
	15	1.5	crushed fresh garlic		0.50
	95	9.80	medium flour		3.50
	40	4.10	curry powder		1.50
	535	55.00	milk	1	3.00
	180	18.50	water		6.50
	20	2.00	salt		0.75
	970	100.00	diced cooked chicken	2	2.50
	120	12.40	mango chutney		4.50
2	070		Gross weight	4	10.00

Curried chicken

COOKING METHOD

1 Place the margarine and crushed fresh garlic into a pan and melt down slowly.
2 Blend together the flour and curry powder, add to the above and cook until a roux is obtained. Remove from the heat.
3 Mix the milk and water together. Add to the above slowly, stirring continuously until a smooth sauce is obtained.
4 Return to the heat and stir continuously until the sauce thickens.
5 Add the salt and stir through.
6 Allow to cool to 21°C (70°F) then add and stir through the diced cooked chicken and mango chutney.
7 The filling is now ready for processing.

Filling for 26 Pasties:

Ingredients for filling

Kilo	Gram	%	Ingredients	lb	oz
	50	5.70	vegetable oil		1.75
	160	18.30	chopped onions		5.75
	5	0.60	crushed garlic		0.25
	875	100.00	minced beef	1	15.25
	70	8.00	chopped green peppers		2.50
	7	0.80	chilli sauce		0.25
	4	0.45	cumin		0.25
	20	2.30	tomato puree		0.75
	40	4.60	medium flour		1.50
	5	0.60	salt		0.25
	700	80.00	drained tinned tomatoes	1	9.00
	200	22.30	drained tinned red kidney beans		7.00
2	136		Gross weight	4	12.50

Mexican minced beef

COOKING METHOD

1 Fry the chopped onions, crushed garlic, minced beef and chopped green peppers in vegetable oil for approximately 3 minutes.
2 Add the chilli sauce, cumin, tomato puree, medium flour and salt to the above and cook for 1 minute.
3 Add the tinned tomatoes and red kidney beans and mix through until thoroughly dispersed.
4 Simmer for 15 minutes.
5 Allow to cool to 21°C (70°F). The filling is now ready for processing.

Filling for 26 Pasties:

Ingredients for filling

Kilo	Gram	%	Ingredients	lb	oz
	375	60.00	diced carrot		13.50
	375	60.00	diced swede		13.50
	250	40.00	chopped onions		9.00
	250	40.00	sliced mushrooms		9.00
	185	30.00	peas		6.50
	625	100.00	mashed potato	1	6.25
	20	3.00	salt		0.75
	5	0.80	pepper		0.25
	5	0.80	mixed herbs		0.25
2	090		Gross weight	4	11.00

Ingredients for filling

Kilo	Gram	%	Ingredients	lb	oz
1	800	100.00	minced beef	4	0.00
	600	33.3	chopped onions	1	5.50
1	500	83.30	water	3	5.50
	45	2.50	salt		1.50
	15	0.80	pepper	1	0.50
	30	1.60	meat extract flavour		1.00
	120	6.60	cornflour		4.25
	150	8.30	water	2	5.25
1	200	66.60	uncooked diced potato	2	11.00
5	460		Gross weight	12	2.50

Vegetable

(See colour plate 5.)

COOKING METHOD

1 Place the diced carrot, diced swede, chopped onions and sliced mushrooms into a pan with sufficient water and bring to the boil.
2 Reduce the heat and allow to simmer for 10 minutes.
3 Remove from the heat and drain the water from the vegetables.
4 Add the peas, mashed potato, salt, pepper and mixed herbs and mix through thoroughly until dispersed.
5 The filling is now ready for processing.

SAVOURY SLICE

This product requires savoury paste for the base and puff pastry for the top, therefore: use recipe A or B for savoury paste (p. 194).

Using the recipe for the half puff pastry, make the puff pastry by the Scotch method.

Processing method

Yield 60

1 Scale 2 at 900 g (2 lb) of savoury paste and shape into a rectangle.
2 Pin out the savoury paste and line two small baking trays measuring 37.5 × 45 cm (15 × 18").
3 Prepare the savoury filling as follows:

Cooking method

- place the minced beef, chopped onions, water, salt, pepper and meat extract flavour into a pan and bring to the boil
- reduce the heat and allow to simmer for 10 minutes
- mix the cornflour and water together, add to the above whilst stirring continuously
- when the filling has thickened, remove from the heat, add the uncooked diced potato and stir through

- allow the filling to cool to 21°C (70°F) before processing begins.

4 Place 2.5 kg (5 lb 9.25 oz) of the savoury filling into each tray and spread evenly until level.
5 Using half of the puff pastry per tray, pin it out and place over the filling.
6 Trim off the excess puff pastry from the top edge.
7 Dock all of the puff pastry surface, then using pastry wheels 6 × 5, mark the pastry into 30 squares.
8 Allow the puff pastry 30 minutes rest before baking.
9 Brush the puff pastry with eggwash and bake at 225°C (440°F) for approximately 35 minutes.
10 When thoroughly cooled, use a sharp knife to cut slices.

APPLE TURNOVERS

Make the puff pastry using the recipe for half puff pastry.

Ingredients for filling

Kilo	Gram	%	Ingredients	lb	oz
1	800	100.00	unsweetened tinned apple	4	0.00
	270	15.00	sugar	1	10.00
	90	5.00	pre-gelatinised starch		3.75
2	160		Gross weight	4	13.25

Processing method

Yield approx 26

1 Pin out the puff pastry to approximately 4 mm ($\frac{3}{16}$") thick.
2 Using a 15 cm (6") diameter plain cutter, cut out the bases.
3 Prepare the apple filling as follows:

Apple turnovers

Mixing method

- chop the apple into small pieces
- mix the sugar and pre-gelatinised starch together, add to the above and mix through thoroughly.

4 Lay out the puff pastry bases in rows, then place approximately 70 g (2.5 oz) of filling into the centre of each puff pastry base.
5 Dampen the edge of half of each puff pastry base with water.
6 Fold one side of the puff pastry over to enclose the filling and seal the join firmly.
7 Brush the top of each turnover with water, then dip into sugar and place onto a tray lined with silicone paper.
8 Allow a rest period of 30 minutes before baking.
9 Using a sharp knife make two vents in the top and bake at 215°C (420°F) for approximately 25 minutes.

Note: For fresh cream apple turnovers, make a slightly smaller turnover and when cool, cut the turnover and fill with a rope of fresh cream.

CREAM SLICE

(See colour plate 13.)

Make the puff pastry using the recipe for three quarter puff pastry.

Materials required for 36 Cream Slices

Kilo	Gram	Ingredients	lb	oz
	800	fondant	1	12
	400	jam		14
1	400	fresh cream	3	4

Processing method

Yield approx 36

1 Pin out the puff pastry to a large rectangle measuring 60 × 72 cm (24 × 29").
2 Mark and cut into six strips measuring 10 × 72 cm (4 × 29").
3 Place the strips onto a tray lined with silicone paper.
4 Dock each strip down the middle only.
5 Allow a rest period of 30 minutes before baking.
6 Bake at 230°C (446°F) for 15–20 minutes.
7 On withdrawal from the oven, place the bases onto a cooling wire.
8 When cool, using a palette knife, spread prepared fondant evenly over the flat side of three puff pastry bases and allow to set.

9 Pipe a zig-zag of jam over the three hollow bases.
10 Pipe a rope of cream within each hollow base.
11 Place each fondant coated top onto a creamed base and mark into 12 equal portions.
12 Using a very sharp knife, cut each prepared base into slices. The knife should be dipped into hot water and cleaned before every cut.

Note: Docking each base down the middle creates a hollow within the baked base. When two bases are placed together, support is given to the cutting process and the cream is prevented from being squeezed out.

CUSTARD SLICE

Make the puff pastry using the recipe for three quarter puff pastry.

Materials required for 36 Custard slices

Kilo	Gram	Ingredients	lb	oz
	800	Lemon fondant	1	12
	400	jam		14
1	400	custard	3	4

Processing method

Yield approx 36

Follow all stages of the processing method for Cream Slices. At stage 10, replace the cream with custard and at stage 11, use lemon coloured and flavoured fondant.

PALMIERS

Make the puff pastry using the recipe for three quarter puff pastry.

Materials required for 36 Palmiers

Kilo	Gram	Ingredients	lb	oz
	400	jam		14
1	400	fresh cream	3	4

Processing method

Yield approx 36 pairs

1 Pin out the puff pastry to a large rectangle 60 cm (24") wide and 4 mm ($\frac{3}{16}$") thick. The length of the rectangle is determined by the thickness.
2 Dampen the surface of the puff pastry and then dredge with caster sugar.
3 Mark and cut into two pieces measuring 30 cm (12") wide.
4 Using the predetermined width of 30 cm (12"), fold each piece as follows:

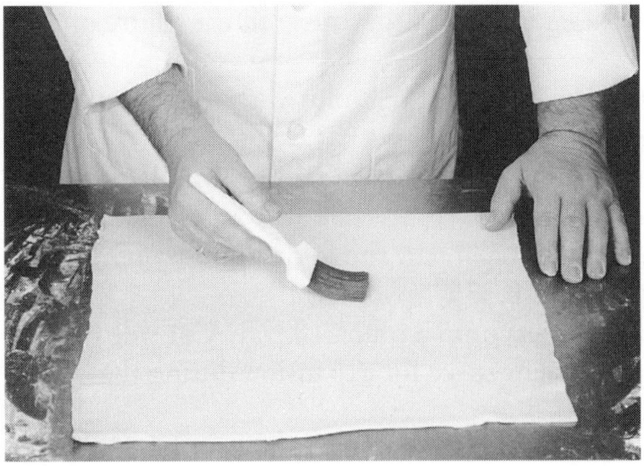

Dampen the surface, dredge with caster sugar and fold

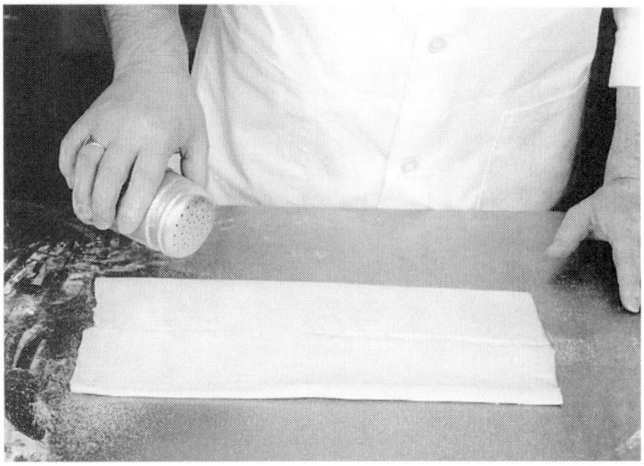

Dampen the surface, dredge with caster sugar and fold

Use a scotch scraper to cut folded puff pastry strip into slices

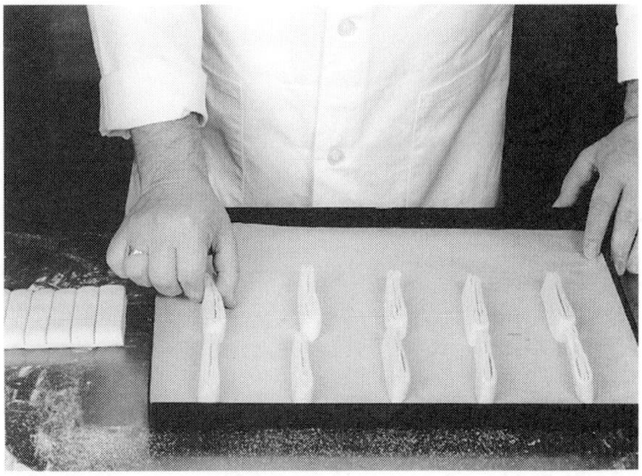

Place Palmiers onto a prepared tray; allow sufficient room for expansion during baking

Palmiers

- fold both ends in until they meet in the centre of the paste
- dampen the surface of the folds with water and then dredge with caster sugar
- fold the whole paste again in half to complete the folding process.

5 Using a scotch scraper, cut the folded puff pastry strip into slices 1 cm (0.375") wide.
6 Place the Palmiers onto a prepared tray. Cut side down allowing sufficient space for expansion during the baking process.
7 Allow a rest period of 30 minutes before baking.
8 Bake at 215°C (420°F) for approximately 20 minutes until a light golden brown colour is obtained.
9 On withdrawal from the oven, place the Palmiers onto a cooling wire.
10 When cool, sandwich two Palmiers together with jam and fresh cream.

CREAM CORONET

Make the puff pastry using the recipe for three quarter puff pastry.

Materials required for 50 Cream Coronets

Kilo	Gram	Ingredients	lb	oz
1	000	royal icing	2	4
	400	red piping jelly		14
	500	jam	1	2
1	800	fresh cream	4	

Processing method

Yield approx 50

1 Pin out the puff pastry to a large rectangle 40 cm (16") wide and 6 mm (0.25") thick. The length of the rectangle is determined by the thickness.
2 Spread slightly softened royal icing evenly over the surface of the puff pastry.
3 Mark and cut into four strips 10 cm (4") wide.
4 Using red piping jelly, pipe thin lines in a criss-cross design over each strip.
5 Mark and cut each strip into slices 6 cm (2.5") wide and place onto a prepared tray.
6 Allow a rest period of 1 hour before baking.
7 Bake at 215°C (420°F) for approximately 25 minutes.
8 On withdrawal from the oven, place the coronets onto a cooling wire.
9 When cool, cut each coronet horizontally through the centre.

10 Pipe a line of jam and a rope of fresh cream onto the base and replace the top.

MILLE-FEUILLE GATEAUX

Make the puff pastry using the recipe for three quarter puff pastry.

Materials required for approx 12 Mille-Feuille

Kilo	Gram	Ingredients	lb	oz
1	200	jam	2	11
2	500	custard cream filling	5	9
1	800	fondant	4	
	700	roast rib almonds	1	9

Processing method

Yield approx 12

1 Pin out the puff pastry until it is 2–3 mm (0.125") thick.
2 Dock the pastry well and evenly.
3 Using a 15 cm (6") diameter plain cutter, cut out the bases.
4 Place the bases onto a prepared tray and allow a rest period of 30 minutes before baking.
5 Bake at 230°C (446°F) for approximately 20 minutes until crisp and golden brown.
6 On withdrawal from the oven, place the bases onto a cooling wire.
7 Prepare a rich custard filling by blending together equal quantities of whipped fresh cream and cold custard.
8 Using three bases, fill and assemble as follows:
- select the most round and flat base for the top
- apply a thin layer of jam and a layer of custard cream to the remaining two bases
- assemble the bases together and place the top in position.

9 Coat the sides of the gateaux with cream custard.
10 Using prepared fondant, apply a marbled design to the top of the gateaux.
11 Mask the sides with nib roast almonds.

Cut out discs

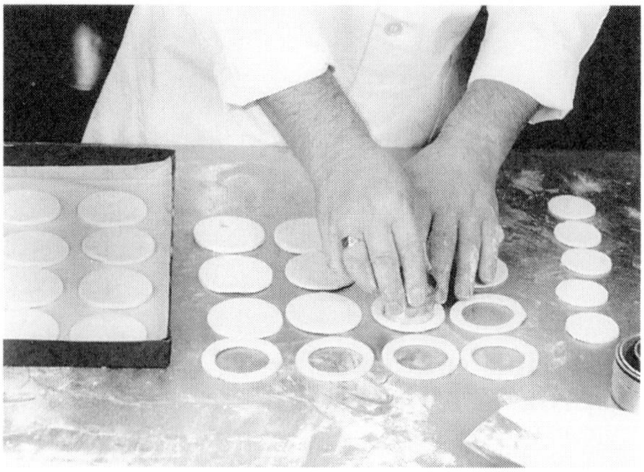

Cut out the centre from half of the discs to form rings

Dampen surface of whole discs with water

Place rings on top of the discs

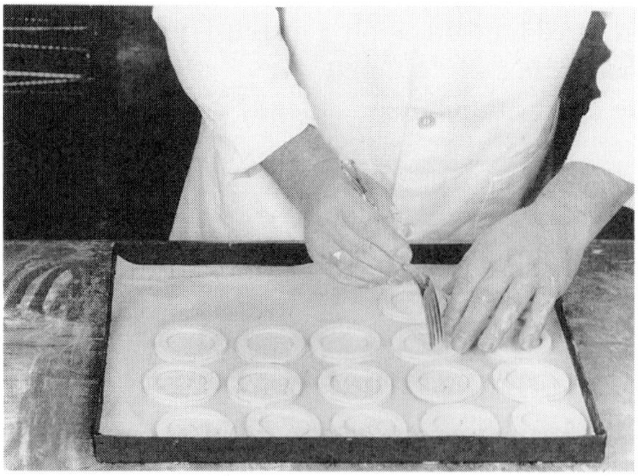

Dock the centres using a fork

Vol au vents

VOL-AU-VENTS

Make the puff pastry using the recipe for full puff pastry.

Processing method

Yield approx 60

1 Pin out the puff pastry until it is 3 mm (0.125") thick.
2 Using a 7.5 cm (3") diameter plain cutter, cut out the discs.
3 Using a 6 cm (2.5") diameter plain cutter, cut out the centre from half of the discs to form rings.
4 Place the whole discs onto a prepared tray and dampen the surface with water.
5 Place the rings on top of the discs, press gently to secure the assembly of the vol-au-vent.
6 Dock the centres using a fork.
7 Brush the top edge with eggwash and allow a rest period of 30 minutes before baking.
8 Bake at 230°C (446°F) for approximately 25 minutes.

Note: The centres that are cut out from the rings, may be brushed with eggwash, rested, baked and used as a decorative lid on filled vol-au-vents.

9 Prepare a basic white sauce as follows:

Ingredients – white sauce

Kilo	Gram	%	Ingredients	lb	oz
	120	12.00	margarine		4.25
	120	12.00	medium flour		4.25
1	000	100.00	fresh milk	2	3.50
	10	1.00	salt		0.50
	2	0.20	pepper		pinch
1	252		Gross weight	2	12.50

Cooking method

- place the margarine into a pan and melt down slowly
- add the flour and cook until a roux is obtained. Remove from the heat
- add the milk slowly to the above while stirring continuously
- when all of the milk has been added, return to the heat to thicken, stirring continuously
- add the salt and pepper and stir through
- allow the sauce to cool to 21°C (70°F).

10 Add one of these fillings to the basic white sauce and stir through until thoroughly dispersed.

i 800 g (1 lb 2.5 oz) diced cooked chicken
400 g (14.5 oz) sliced cooked mushrooms

ii 1 kg (2 lb 3.5 oz) diced cooked ham
200 g (7.5 oz) sweetcorn

iii 1.2 kg (2 lb 10 oz) peeled cooked prawns
iv 900 g (2 lb) grated cheddar cheese
300 g (10.75 oz) chopped onions.

11 Place sufficient filling into each vol-au-vent.
12 The vol-au-vents can be garnished with baked lids, parsley, tomatoes, cucumber or chopped spring onions.

CREAM HORNS

This product can be made from half puff pastry or from puff pastry trimmings.

Processing method

Yield approx 36

1 Pin out the puff pastry to a large rectangle 60 cm (24") wide and 2 mm (0.125") thick. The length of the rectangle is determined by the thickness.
2 Using pastry wheels, mark and cut into thin strips measuring 60 × 2.5 cm (24 × 1").
3 Dampen the surface of the strips with water.
4 Carefully wrap the strip around a clean, greased horn mould. The wrapping must begin at the pointed end of the mould, working towards the open end. Ensure the puff pastry strip overlaps itself sufficiently to secure the shape.
5 Dampen the surface of the horn with water, then roll in caster sugar.
6 Place the horns onto a prepared tray and allow a rest period of 30 minutes before baking.
7 Bake at 215°C (420°F) for approximately 25 minutes.
8 On withdrawal from the oven, release the horns from the mould and place onto a cooling wire.
9 When cool, pipe a line of jam up the inside of the horn, fill with fresh cream and pipe a rosette at the open end.

ECCLES CAKES

This product can be made from half puff pastry or from puff pastry trimmings.

Ingredients for filling

Kilo	Gram	%	Ingredients	lb	oz
	450	100.00	currants	1	0.00
	160	35.00	brown sugar		5.75
	225	50.00	cake crumbs		8.00
	5	1.10	mixed spice		0.25
	110	24.40	melted butter		4.00
	950		Gross weight	2	2.00

Processing method

Yield approx 36

1 Pin out the puff pastry to a 62 cm (25") square approximately 4 mm ($\frac{3}{16}$") thick.
2 Using pastry wheels, mark and cut the puff pastry into 10 cm (4") squares.
3 Prepare the Eccles filling as follows:

Mixing method

- place all the ingredients into a bowl and mix together thoroughly.

4 Place approximately 25 g (1 oz) of Eccles filling into the centre of each square.
5 Bring each corner of the square to the centre, gather in the remaining pastry and secure together to completely enclose the filling.
6 Flatten slightly, turn over and pin out to 8 cm (3") diameter.
7 Brush the tops with water and dip into caster sugar.
8 Place the Eccles onto a prepared tray.
9 Using a sharp knife, make two vents in the top.
10 Allow a rest period of 30 minutes before baking.
11 Bake at 215°C (420°F) for approximately 20 minutes.

C H A P T E R

eleven

Powder aerated products

The term 'powder aerated products' refers to the influence of baking powder upon the volume, shape and general character of the product. The popularity of aerated products has been maintained by the continued success of the scone. The vast majority of bakers within the UK will include one or more types of scone within their daily production schedule. Bakers supply the high demand for scones to a variety of outlets, including supermarkets, coffee shops and other eating areas. To be enjoyed at their best, scones should be produced and consumed on the same day. It is possible to produce a wide range of scones from a basic recipe by:

- adding fruit
- using brown flour to replace white flour
- producing different shapes
- baking on a hot-plate instead of in an oven.

CHARACTERISTICS OF SCONES

In general, most types of scones should have the following characteristics:

- a good volume, with even expansion
- a golden brown colour
- a smooth crust surface
- a creamy crumb colour
- a slight openness to the texture.

The aim of mixing

- to disperse and dissolve all of the ingredients
- to prevent the complete formation of gluten forming proteins
- to form a smooth, clear dough.

Basic ingredients

The basic ingredients required to make scones are:

- medium strength flour
- baking powder
- soft fats
- sugar
- milk.

Note: Egg can be included to improve the volume, colour, eating quality, nutritional value and shelf life of a scone.

Temperature of ingredients

Prior to mixing scone doughs, the dry ingredients and fat should be held at 16–21°C (61–70°F). This will assist in the mixing process and the consistency of the scone dough. However, the milk and any other liquid must be chilled. The cold liquids ensure the dough remains cool, thus preventing the baking powder from emitting carbon dioxide gas before the product reaches the baking stage. This will ensure a full volume is obtained.

MIXING METHODS

This is an outline for each of the mixing methods used to make scone dough. A more detailed description of each method can be found in the recipes for scones.

Rub-in method

1 Sieve together the dry ingredients.
2 Rub the fat through the dry ingredients to a crumble.
3 Mix together the sugar and liquids and add to the above.
4 Mix to a smooth, clear dough.

Note: Add fruit when the dough is half clear.

Blending method

1 Sieve together the dry ingredients.
2 Mix together the soluble ingredients and liquids.
3 Add the solution slowly to the dry ingredients.
4 Mix to a smooth, clear batter.

High speed method

Using a high speed mixing machine, place all of the ingredients into the mixing chamber and mix for 15–20 seconds. Fruit should be added and mixed through during the final five seconds of the mixing time.

Points to consider when processing scones

1 Never use warm liquids – all liquids must be chilled.
2 Do not overmix.
3 Keep scraps to a minimum, add at the rate of 10% to freshly made scone dough.
4 Do not over-handle the scone dough.
5 Avoid excessive dusting.
6 Do not pin scone doughs too thin.
7 Minimise trimmings by cutting out scones as close together as possible.
8 Accurate scaling is essential to ensure that the yield is obtained and a uniform product is produced.
9 Allow a rest period of 15 minutes prior to baking.

Storage of unbaked scones

Unbaked scones can be stored under cool, humid conditions in a retarder for 16–24 hours. This offers the baker the following advantages:

1 The opportunity to build up stock levels and even out production.
2 Fresh scones at the point of sale.

Baking of scones

Scones can be baked in the oven or on a hot-plate. In general the baking temperature is as follows:

- oven – 225°C (440°F)
- hot-plate – moderate.

DURING THE BAKING PROCESS

During the initial stages of the baking process, the heat will penetrate the scone units and activate the moistened baking powder. The baking powder will then produce carbon dioxide gas which steadily lifts the scone to its full volume. The dough coagulates, and finally the crust colour is formed.

The baking temperature will depend upon the following:

- shape, size and depth
- density
- sugar content
- product characteristics.

Cooling

Scones which are wrapped or finished with jam and fresh cream must be thoroughly cooled prior to processing. However, in some outlets scones are sold served warm and do not require a long cooling period.

Shelf life

The freshness can be retained and the staling process can be delayed by closely wrapping the products in airtight packaging.

OVEN CHART

Product	Baking temperature in °C (°F)	Baking time in minutes	Additional control procedures
Plain Scones	225 (440)	15–20	Open damper for final 5 mins
Fruited Scones	225 (440)	15–20	" " " "
Scone Rounds	225 (440)	15–20	" " " "
Hot-Plate Scones	Moderate hot plate	10	None
Cheese Scones	225 (440)	15–20	Open damper for final 5 mins
Potato Scones	Moderate hot plate	10	None
Drop Scones	Moderate hot plate	10	None
Ring Doughnuts	190 (374)	2–3	None

RECIPES FOR POWDER AERATED PRODUCTS

PLAIN AND FRUITED SCONES, AND SCONE ROUNDS – RUB-IN PROCESS

(See colour plate 21.)

Note: To produce Brown Scones and Scone Rounds, simply:

- replace the medium flour with brown flour
- increase the cold milk to 500 g (1 lb 1.75 oz).

Ingredients

Kilo	Gram	%	Ingredients	lb	oz
1	000	100.00	medium 2 flour	3.	50
	60	6.00	baking powder		2.00
	190	19.00	shortening		6.75
	190	19.00	caster sugar		6.75
	440	44.00	cold milk		15.75
	120	12.00	cold egg		4.25
	5	0.50	vanilla essence		0.25
	5	0.50	egg colour		0.25
2	010		Gross weight	4	7.50
1	929		Net weight	4	4.50

Production Points

Scone dough temperature	**Cool**
Scaling weight:	
scones	**55 g (2 oz)**
rounds	**260 g (9.25 oz)**
Yield:	
plain scones	**35**
fruit scones	**38**
plain rounds	**7**
fruit rounds	**8**
Baking temperature	**225°C (440°F)**
Baking time	**15–20 mins**

Mixing method for Plain Scones

1 Sieve together the flour and baking powder and place in a mixing bowl.
2 Add the shortening to the dry ingredients. Using a beater, mix on slow speed until a crumbly consistency is obtained.
3 Dissolve the sugar in the cold milk, cold egg, vanilla essence and egg colour, and add to the above.
4 Mix on slow speed until a smooth clear dough is obtained. Do not overmix the scone dough at this stage.

Mixing method for Fruited Scones

1 Follow stages 1, 2 and 3 for Plain Scones.
2 Mix on slow speed until the dough is half clear.
3 Add the fruit content and mix on slow speed until a clear dough is obtained and the fruit is thoroughly dispersed. Do not overmix the scone dough at this stage.

FRUIT ADDITIONS TO BASIC SCONE DOUGH

To produce a range of fruited scones or scone rounds, add one of the following quantities of fruit to the plain scone dough recipe:

- 200 g (7 oz) currants
- 200 g (7 oz) sultanas
- 200 g (7 oz) glace cherries.

Processing method for Plain and Fruited Scones

1 Pin out the scone dough to approximately 2 cm (0.75") thick.
2 Using a 6–7 cm (2.5–2.75") diameter round plain cutter, cut out the scones.
3 Place the scones onto a greased baking tray.
4 Brush the tops of the scones with eggwash.
5 Allow the scones to rest for 15 minutes before baking.
6 Bake at 225°C (440°F) for 15–20 minutes.
7 On withdrawal from the oven, place the scones onto a cooling wire until cool.

Processing method for Plain and Fruited Scone Rounds

1 Scale 7 or 8 at 260 g (9.25 oz) and mould round.
2 Pin out the scone dough piece to a flat round shape 2 cm (0.75") thick.
3 Place the rounds onto a greased baking tray and using a scotch scraper cut each round into four equal segments.
4 Brush the tops of the rounds with eggwash.
5 Allow the rounds to rest for 15 minutes before baking.
6 Bake at 225°C (440°F) for 15–20 minutes.
7 On withdrawal from the oven, place the rounds onto a cooling wire until cool.

HOT PLATE SCONES

Yield approx 75

Preparation of the hot plate

Before production can begin the hot plate should be prepared in the following way:

1 Cleaned and polished with a soft cloth.
2 Lightly greased.
3 Lit and adjusted to the appropriate setting to obtain the correct baking temperature.

Note:

- Stage 1 of preparing the hot plate must be performed between the baking of each batch of scones.

- Great care must be taken to ensure the baking surface of the hot plate is never scratched to prevent the scones sticking during the baking process.

Recipe and mixing method

1 Make a scone dough using the recipe and appropriate mixing method for Plain and Fruited Scones and Scone Rounds.
2 To produce a range of hot plate scones, use the fruit additions given for Plain and Fruited Scones.

Hot plate scones

Processing method

1 Pin out the scone dough piece to approximately 1 cm (0.25") thick.
2 Using a 6–7 cm (2.5–2.75") diameter round plain cutter, cut out the scones.
3 Place the scones onto the prepared hot-plate in rows, allowing sufficient space for turning.
4 When the scones are half-baked, using a palette knife, turn the scones over to complete the baking process.
5 When the scones are fully baked, remove from the hot-plate and place onto a cooling wire.

CHEESE SCONES – RUB-IN PROCESS

Ingredients

Kilo	Gram	%	Ingredients	lb	oz
1	000	100.00	medium flour	2	3.50
	60	6.00	baking powder		2.00
	2	0.20	dry mustard		pinch
	250	25.00	cake margarine		9.00
	440	44.00	cold milk		15.75
	140	14.00	cold egg		5.00
	200	20.00	grated cheddar cheese		7.00
2	092		Gross weight	4	10.25
2	008		Net weight	4	7.25

Production Points

Scone dough temperature	**Cool**
Scaling weight	**55 g (2 oz)**
Yield	**36**
Baking temperature	**225°C (440°F)**
Baking time	**15–20 mins**

Mixing method

1 Sieve together the flour, baking powder and dry mustard and place into a mixing bowl.
2 Add the cake margarine to the dry ingredients and using a beater, mix on slow speed until a crumbly consistency is obtained.
3 Mix together the cold milk and cold egg and add to the above. Mix on slow speed until the dough is half clear.
4 Add the grated cheddar cheese and mix on slow speed until a clear dough is obtained and the cheese is thoroughly dispersed.

Note: Do not overmix the scone dough at this stage.

Processing method

Follow stages 1–7 of the processing method for Plain and Fruited Scones.

POTATO SCONES – RUB-IN PROCESS

Ingredients

Kilo	Gram	%	Ingredients	lb	oz
	500	100.00	medium flour	1	1.75
	15	3.00	baking powder		0.50
	5	1.00	salt		0.25
	220	44.00	cake margarine or butter		8.00
	220	44.00	cold milk		8.00
	60	12.00	cold egg		2.00
	500	100.00	cold mashed potato	1	1.75
1	520		Gross weight	3	6.25
1	460		Net weight	3	4.00

Production Points

Scone dough temperature	**Cool**
Scaling weight	**55 g (2 oz)**
Yield	**27**
Baking temperature	**Moderate hot-plate**
Baking time	**10–15 mins**

Mixing method

1 Sieve together the flour, baking powder and salt and place into a mixing bowl.
2 Add the cake margarine or butter to the dry ingredients. Using a beater, mix on slow speed until a crumble consistency is obtained.
3 Mix together the cold milk and cold egg and add to the above, with the mashed potato.
4 Mix on slow speed until a smooth clear dough is obtained.

Processing method

1 Pin out the scone dough to approximately 0.5 cm ($\frac{3}{16}$") thick.
2 Using a 8 cm (3.25") diameter round plain cutter, cut out the scones.
3 Place the scones onto a lightly greased moderate hot-plate in rows, allowing sufficient space for turning.
4 When the scones are half-baked, using a palette knife, turn the scones over to complete the baking process.
5 When the scones are fully baked, remove from the hot-plate and place onto a cooling wire.

DROP SCONES – BLENDING PROCESS

Ingredients

Kilo	Gram	%	Ingredients	lb	oz
	500	100.00	medium flour	1	1.75
	25	5.00	baking powder		1.00
	150	30.00	caster sugar		5.50
	7	1.40	salt		0.25
	70	14.00	egg		2.50
	450	90.00	milk	1	0.00
	2	0.40	egg colour		0.12
	35	7.00	vegetable oil or melted butter		1.25
1	239		Gross weight	2	12.25
1	190		Net weight	2	10.50

Production Points

Batter temperature	**Cool**
Scaling weight	**approx 35 g (1.25 oz)**
Yield	**approx 34**
Baking temperature	**Moderate hot-plate**
Baking time	**8–10 mins**

Mixing method

1. Sieve together the flour and baking powder and place into a mixing bowl.
2. Mix together the caster sugar, salt, egg, milk and egg colour. Using a whisk, add the solution to the dry ingredients in a slow, steady stream on slow speed. Scrape down.
3. Whisk on slow speed for 2–3 minutes until a smooth, clear batter is obtained.
4. Add the vegetable oil or melted butter, whisk on slow speed for 10 seconds. Scrape down. Whisk on slow speed for 20 seconds until thoroughly dispersed.

Processing method

1. The hot-plate must be clean, polished, lightly greased and set at a moderate temperature.
2. Using a savoy bag and plain tube, pipe approximately 34 drops, weighing approximately 35 g (1.25 oz) onto the hot-plate in neat rows. Allow sufficient space for turning.
3. When the drop scones are half-baked, using a wide palette knife, turn the scones over to complete the baking process.
4. When the scones are fully baked, remove from the hot-plate and place onto a cooling wire.

RING DOUGHNUTS – BLENDING PROCESS

Ingredients

Kilo	Gram	%	Ingredients	lb	oz
1	000	100.00	bread flour	2	3.50
	30	3.00	baking powder		1.00
	310	31.00	caster sugar		11.00
	155	15.50	cold egg		5.50
	750	75.00	cold milk	1	10.75
	155	15.50	vegetable oil		5.50
2	400		Gross weight	5	5.25
2	304		Net weight	5	1.75

Production Points

Batter temperature	**Cool**
Scaling weight	**approx 50 g (1.75 oz)**
Yield	**approx 40**
Frying temperature	**190°C (374°F)**
Frying time	**2–3 mins**

Mixing method

1 Sieve together the flour and baking powder and place into a mixing bowl.
2 Dissolve the sugar into the cold egg, cold milk and vegetable oil.
3 Using a beater, add the solution to the dry ingredients in a slow, steady stream on slow speed. Scrape down.
4 Mix on slow speed for 30–60 seconds until a smooth, clear batter is obtained. Do not overmix the batter at this stage.

Processing method

1 Fill the hopper of a ring doughnut depositing machine and proceed to deposit the shaped batter into the hot frying oil.
2 Halfway through the frying process, turn the ring doughnuts over to complete the frying process.
3 When frying is complete remove the doughnuts from the fryer, place onto a draining wire and allow to drain for 1 minute.
4 Roll the ring doughnuts in caster sugar.

C H A P T E R

twelve

Cakemaking processes

For the majority of people, eating a confectionery product is one of life's pleasures. Tastes may differ, but the enjoyment of consuming one's personal favourite cake is a luxury. An extensive range of confectionery products is produced to meet the varied demands of the general public. New products are continually being developed, but established products such as Madeira Cake, for example, prove that a product can remain popular for many years.

CHARACTERISTICS OF CAKE AND SPONGE PRODUCTS

The density of a cake will vary according to the type of cake. A Madeira Cake and a Swiss Roll will have a light, porous eating quality, whereas a Christmas Cake will have a rich, heavy eating quality. However, most cakes and sponge products will have some of the following characteristics:

- a good volume and uniform shape
- an even crust colour
- a thin crust
- a clean and bright crumb colour
- regular and evenly distributed cells to form a mellow crumb structure
- sufficient moisture to the crumb to make a cake enjoyable to the palate
- a fine flavour and aroma.

Categories of cake and sponge products

Cake and sponge products can be broadly divided into seven categories:

1 Plain cake – eg Genoese, Angel Cake.
2 Lightly fruited cake – eg Sultana Cake, Cherry Cake.
3 Heavily fruited cake – eg Dundee Cake, Wedding Cake.
4 Decorated cake – eg Fondant Dips, Bar Gateaux.
5 Light sponge – eg Swiss Rolls.
6 Medium sponge – eg Plain and Chocolate Sponge Cakes.
7 Heavy sponge – eg Sponge Drops and Fingers.

Cakes for occasions

Certain occasions and events throughout the year demand a particular type of decorated cake. Here are some examples:

- Birthday Cakes
- Wedding Cakes
- Novelty Cakes
- Anniversary Cakes
- Christening Cakes
- Valentine Cakes
- Mothers Day Cakes

- Christmas Cakes
- Simnel Cakes for Easter.

THE PROCESSES

Skill, knowledge and judgment are required to produce cake and sponge products successfully. A command of the most common mixing processes is essential. There are five major processes used to produce cake and sponge products:

1 Cake products
   - the Sugar Batter Process
   - the Blending Process.

2 Sponge products
   - the Traditional Process
   - the Emulsified Process
   - the Delayed Soda Process.

The aim of mixing

- to disperse and dissolve all ingredients
- to form an emulsion
- to incorporate air into the batter or sponge.

Basic ingredients

The basic ingredients required to make cake and sponge products are:

Cake:

- soft flour
- soft fat
- sugar
- egg

Sponge:

- soft flour
- sugar
- egg

Batter temperature

To ensure that a cake and sponge batter is a stable emulsion, the final batter temperature should be 18–21°C

(64–70°F). It is therefore necessary to increase the temperature of the egg and other liquids to 21°C (70°F) before addition.

MIXING METHODS

This is an outline for each of the mixing methods used to make cake and sponge batters. A more detailed description of each method can be found in the recipes for cakes and sponge products.

Cakes

SUGAR BATTER METHOD

1 Beat together the sugar and fat until light.
2 Add the egg in five additions. Beat each addition in thoroughly.
3 Sieve together the dry ingredients, add to above and mix through until a smooth clear batter is obtained.

Note: Milk and fruit should be added when the batter is half clear.

BLENDING METHOD

1 Sieve together the dry ingredients. Add the fat and mix to a crumble or paste consistency.
2 Add the milk and mix until a paste is formed.
3 Add the egg slowly and mix until a smooth batter is obtained.
4 Add fruit and mix through until thoroughly dispersed.

HIGH SPEED METHOD

Using a high speed mixing machine, place all of the ingredients into the mixing chamber and mix for 15–20 seconds. Fruit should be added and mixed through during the final 5 seconds of the mixing time.

Sponges

TRADITIONAL METHOD

1 Whisk together the egg and sugar to a full sponge.
2 Sieve the flour and carefully fold through the sponge.
3 Process immediately.

EMULSIFIED METHOD

1 Mix together the egg, water and emulsifier.
2 Sieve together the dry ingredients, add to above and blend through.
3 Whisk on top speed for 3 minutes.
4 Whisk the remaining water through until thoroughly dispersed.

DELAYED SODA

1 Blend together the liquids and sieved dry ingredients.
2 Whisk on top speed for 20 minutes.
3 Mix together the bicarbonate of soda and remaining water, add to above and mix through until thoroughly dispersed.

Points to consider when processing cake and sponge products

CAKE

1 Prepare all ingredients correctly before addition.
2 Strictly adhere to the mixing speed and times.
3 Scrape down regularly to ensure a smooth, lump free batter is obtained.
4 Once the flour has been added to the mix, do not overmix and toughen.
5 Large bowls of cake batter should be scraped down throughout the scaling process to prevent discoloration and streaks occurring in the cake crumb of the final number of cakes scaled off.
6 Prepare tins correctly to ensure the product can be released without damage.
7 Accurate scaling is essential to ensure the yield is obtained and a uniform product is produced.

SPONGES

1 All weighing and mixing equipment must be free from grease.
2 Prepare all ingredients correctly before additions.
3 Strictly adhere to the mixing speed and times.
4 Once the flour has been added during the traditional method, do not overmix or over-handle to prevent loss of aeration and bake immediately.
5 Accurate scaling is essential to ensure that the yield is obtained and a uniform product is produced.

6 Ensure the sponge is spread evenly over the baking tray for Swiss Roll.
7 Prepare tins correctly to ensure the product can be released without damage.

Baking of cakes and sponges

A general guide to the baking temperature of cake and sponge products is:

- 170°C (340°F) – Wedding Cake, Angel Cake
- 182°C (360°F) – Madeira Cake
- 190°C (374°F) – American Muffins
- 204°C (400°F) – Sponge Cakes
- 240°C (464°F) – Swiss Rolls.

DURING THE BAKING PROCESS

During the baking of cake and sponge products, the heat will penetrate the batter. The heat causes the incorporated air and egg to expand, and activates the moistened baking powder which then produces carbon dioxide gas. Together they steadily lift the product to its full volume. The batter gelatinises and coagulates, and the crust colour emerges as the sugar begins to caramelise until the product is thoroughly baked. The baking process can take as short a time as 7 minutes to as long as 4½ hours. However, the final objective is always the same: to produce a moist product with a pleasant flavour.

To achieve this objective, the appropriate baking temperature should be used and this will depend upon the following considerations.

- shape, size and depth
- density
- sugar content
- product characteristics.

In conjunction with the appropriate baking temperature, a fully loaded oven can benefit the baking process. The humidity generated from the products assist in obtaining a good shape and an even bake.

PROTECTION DURING BAKING

Large cakes such as Genoa Slab and Christmas Cake take a long time to bake and therefore require protection from the heat. The protection will ensure the interior is fully baked while a good even crust colour is obtained. The areas of the cake which require protection are the base and sides. They should be protected as follows:

1 Base – Hardboard, cardboard or thick paper placed on the baking tray under the cake tin, hoop or slab frame.
2 Sides – Card or thick paper secured around the outside of the tin or hoop.

Note: Cake frames made from wood do not require any protection during the baking process.

Finally, great care must be taken to avoid disturbing cake and sponge products during the baking process, which could cause them to collapse.

Cooling

On withdrawal from the oven, cake and sponge products should be allowed to cool on the tray in the tin, hoop or frame until they can be handled without being damaged. Cakes and sponges which are to be wrapped or finished must be thoroughly cooled prior to processing.

Final decoration

Cake and sponge products are decorated with suitable finishing materials to enhance their appearance, add flavour and improve the general eating qualities. Finishing techniques range from the most simple to highly intricate designs. Nevertheless, the practical application of the finish or design should be reproduced consistently to a good standard to maintain the quality and appeal of the product.

Finally, cake and sponge products provide the baker and confectioner with the opportunity to be creative.

OVEN CHARTS

Cakes

Product	Baking temperature in °C (°F)	Baking time in minutes	Additional control procedures
Cup Cakes	204 (400)	20	Open damper for final 5 mins
Madeira Cake	182 (360)	50–60	" " " " 10 mins
Loaf Cake	182 (360)	45–60	" " " "
Gateau Bases	190 (374)	25	" " " " 5 mins
Chocolate Gateau Bases	190 (374)	25	" " " "
Dundee Cake	182 (360)	75	" " " " 10 mins
Dundee Slab Cake	177 (350)	120	" " " " 15 mins
Simnel Cake	182 (360)	60–75	" " " " 10 mins
Christmas Cake	171 (340)	150–180	" " " "
Birthday Cake	171 (340)	150–180	" " " "
Wedding Cake			
Top	165 (330)	120–135	" " " "
Middle	165 (330)	180–210	" " " "
Bottom	165 (330)	240–270	" " " "
Genoese	190 (374)	30	" " " " 5 mins
High Ratio Gateau Bases	190 (374)	25	" " " "
Farmhouse Cake	180 (356)	60–75	" " " " 10 mins
Mixed Fruit Cake	180 (356)	60–75	" " " "
Ginger Cake	180 (356)	45–60	" " " "
Ginger Squares	180 (356)	25–30	" " " " 5 mins
Genoa Slab	175 (346)	120	" " " " 10 mins
Angel Cake	170 (338)	75–90	" " " "
Carrot Cake Squares	190 (374)	25	" " " " 5 mins
American Muffins	190 (374)	25	4 " " "

Sponge products

Product	Baking temperature in °C (°F)	Baking time in minutes	Additional control procedures
Plain Sponge Cake	204 (400)	20–25	Open damper for final 5 mins
Sponge Curls	240 (464)	7	" " " 2 mins
Sponge Drops & Fingers	240 (464)	7	" " " "
Chocolate Sponge Cake	204 (400)	20–25	" " " 5 mins
Plain Swiss Roll	240 (464)	8	" " " 2 mins
Chocolate Swiss Roll	240 (464)	8	" " " "

RECIPES USING THE SUGAR BATTER PROCESS

CUP CAKES

Ingredients

Kilo	Gram	%	Ingredients	lb	oz
	470	67.00	caster sugar	1	0.75
	350	50.00	cake margarine		12.50
	120	17.00	shortening		4.25
	590	84.00	egg at 21°C (70°F)	1	5.00
	5	0.70	vanilla essence		0.25
	5	0.70	egg colour		0.25
	700	100.00	cake flour	1	9.00
	20	3.00	baking powder		0.75
	120	17.00	milk		4.25
2	380		Gross weight	5	5.00
2	284		Net weight	5	1.50

Production Points

Batter temperature	**21°C (70°F)**
Scaling weight	**35–40 g (1.25–1.50 oz)**
Yield	**60**
Baking temperature	**204°C (400°F)**
Baking time	**approx 20 mins**

Mixing method

1. Place the caster sugar, cake margarine and shortening into a mixing bowl.
2. Using a beater, blend together on slow speed, then beat on top speed for up to 10 minutes until light and aerated.
3. Mix together the egg, vanilla essence and egg colour, then add to the above in five additions. Each addition must be blended through on slow speed, the mixture scraped down, then the egg solution beaten in on top speed for 15 seconds.
4. Sieve together the flour and baking powder and add to the above. Mix through on slow speed until the batter is half clear.
5. Add the milk to the above and mix through on slow speed for 5 seconds. Scrape down.
6. Mix on slow speed for approximately 30 seconds until a smooth, clear batter is obtained. Do not overmix the batter at this stage.

Processing method

1. Using a savoy bag and plain tube, pipe 60 at 35–40 g (1.25–1.50 oz) of batter into a paper case supported by a bun frame or tin.
2. Bake at 204°C (400°F) for approximately 20 minutes.
3. On withdrawal from the oven, place the cup cake onto a cooling wire.

Finishing methods

BEFORE BAKING

The cup cakes can be decorated with a variety of ingredients such as flaked nuts, chopped cherries, chocolate chips, desiccated coconut, etc.

AFTER BAKING

The cup cakes can be decorated with coloured and flavoured fondant, chocolate flavoured coating, buttercream and fresh cream. Motifs and characters popular with children can be used to decorate this product.

MADEIRA CAKE

Ingredients

Kilo	Gram	%	Ingredients	lb	oz
	480	80.00	caster sugar	1	1.25
	360	60.00	cake margarine or butter		13.00
	120	20.00	shortening		4.25
	480	80.00	egg at 21°C (70°F)	1	1.25
	30	5.00	glycerine		1.00
	1	0.16	lemon essence		0.06
	3	0.50	vanilla essence	1	0.12
	1	0.16	almond essence		0.06
	2	0.33	egg colour		0.12
	600	100.00	cake flour	1	5.50
	10	1.60	baking powder		0.50
	110	18.00	milk at 21°C (70°F)		4.00
2	197		Gross weight	4	15.00
2	109		Net weight	4	12.00

Production Points

Batter temperature	**21°C (70°F)**
Deep hoop/tin	**15 cm (6") diameter round**
Scaling weight	**420 g (15 oz)**
Yield	**5**
Baking temperature	**182°C (360°F)**
Baking time	**50–60 mins**

Mixing method

1. Place the caster sugar, cake margarine or butter and shortening into a mixing bowl.
2. Using a beater, blend together on slow speed, then beat on top speed for up to 10 minutes until light and aerated.
3. Mix together the egg, glycerine, lemon essence, vanilla essence, almond essence and egg colour, then add to the above in five additions. Each addition must be blended through on slow speed, the mixture scraped down, then the egg solution beaten in on top speed for 15 seconds.
4. Sieve together the flour and baking powder and add to the above. Mix through on slow speed until the batter is half clear.
5. Add the milk to the above and mix through on slow speed for 5 seconds. Scrape down.
6. Mix on slow speed for approximately 30 seconds until a smooth, clear batter is obtained. Do not overmix the batter at this stage.

Processing method

1. Scale 5 at 420 g (15 oz) into deep 15 cm (6") diameter round hoops or tins lined with a paper case.
2. Moisten the back of the hand with milk and level the top of the batter.
3. Bake at 182°C (360°F) for 50–60 minutes.
4. On withdrawal from the oven, allow the Madeira Cakes to cool in the hoop or tin until they can be handled without being damaged.
5. Now place the Madeira Cakes onto a cooling wire.

LOAF CAKE SELECTION

Ingredients

Kilo	Gram	%	Ingredients	lb	oz
	400	80.00	caster sugar		14.25
	300	60.00	cake margarine or butter		10.75
	100	20.00	shortening		3.50
	350	70.00	egg at 21°C (70°F)		12.50
	25	5.00	glycerine		1.00
	5	1.00	vanilla essence		0.25
	500	100.00	cake flour	1	2.00
	15	3.00	baking powder		0.50
	120	24.00	milk at 21°C (70°F)		4.25
1	815		Gross weight	4	1.00
1	742		Net weight	3	14.50

Production Points

Batter temperature	**21°C (70°F)**
Tin	**Small loaf tin**
Scaling weight	**Refer to Additions (below)**
Yield	**Refer to Additions (below)**
Baking temperature	**182°C (360°F)**
Baking time	**45–60 mins**

(See colour plate 7.)

Mixing method

1 Place the caster sugar, cake margarine or butter and shortening into a mixing bowl.
2 Using a beater, blend together on slow speed, then beat on top speed for up to 10 minutes until light and aerated.
3 Mix together the egg, glycerine and vanilla essence, almond essence, then add to the above in five additions. Each addition must be blended through on slow speed, the mixture scraped down, then the egg solution beaten in on top speed for 15 seconds.
4 Sieve together the flour and baking powder and add to the above. Mix through on slow speed until the batter is half clear.
5 Add the fruit or nut content to above. While this is mixing on slow speed for 5–10 seconds, pour the milk into the batter. Scrape down.
6 Mix on slow speed for approximately 30 seconds until the fruit or nut is thoroughly dispersed. Do not overmix the batter at this stage.

Processing method

1 Scale 5 at the appropriate weight into the small loaf tin lined with a paper case.
2 Moisten the back of the hand with milk and level the top of the batter.
3 Sprinkle the appropriate finishing material over the batter.
4 Bake at 182°C (360°F) for 45–60 minutes.
5 On withdrawal from the oven, allow the loaf cakes to cool in the tin until they can be handled without being damaged.
6 Now place the loaf cakes onto a cooling wire.

Additions to basic cake batter

CURRANT

Yield 5

1 At stage 5 of the mixing method, add 530 g (1 lb 3 oz) currants.
2 At stage 1 of the processing method, scale 5 at 450 g (1 lb).

3 At stage 3 of the processing method, sprinkle flaked almonds or caster sugar over the batter.

SULTANA

Yield 5

1 At stage 5 of the mixing method, add 530 g (1 lb 3 oz) sultanas.
2 At stage 1 of the processing method, scale 5 at 450 g (1 lb).
3 At stage 3 of the processing method, sprinkle flaked almonds or caster sugar over the batter.

CHERRY

Yield 5

1 At stage 5 of the mixing method add 530 g (1 lb 3 oz) halved glacé cherries that have been washed, dried and dusted with medium strength flour.
2 At stage 1 of the processing method, scale 5 at 450 g (1 lb).
3 At stage 3 of the processing method, sprinkle nib sugar over the batter.

COCONUT

Yield 5

1 At stage 5 of the mixing method, add 400 g (14.25 oz) desiccated coconut.
2 At stage 1 of the processing method, scale 5 at 425 g (15.25 oz).
3 At stage 3 of the processing method, sprinkle desiccated coconut over the batter.

DATE AND WALNUT

Yield 5

1 At stage 5 of the mixing method, add 400 g (14.25 oz) chopped dates and 130 g (4.50 oz) broken walnuts.
2 At stage 1 of the processing method, scale 5 at 450 g (1 lb).
3 At stage 3 of the processing method, sprinkle demerara sugar over the batter.

GATEAU BASES

Ingredients

Kilo	Gram	%	Ingredients	lb	oz
	235	71.00	caster sugar		8.50
	90	27.00	cake margarine or butter		3.25
	95	28.00	shortening		3.50
	230	70.00	egg		8.25
	5	1.50	colour		0.25
	5	1.50	flavour		0.25
	330	100.00	cake flour		11.75
	15	4.50	baking powder		0.50
	5	1.50	salt		0.25
	135	41.00	milk		4.75
1	145		Gross weight	2	9.25
1	099		Net weight	2	7.50

Production Points

Batter temperature	**21°C (70°F)**
Shallow tin	**15 cm (6") diameter round**
Scaling weight	**265 g (9.25 oz)**
Yield	**4**
Baking temperature	**190°C (374°F)**
Baking time	**approx 25 mins**

Note: This batter may be coloured and flavoured as required.

Mixing method

1 Place the caster sugar, cake margarine or butter and shortening into a mixing bowl.
2 Using a beater, blend together on slow speed, then beat on top speed for up to 10 minutes until light and aerated.
3 Mix together the egg, colour and flavour then add to the above in five additions. Each addition must be blended through on slow speed, the mixture scraped down, then the egg solution beaten in on top speed for 15 seconds.
4 Sieve together the flour, baking powder and salt and add to above. Mix through on slow speed until the batter is half clear.
5 Add the milk to the above and mix through on slow speed for 5 seconds. Scrape down.
6 Mix on slow speed for approximately 30 seconds until a smooth, clear batter is obtained. Do not overmix the batter at this stage.

Processing method

1 Scale 4 at 250 g (9 oz) of batter into shallow 15 cm (6") diameter round tins and level slightly.
2 Bake at 190°C (374°F) for approximately 25 minutes.
3 On withdrawal from the oven, allow the gateau bases to cool in the tin until they can be handled without being damaged.
4 Now place the gateau bases onto a cooling wire.

Note: For larger gateau bases, increase the recipe and use the following scaling weights:

17.50 cm (7") scale at 350 g (12.5 oz)
20 cm (8") scale at 425 g (15 oz)
22.50 cm (9") scale at 570 g (1 lb 4.25 oz)
25 cm (10") scale at 700 g (1 lb 9 oz)

CHOCOLATE GATEAU BASES

Ingredients

Kilo	Gram	%	Ingredients	lb	oz
	270	71.00	caster sugar		9.75
	105	27.00	cake margarine or butter		3.75
	110	28.00	shortening		4.00
	290	76.00	egg at 21°C (70°F)		10.25
	5	1.30	chocolate compound		0.25
	380	100.00	cake flour		13.50
	15	4.00	baking powder		0.50
	5	1.30	salt		0.25
	35	9.00	cocoa powder		1.25
	170	44.00	milk		6.00
1	385		Gross weight	3	1.50
1	329		Net weight	2	15.50

Production Points

Batter temperature	**21°C (70°F)**
Shallow tin	**15 cm (6") diameter round**
Scaling weight	**260 g (9.25 oz)**
Yield	**5**
Baking temperature	**190°C (374°F)**
Baking time	**approx 25 mins**

Mixing method

1 Place the caster sugar, cake margarine or butter and shortening into a mixing bowl.
2 Using a beater, blend together on slow speed, then beat on top speed for up to 10 minutes until light and aerated.
3 Mix together the egg and chocolate compound, then add to the above in five additions. Each addition must be blended through on slow speed, the mixture scraped down, then the egg solution beaten in on top speed for 15 seconds.
4 Sieve together the flour, baking powder, salt and cocoa powder and add to above. Mix through on slow speed until the batter is half clear.
5 Add the milk to the above and mix through on slow speed for 5 seconds. Scrape down.
6 Mix on slow speed for approximately 30 seconds until a smooth, clear batter is obtained. Do not overmix the batter at this stage.

Processing method

1 Scale 5 at 260 g (9.25 oz) of batter into shallow 15 cm (6") diameter round tins and level slightly.
2 Bake at 190°C (374°F) for approximately 25 minutes.
3 On withdrawal from the oven, allow the chocolate gateau bases to cool in the tin until they can be handled without being damaged.
4 Now place the chocolate gateau bases onto a cooling wire.

Note: For larger chocolate gateau bases, increase the recipe and use the following scaling weights:

17.50 cm (7") scale at 350 g (12.50 oz)
20 cm (8") scale at 425 g (15 oz)
22.50 cm (9") scale at 570 g (1 lb 4.25 oz)
25 cm (10") scale at 700 g (1 lb 9 oz)

DUNDEE CAKE AND SLAB

Ingredients

Kilo	Gram	%	Ingredients	lb	oz
	170	28.30	caster sugar		6.00
	325	54.20	brown sugar		11.50
	325	54.20	butter or cake margarine		11.50
	170	28.30	shortening		6.00
	600	100.00	egg at 21°C (70°F)	1	5.50
	50	8.30	glycerine		1.75
	12	2.00	caramel colour		0.50
	12	2.00	vanilla essence		0.50
	12	2.00	almond essence		0.50
	15	2.50	rum		0.50
	600	100.00	medium flour	1	5.50
	7	1.20	baking powder		0.25
	120	20.00	ground almonds		4.25
1	440	240.00	sultanas	3	3.50
	30	5.00	lemon zest and juice		1.00
	30	5.00	orange zest and juice		1.00
3	918		Gross weight	8	11.75
3	761		Net weight	8	6.00

Mixing method

1. Place the caster sugar, brown sugar, butter or cake margarine and shortening into a mixing bowl.
2. Using a beater, blend together on slow speed, then beat on top speed for up to 10 minutes until light and aerated.
3. Mix together the egg, glycerine, caramel colour, vanilla essence, almond essence and rum, then add to the above in five additions. Each addition must be blended through on slow speed, the mixture scraped down, then the egg solution beaten in on top speed for 15 seconds.
4. Sieve together the flour, baking powder and ground almonds and add to above. Mix through on slow speed until the batter is half clear.
5. Mix together the sultanas, lemon zest and juice and orange zest and juice, add to the above and mix through on slow speed for 5 seconds. Scrape down.
6. Mix on slow speed for approximately 30 seconds until the fruit is thoroughly dispersed. Do not overmix the batter at this stage.

Dundee cake

Production Points

Batter temperature	**21°C (70°F)**
Deep hoop/tin	**15 cm (6") diameter round**
Frame	**25 × 20 × 7.5 cm (10 × 8 × 3")**
Scaling weight:	
cake	**750 g (1 lb 10.75 oz)**
slab	**1850 g (4 lb 4 oz)**
Yield:	
cake	**5**
slab	**2**
Baking temperature:	
cake	**182°C (360°F)**
slab	**177°C (350°F)**
Baking time:	
cake	**approx 1 hour 15 mins**
slab	**approx 2 hours**

Processing methods

CAKES

1. Scale 5 at 750 g (1 lb 10.75 oz) into deep 15 cm (6") diameter round hoops or tins lined with greaseproof paper.
2. Moisten the back of the hand with milk, and press the batter until it fills the tin or hoop and a flat level surface is obtained.
3. Starting at the edge, decorate the cake by placing rings of split almonds on the top.
4. Bake at 182°C (360°F) for approximately 1 hour 15 minutes.

   Note: These cakes require protection during the baking stage as described on p. 263.

5. On withdrawal from the oven, allow the Dundee Cakes to cool in the hoop or tin until they can be handled without being damaged.

SLABS

1. Scale 2 at 1850 g (4 lb 4 oz) into a standard slab frame lined with greaseproof paper.
2. Moisten the back of the hand with milk, and press the batter until it fills the frame and a flat, level surface is obtained.
3. Decorate the slab by placing neat rows of split almonds on the top.
4. Bake at 177°C (350°F) for approximately 2 hours.

   Note: These slabs require protection during the baking stage as described on p. 263.

5. On withdrawal from the oven, allow the Dundee Slabs to cool in the slab frame until they can be handled without being damaged.
6. When cool, remove the slabs from the frame. Mark and cut into five equal portions and wrap.

SIMNEL CAKE

Ingredients

Kilo	Gram	%	Ingredients	lb	oz
	135	41.50	caster sugar		4.75
	135	41.50	brown sugar		4.75
	160	49.20	cake margarine or butter		5.75
	110	33.80	shortening		4.00
	345	106.00	egg at 21°C (70°F)		12.25
	25	7.70	glycerine		1.00
	325	100.00	medium flour		11.50
	5	1.50	baking powder		0.25
	50	15.40	ground almonds		1.75
	5	1.50	mixed spice		0.25
	270	83.00	sultanas		9.50
	270	83.00	currants		9.50
	110	33.80	halved glacé cherries		4.00
	55	16.90	mixed peel		2.00
2	000		Gross weight	4	7.25
1	920		Net weight	4	4.25

Production Points

Batter temperature	**21°C (70°F)**
Deep hoop/tin	**15 cm (6") diameter round**
Scaling weight:	
batter	**480 g (1 lb 1 oz)**
marzipan	**100 g (3.50 oz)**
Yield	**4**
Baking temperature	**182°C (360°F)**
Baking time	**1 hour–1 hour 15 mins**

Mixing method

1. Place the caster sugar, brown sugar, cake margarine or butter and shortening into a mixing bowl.
2. Using a beater, blend together on slow speed, then beat on top speed for up to 10 minutes until light and aerated.
3. Mix together the egg and glycerine, then add to the above in five additions. Each addition must be blended through on slow speed, the mixture scraped down, then the egg solution beaten in on top speed for 15 seconds.
4. Sieve together the flour, baking powder, ground almonds and mixed spice and add to above. Mix through on slow speed until the batter is half clear.
5. Mix together the sultanas, currants, halved glacé cherries and mixed peel, add to the above and mix through on slow speed for 5 seconds. Scrape down.
6. Mix on slow speed for approximately 30 seconds until the fruit is thoroughly dispersed. Do not overmix the batter at this stage.

Processing methods

1. Scale 4 at 240 g (8.50 oz) of batter into deep 15 cm (6") diameter round hoops or tins lined with greaseproof paper. Flatten and level the batter.
2. Scale 4 at 100 g (3.50 oz) marzipan, mould round, pin out and fit over the batter within the hoop or tin.
3. Scale 4 at 240 g (8.50 oz) of batter over the marzipan.
4. Using milk on the back of the hand, press the batter until it fills the hoop or tin and a level, flat surface is obtained.
5. Bake at 182°C (360°F) for 1–1$^1/_4$ hours.

   Note: These cakes require protection during the baking stage as described on p. 263.

6. On withdrawal from the oven, allow the Simnel Cakes to cool in the hoop or tin until they can be handled without being damaged.

Finishing method

1. When cool, brush the top of the cake with boiled apricot puree.
2. Decorate the top edge with shaped or plaited marzipan.

3 To obtain a golden brown colour, subject the marzipan to flash heat by using a very hot oven, a grill, or even a blow torch.
4 Flood the centre of the top of the cake with fondant and allow it to set.
5 Using royal icing, pipe the word 'SIMNEL' onto the fondant.
6 Edible and inedible Easter motifs can be used to enhance the general appearance of this product.

Note: The use of a very high quality marzipan is essential to the successful finishing of this product. The marzipan must be able to maintain its form and shape during the heating and colouring stage of the finishing method.

CHRISTMAS CAKE OR BIRTHDAY CAKE

Ingredients

Kilo	Gram	%	Ingredients	lb	oz
	160	39.00	caster sugar		5.75
	160	39.00	brown sugar		5.75
	230	56.00	cake margarine or butter		8.25
	75	8.30	shortening		3.75
	410	100.00	egg at 21°C (70°F)		14.75
	10	2.40	vanilla essence		0.50
	30	7.30	glycerine		1.00
	410	100.00	medium flour		14.75
	50	12.20	ground almonds		1.75
	15	3.60	mixed spice		0.50
	600	146.40	currants	1	5.25
	600	146.40	sultanas	1	5.25
	260	63.40	halved glacé cherries		9.25
	120	29.30	mixed peel		4.25
3	130		Gross weight	7	0.75
3	004		Net weight	6	11.25

Mixing method

1 Place the caster sugar, brown sugar, cake margarine or butter and shortening into a mixing bowl.
2 Using a beater, blend together on slow speed, then beat on top speed for up to 10 minutes until light and aerated.
3 Mix together the egg, vanilla essence and glycerine, then add to the above in five additions. Each addition must be blended through on slow speed, the mixture scraped down, then the egg solution beaten in on top speed for 15 seconds.
4 Sieve together the flour, ground almonds and mixed spice and add to above. Mix through on slow speed until the batter is half clear.
5 Mix together the currants, sultanas, halved glacé cherries and mixed peel, add to the above and mix through on slow speed for 5 seconds. Scrape down.
6 Mix on slow speed for approximately 30 seconds until the fruit is thoroughly dispersed. Do not overmix the batter at this stage.

Processing method

1 Scale 2 at 1500 g (3 lb 5.50 oz) of batter into the deep hoops, tins or frames lined with greaseproof paper.
2 Moisten the back of the hand with milk, and press the

Production Points

Batter temperature	**21°C (70°F)**
Deep hoop/tin	**20 cm (8") diameter round**
Tin/frame	**17.5 cm (7") square**
Scaling weight	**1500 g (3 lb 5.50 oz)**
Yield	**2**
Baking temperature	**171°C (340°F)**
Baking time	**2½–3 hours**

batter until it fills the hoop, tin or frame and a flat surface is obtained.

3 Bake at 171°C (340°F) for 2½–3 hours.

Note: These cakes require protection during the baking stage as described on p. 263.

4 On withdrawal from the oven, allow the Christmas or Birthday Cake to cool in the hoop, tin or frame until they can be handled without being damaged.

Maturing process

This type of rich fruit cake requires a period of time to mature. It is therefore necessary to make this cake 4–6 weeks in advance. During the maturing process, the moistness and flavour can be enhanced by the addition of a spirit. The spirits suitable are Brandy, Rum and Sherry. To apply the spirit to the cake, use a thin needle to pierce the whole surface area, then pour a small quantity of the spirit over the cake so it is absorbed through the fine holes. Finally, it is important to keep rich fruit cakes wrapped in greaseproof paper and stored in cool, airtight conditions.

WEDDING CAKE

Ingredients

Kilo	Gram	%	Ingredients	lb	oz
	735	100.00	Barbados sugar	1	10.25
	735	100.00	butter	1	10.25
	55	7.50	shortening		2.00
	945	129.00	egg at 21°C (70°F)	2	1.75
	10	1.40	vanilla essence		0.50
	10	1.40	almond essence		0.50
	735	100.00	medium flour	1	10.25
	235	32.00	ground almonds		8.50
	10	1.40	mixed spice		0.50
	5	0.70	nutmeg		0.25
	5	0.70	ground ginger		0.25
	5	0.70	cinnamon		0.25
2	360	321.00	currants	5	4.00
1	050	143.00	sultanas	2	5.50
	525	71.40	halved glacé cherries	1	2.75
	630	85.70	mixed peel	1	6.50
	60	8.10	lemon zest and juice		2.00
	60	8.10	orange zest and juice		2.00
	60	8.10	rum		2.00
8	230		Gross weight	18	6.00
7	900		Net weight	17	10.00

Mixing method

1 Place the Barbados sugar, butter and shortening into a mixing bowl.
2 Using a beater, blend together on slow speed, then beat on top speed for up to 10 minutes until light and aerated.
3 Mix together the egg, vanilla essence and almond essence, then add to the above in five additions. Each addition must be blended through on slow speed, the mixture scraped down, then the egg solution beaten in on top speed for 15 seconds.
4 Sieve together the flour, ground almonds, mixed spice, nutmeg and cinnamon and add to above. Mix through on slow speed until the batter is half clear.
5 Mix together the currants, sultanas, halved glacé cherries, mixed peel, zest and juice of the lemon and orange and rum, add to the above and mix through on slow speed for 5 seconds. Scrape down.
6 Mix on slow speed for approximately 30 seconds until the fruit is thoroughly dispersed. Do not overmix the batter at this stage.

Processing method

1 For a round or square Wedding Cake, scale the batter as follows into a hoop, tin or frame lined with greaseproof paper.

   - Top – 1450 g (3 lb 3.50 oz)
   - Middle – 2700 g (6 lb)
   - Bottom – 3750 g (8 lb 5.50 oz)

2 Moisten the back of the hand with milk, and press the batter until it fills the hoop, tin or frame and a level, flat surface is obtained.
3 Bake each tier at 165–171°C (330–340°F) for the appropriate time:

   - Top – 2–2½ hours
   - Middle – 3–3½ hours
   - Bottom – 4–4½ hours

   Note: These cakes require protection during the baking stage as described on p. 263.

Production Points

Batter temperature	**21°C (70°F)**	
Hoop or tin/frame:		
Tier	**Round**	**Square**
Top	**17.5 cm (7")**	**15 cm (6")**
Middle	**22.5 cm (9")**	**20 cm (8")**
Bottom	**27.5 cm (11")**	**25 cm (10")**
Scaling weight:		
Top	**1450 g (3 lb 3.50 oz)**	
Middle	**2700 g (6 lb)**	
Bottom	**3750 g (8 lb 5.50 oz)**	
Yield	**1 three tier wedding cake**	
Baking temperature	**165–171°C (330–340°F)**	
Baking time:		
Top	**2–2½ hours**	
Middle	**3–3½ hours**	
Bottom	**4–4½ hours**	

Note: To improve the moistness and flavour of the wedding cake, mix together the currants, sultanas, halved glacé cherries, mixed peel, zest and juice of the lemon and orange and the rum. Cover and allow to stand for 24 hours prior to beginning the mixing process. This will enable the fruit to absorb the moisture and flavour of the juices and rum.

4 On withdrawal from the oven, allow the Wedding Cakes to cool in the hoop, tin or frame until they can be handled without being damaged.

(See overleaf for recipes using the blending process.)

RECIPES USING THE BLENDING PROCESS

GENOESE

Ingredients

Kilo	Gram	%	Ingredients	lb	oz
1	000	100.00	high ratio cake flour	2	4.00
	25	2.50	baking powder		1.00
	25	2.50	salt		1.00
1	300	130.00	caster sugar	2	14.25
	750	75.00	high ratio shortening	1	10.75
	450	45.00	milk at 18°C (64°F)	1	0.00
	750	75.00	egg at 18°C (64°F)	1	10.75
	50	5.00	milk at 18°C (64°F)		1.75
	10	1.00	colour		0.50
	10	1.00	flavour		0.50
4	370		Gross weight	9	12.50
4	195		Net weight	9	6.50

Production Points

Batter temperature	**18°C (64°F)**
Tray	**4-sided large tray**
Scaling weight	**4200 g (9 lb 6 oz)**
Yield	**1 large baking tray 75 × 45 cm (30 × 18")**
Baking temperature	**190°C (374°F)**
Baking time	**30 mins**

To produce Chocolate Genoese, simply:

- add 200 g (7 oz) cocoa powder with the dry ingredients
- increase the first amount of milk to 500 g (1 lb 1.75 oz)
- add 20 g (0.75 oz) of chocolate compound.

Mixing method

1 Sieve together the flour, baking powder, salt and caster sugar and place into a mixing bowl.
2 Add the high ratio shortening to the dry ingredients and using a beater mix on slow speed until a crumble consistency is obtained.
3 Add the first amount of milk in a steady stream on slow speed until a paste is formed. Scrape down. Mix on slow speed for 1 minute.
4 Mix together the egg, the second amount of milk, colour and flavour. Add half of the solution in a slow stream on a slow speed to ensure a smooth batter is obtained. Scrape down.
5 Add the remainder of the solution in a slow stream on slow speed. Scrape down.
6 Mix on slow speed for 3 minutes to form a smooth, clear batter.

Processing method

1 Scale 1 at 4200 g (9 lb 6 oz) of batter onto a large four-sided baking tray lined with greaseproof paper.
2 Spread the batter over the tray until even and level.
3 Bake at 190°C (374°F) for 30 minutes.
4 On withdrawal from the oven, allow the Genoese to cool in the tray until it can be handled without being damaged.

HIGH RATIO GATEAU BASES

Ingredients

Kilo	Gram	%	Ingredients	lb	oz
	350	100.00	high ratio cake flour		12.50
	15	4.30	baking powder		0.50
	35	10.00	rice flour		1.25
	25	7.10	milk powder		1.00
	265	75.70	high ratio shortening		9.50
	425	121.00	caster sugar		15.25
	10	2.80	salt		0.25
	145	41.40	milk at 18°C (64°F)		5.25
	7.5	2.10	colour		0.25
	7.5	2.10	flavour		0.25
	320	91.40	egg at 18°C (64°F)		11.50
	110	31.40	milk at 18°C (64°F)		4.00
1	715		Gross weight	3	13.50
1	646		Net weight	3	11.00

Production Points

Batter temperature	**18°C (64°F)**
Shallow tin	**15 cm (6") diameter round**
Scaling weight	**260 g (9.25 oz)**
Yield	**6**
Baking temperature	**190°C (374°F)**
Baking time	**25 mins**

Note: The batter may be coloured and flavoured as required.

Mixing method

1. Sieve together the flour, baking powder, rice flour and milk powder and place into a mixing bowl.
2. Add the high ratio shortening to the dry ingredients and using a beater mix on slow speed until a crumble consistency is obtained.
3. Mix together the caster sugar, salt, the first amount of milk, colour and flavour. Add to above in a steady stream on slow speed until a paste is formed. Scrape down. Mix on slow speed for 1 minute.
4. Mix together the egg and the second amount of milk. Add half of the solution in a slow stream on a slow speed to ensure a smooth batter is obtained. Scrape down.
5. Add the remainder of the solution in a slow stream on slow speed. Scrape down.
6. Mix on slow speed for 3 minutes to form a smooth, clear batter.

Processing method

1. Scale 6 at 270 g (9.5 oz) of batter into shallow 15 cm (6") diameter round tins and level slightly.
2. Bake at 190°C (374°F) for 25 minutes.
3. On withdrawal from the oven, allow the gateau bases to cool in the tin until they can be handled without being damaged.
4. Now place the gateau bases onto a cooling wire.

Note: For large gateau bases, increase the recipe and use the following scaling weights:

17.5 cm (7") scale at 340 g (12 oz)
20 cm (8") scale at 400 g (14.25 oz)
22.5 cm (9") scale at 530 g (1 lb 2.75 oz)
25 cm (10") scale at 650 g (1 lb 7 oz)

FARMHOUSE CAKE

Ingredients

Kilo	Gram	%	Ingredients	lb	oz
	500	100.00	bread flour	1	1.75
	10	2.00	baking powder		0.50
	5	1.00	salt		0.25
	20	4.00	milk powder		0.75
	170	34.00	granulated sugar		6.00
	160	32.00	brown sugar		5.75
	3	0.60	mixed spice		0.12
	360	72.00	shortening		13.00
	170	34.00	egg at 21°C (70°F)		6.00
	10	2.00	glycerine		0.50
	180	36.00	water		6.50
	250	50.00	currants		9.00
	200	40.00	sultanas		7.00
	50	10.00	halved glacé cherries		2.00
2	088		Gross weight	4	11.25
2	005		Net weight	4	8.25

Production Points

Batter temperature	**21°C (70°F)**
Deep tin/hoop	**15 cm (6") diameter round**
Scaling weight	**500 g (1 lb 1.75 oz)**
Yield	**4**
Baking temperature	**180°C (356°F)**
Baking time	**1 hour–1 hour 15 mins**

Mixing method

1 Sieve together the flour, baking powder, salt, milk powder, granulated sugar, brown sugar and mixed spice and place into a mixing bowl.
2 Add the shortening to the dry ingredients. Use a beater to mix on slow speed until a crumble consistency is obtained.
3 Mix together the egg and glycerine. Add to the above in a slow, steady stream on slow speed until a paste is formed. Scrape down. Mix on medium speed for 1 minute.
4 Add the water slowly on slow speed. Scrape down, and mix on medium speed for 30 seconds.
5 Add the currants, sultanas and halved glacé cherries, and mix through on slow speed until thoroughly dispersed. Do not overmix the batter at this stage.

Processing method

1 Scale 4 at 500 g (1 lb 1.75 oz) of batter into deep 15 cm (6") diameter round tins or hoops, lined with a paper case.
2 Moisten the back of the hand with milk, and level the top of the batter.
3 Dredge the surface of the batter with demerara sugar.
4 Bake at 180°C (356°F) for 1 hour–1 hour 15 minutes.

Note: These cakes require protection during the baking stage as described on p. 263.

5 On withdrawal from the oven, allow the farmhouse cakes to cool in the tin or hoop until they can be handled without being damaged.

Farmhouse cake

MIXED FRUIT CAKE

Ingredients

Kilo	Gram	%	Ingredients	lb	oz
	330	100.00	cake flour		11.75
	10	3.00	baking powder		0.50
	5	1.50	salt		0.25
	25	7.60	milk powder		1.00
	330	100.00	caster sugar		11.75
	330	100.00	sieved cake crumbs		11.75
	190	57.50	shortening		6.75
	235	71.20	egg at 21°C (70°F)		8.50
	235	71.20	water		8.50
	25	7.60	glycerine		1.00
	5	1.50	egg colour		0.25
	210	63.60	currants		7.50
	130	39.40	sultanas		4.50
	40	12.10	mixed peel		1.50
2	100		Gross weight	4	11.50
2	016		Net weight	4	8.50

Mixing method

1 Sieve together the flour, baking powder, salt, milk powder, caster sugar and cake crumbs and place into a mixing bowl.
2 Add the shortening to the dry ingredients and using a beater mix on slow speed until a crumble consistency is obtained.
3 Mix together the egg, water, glycerine and egg colour. Add to the above in a steady stream on slow speed until a paste is formed. Scrape down.
4 Mix on medium speed for 2–3 minutes until a smooth batter is obtained.
5 Add the currants, sultanas and mixed peel and mix through on slow speed until thoroughly dispersed. Do not overmix the batter at this stage.

Processing method

1 Scale 4 at 500 g (1 lb 1.75 oz) of batter into deep 15 cm (6") diameter round tins or hoops, lined with a paper case.
2 Moisten the back of the hand with milk, and level the top of the batter.
3 Dredge the surface of the batter with caster sugar.

Production Points

Batter temperature	**21°C (70°F)**
Deep tin/hoop	**15 cm (6") diameter round**
Scaling weight	**500 g (1 lb 1.75 oz)**
Yield	**4**
Baking temperature	**180°C (356°F)**
Baking time	**1 hour–1 hour 15 mins**

4 Bake at 180°C (356°F) for 1–1 hour 15 minutes.

Note: These cakes require protection during the baking stage as described on p. 263.

5 On withdrawal from the oven, allow the cakes to cool in the tins or hoops until they can be handled without being damaged.

GINGER CAKE AND SQUARES

Ingredients

Kilo	Gram	%	Ingredients	lb	oz
	585	100.00	medium flour	1	5.00
	235	40.00	sieved cake crumbs		8.50
	12.5	3.00	ground ginger		0.50
	5	1.00	mixed spice		0.25
	235	40.00	water		8.50
	235	40.00	vegetable oil		8.50
	235	40.00	golden syrup		8.50
	115	20.00	treacle		4.00
	295	50.00	brown sugar		10.50
	60	10.00	cold water		2.00
	115	20.00	egg		4.00
	6	1.00	bicarbonate of soda		0.25
2	138		Gross weight	4	12.00
2	052		Net weight	4	9.00

Mixing method

1 Sieve together the flour, cake crumbs, ground ginger and mixed spice and place into a mixing bowl.
2 Mix together the water, vegetable oil, golden syrup, treacle and brown sugar, until a smooth solution is obtained.
3 Using a beater, add the solution to the dry ingredients in a slow steady stream on slow speed. Scrape down.
4 Mix on medium speed for 5 minutes until a smooth batter is obtained.
5 Mix together the cold water, egg and bicarbonate of soda, add to the above and mix on slow speed. Scrape down.
6 Mix on slow speed for 1 minute until a smooth, clear batter is obtained.

Production Points

Batter temperature	**18°C (64°F)**
Tin	**Small loaf tin**
Tray	**4-sided small baking tray, 45 × 37.5 cm (18 × 15")**
Scaling weight:	
cake	**340 g (12 oz)**
squares	**2 kg (4 lb 7.5 oz)**
Yield:	
cake	**6**
squares	**30**
Baking temperature	**180°C (356°F)**
Baking time:	
cake	**45–60 mins**
squares	**25–30 mins**

Processing methods

CAKES

1. Scale 5 at 340 g (12 oz) of batter into small loaf tins, lined with paper cases.
2. Sprinkle flaked almonds over the surface of the batter.
3. Bake at 180°C (356°F) for 45–60 minutes.
4. On withdrawal from the oven, allow the cakes to cool in the tin until they can be handled without being damaged.

SQUARES

1. Scale 2 kg (4 lb 7.5 oz) of batter into a small four sided baking tray, lined with greaseproof paper.
2. Spread the batter over the tray until even and level.
3. Bake at 180°C (356°F) for 25–30 minutes.
4. On withdrawal from the oven, allow the cakes to cool in the tray until they can be handled without being damaged.
5. When cool, remove the cake from the baking tray.
6. Spread prepared water icing, evenly over the top of the cake and allow to set.
7. Using pastry wheels, 6 × 5, mark the surface of the cake.
8. Using a sharp, clean knife, cut into squares.

GENOA SLAB

Ingredients

Kilo	Gram	%	Ingredients	lb	oz
	600	100.00	high protein cake flour	1	5.50
	10	1.66	baking powder		0.50
	540	90.00	caster sugar	1	3.75
	225	37.50	cake margarine		8.00
	225	37.50	shortening		8.00
	115	19.20	milk at 21°C (70°F)		4.00
	20	3.30	glycerine		0.75
	5	0.80	egg colour		0.25
	5	0.80	vanilla essence		0.25
	540	90.00	egg at 21°C (70°F)	1	3.25
	290	48.30	currants		10.50
	240	40.00	sultanas		8.50
	225	37.50	halved glacé cherries		8.00
3	040		Gross weight	6	12.75
2	918		Net weight	6	8.25

Production Points

Batter temperature	**21°C (70°F)**
Frame	**25 × 20 × 7.5 cm (10 × 8 × 3")**
Scaling weight	**1450 g (3 lb 3.5 oz)**
Yield	**2**
Baking temperature	**175°C (346°F)**
Baking time	**1 hour 15–30 mins**

Mixing method

1. Sieve together the flour, baking powder and caster sugar and place into a mixing bowl.
2. Add the cake margarine and shortening to the dry ingredients and, using a beater, mix on slow speed until a crumble consistency is obtained.
3. Mix together the milk, glycerine, egg colour and vanilla essence. Add to the above in a slow, steady stream on slow speed until a paste is formed. Scrape down.
4. Add half of the egg in a slow, steady stream on slow speed to ensure that a smooth batter is obtained. Scrape down.
5. Add the remainder of the egg in a slow, steady stream on slow speed. Scrape down.
6. Mix on slow speed for 3 minutes to form a smooth, clear batter.
7. Add the currants, sultanas and halved glacé cherries and mix through on slow speed until thoroughly dispersed. Do not overmix the batter at this stage.

Processing method

1. Scale 2 at 1450 g (3 lb 3.5 oz) of batter into a standard slab frame, lined with greaseproof paper.
2. Moisten the back of the hand with milk, and press the batter until it fills the frame and a flat, level surface is obtained.
3. Sprinkle strip almonds over the surface of the batter.
4. Bake at 175°C (346°F) for 1 hour 15–30 minutes.

   Note: These slabs require protection during the baking stage as described on p. 263.

5. On withdrawal from the oven, allow the Genoa Slabs to cool in the slab frame until they can be handled without being damaged.
6. When cool, remove the slabs from the frame, mark and cut into five equal portions and wrap.

VARIETIES OF ANGEL CAKE

To produce Chocolate Angel Cake, simply:

- add 140 g (5 oz) cocoa powder with the dry ingredients
- increase the egg whites to 600 g (1 lb 5.5 oz)
- increase the milk to 205 g (7.5 oz).

Other varieties: add the appropriate colour and flavour.

Ingredients

Kilo	Gram	%	Ingredients	lb	oz
	570	100.00	high ratio cake flour	1	4.25
	17	2.98	baking powder		0.50
	5	0.90	cream powder		0.25
	10	1.75	salt		0.50
	680	119.00	caster sugar	1	8.25
	45	7.90	milk powder		1.50
	430	75.40	high ratio shortening		15.50
	570	100.00	egg white at 18°C (64°F)	1	4.25
	190	33.30	milk at 18°C (64°F)		6.75
	15	2.63	colour		0.50
	15	2.63	flavour		0.50
2	547		Gross weight	5	10.75
2	445		Net weight	5	7.25

Production Points

Batter temperature	**18°C (64°F)**
Frame	**25 × 20 × 7.5 cm (10 × 8 × 3")**
Scaling weight	**1200 g (2 lb 11 oz)**
Yield	**2**
Baking temperature	**170°C (338°F)**
Baking time	**1 hour 15–30 mins**

Mixing method

1. Sieve together the flour, baking powder, cream powder, salt, caster sugar and milk powder and place into a mixing bowl.
2. Add the high ratio shortening to the dry ingredients and using a beater mix on slow speed until a paste is formed.
3. Mix together the egg white, milk, colour and flavour. Add one third of the solution in a slow, steady stream on slow speed. Scrape down. Mix on medium speed for 1 minute.
4. Add remaining solution in a slow, steady stream on slow speed over 2 minutes. Scrape down.
5. Mix on medium speed for 2 minutes to form a smooth, clear batter. Do not overmix the batter at this stage.

Processing method

1. Scale 2 at 1200 g (2 lb 11 oz) of batter into a standard slab frame, lined with greaseproof paper.
2. Moisten the back of the hand with milk, and press the batter until it fills the frame and a flat, level surface is obtained.
3. Bake at 170°C (338°F) for 1 hour 15–30 minutes.

   Note: These slabs require protection during the baking stage as described on p. 263.

4. On withdrawal from the oven, allow the slabs to cool in the slab frame until they can be handled without being damaged.
5. When cool, remove the slabs from the frame, and cut twice, horizontally into three pieces.
6. Assemble the Angel Cake slabs into colour combinations using jam, curd and buttercream.
7. Mark and cut into five equal portions and wrap.

CARROT CAKE SQUARES

Ingredients

Kilo	Gram	%	Ingredients	lb	oz
	405	100.00	high ratio cake flour		14.50
	20	4.94	baking powder		0.75
	5	1.20	salt		0.25
	10	2.50	cinnamon		0.50
	600	148.00	caster sugar	1	5.25
	360	89.00	egg at 18°C (64°F)		12.75
	405	100.00	vegetable oil		14.50
	675	167.00	grated carrot	1	8.00
	135	33.30	chopped walnuts		5.00
2	615		Gross weight	5	13.50
2	510		Net weight	5	9.75

Production Points

Batter temperature	**18°C (64°F)**
Tray	**4-sided small baking tray 45 × 37.5 cm (18 × 15")**
Scaling weight	**2500 g (5 lb 9.25 oz)**
Yield	**30 squares**
Baking temperature	**190°C (374°F)**
Baking time	**25 mins**

(See colour plate 24.)

Mixing method

1. Sieve together the flour, baking powder, salt, and cinnamon and place into a mixing bowl.
2. Mix together the caster sugar, egg and vegetable oil. Using a beater add the solution to the dry ingredients in a slow, steady stream on slow speed. Scrape down.
3. Mix on slow speed for 5 minutes until a smooth batter is obtained.
4. Add the grated carrot and chopped walnuts and mix through on slow speed until thoroughly dispersed.

Processing method

1. Scale 2500 g (5 lb 9.25 oz) of batter onto a small four-sided baking tray, lined with greaseproof paper.
2. Spread the batter over the tray until even and level.
3. Bake at 190°C (374°F) for 25 minutes.
4. On withdrawal from the oven, allow the carrot cake to cool in the tray until it can be handled without being damaged.
5. When cool, remove the carrot cakes from the baking tray.
6. Spread plain or yoghurt flavoured buttercream over the surface of the cake and comb scrape.
7. Using pastry wheels, 6 × 5, mark the surface of the cake.
8. Using a clean, sharp knife cut into squares.

Note: The top of each square can be decorated with a small marzipan carrot or a prepared carrot motif.

American muffins

AMERICAN MUFFINS

Ingredients

Kilo	Gram	%	Ingredients	lb	oz
	700	100.00	medium flour	1	9.00
	30	4.30	baking powder		1.00
	10	1.40	salt		0.25
	250	37.50	caster sugar		9.00
	320	45.70	egg at 21°C (70°F)		11.50
	300	42.80	milk at 21°C (70°F)		10.75
	120	17.10	corn oil		4.25
	10	1.40	vanilla essence		0.50
1	740		Gross weight	3	14.25
1	670		Net weight	3	11.75

Production Points

Batter temperature	**21°C (70°F)**
Tin	**Small deep tin**
Scaling weight	**80 g (3 oz)**
Yield:	
plain	**20**
with additions	**24**
Baking temperature	**190°C (374°F)**
Baking time	**25 mins**

Mixing method

1. Sieve together the flour, baking powder, salt and caster sugar and place into a mixing bowl.
2. Mix together the egg, milk, corn oil and vanilla essence. Using a beater add the solution to the dry ingredients in a slow, steady stream on slow speed. Scrape down.
3. Mix on slow speed for 3 minutes until a smooth, clear batter is obtained. For Plain American Muffins, the batter is now ready for processing.
4. Add the fruit, nut or chocolate content to the batter and mix through on slow speed until thoroughly dispersed. Do not overmix the batter at this stage.

Processing method

1. Using a savoy bag and plain tube, pipe 20 or 24 at 80 g (3 oz) of batter into a paper case, supported by a small deep tin.
2. Bake at 190°C (374°F) for 25 minutes.
3. On withdrawal from the oven, place the muffins onto a cooling wire.

Note: To make additions to the basic muffin batter, add any one of the following ingredients at stage 4 of the mixing method:

- 300 g (10.75 oz) Raisins
- 300 g (10.75 oz) Chopped Apple
- 300 g (10.75 oz) Bilberries
- 150 g (5.5 oz) Raisins and 150 g (5.5 oz) Chopped Pecans
- 300 g (10.75 oz) Chocolate Chips.

RECIPES USING THE TRADITIONAL PROCESS

PLAIN SPONGE CAKES

Ingredients

Kilo	Gram	%	Ingredients	lb	oz
	375	125.00	egg at 21°C (70°F)		13.50
	300	100.00	caster sugar		10.75
	300	100.00	cake flour		10.75
	975		Gross weight	2	3.00
	935		Net weight	2	1.50

Production Points

Sponge temperature	**21°C (70°F)**
Shallow tin	**15 cm (6") diameter round**
Scaling weight	**200 g (7 oz)**
Yield	**4**
Baking temperature	**204°C (400°F)**
Baking time	**20–25 mins**

Mixing method

1 Prior to weighing and mixing, wash and rinse all equipment and allow to drain.
2 Place the egg and caster sugar into a mixing bowl and using a whisk, whisk on slow speed to blend them together.
3 Whisk on top speed for 10–20 minutes until a full sponge is obtained.
4 Sieve the flour, add to above and fold through carefully by hand or on slow speed until the sponge is clear and remains aerated.

Note:

- at this stage, do not overmix the flour through the sponge
- this sponge must be processed and baked immediately.

Processing method

1 Scale 4 at 200 g (7 oz) of sponge into shallow 15 cm (6") diameter round tins that have been greased and floured.
2 Bake at 204°C (400°F) for 20–25 minutes.
3 On withdrawal from the oven, allow the sponge cakes to cool in the tin for a few minutes, until they can be removed from the tin without being damaged.
4 Now place the sponge cakes onto a cooling wire.
5 When cool, split the sponge horizontally into two and sandwich together using jam and fresh cream.
6 Dredge the top of the sponge with icing sugar.

Note:

- this is a perishable product and must be stored or displayed under refrigerated conditions
- for larger sponge cake bases, increase the recipe and use the following scaling weights:
  17.50 cm (7") scale at 245 g (8.5 oz)
  20 cm (8") scale at 390 g (14 oz)
  22.50 cm (9") scale at 520 g (1 lb 2.5 oz)
  25 cm (10") scale at 600 g (1 lb 5.25 oz)

SPONGE CURLS

Ingredients

Kilo	Gram	%	Ingredients	lb	oz
	405	202.00	egg at 21°C (70°F)		14.50
	70	35.00	egg yolk		2.50
	245	122.00	caster sugar		8.75
	40	20.00	glycerine		1.25
	200	100.00	high ratio cake flour		7.25
	960		Gross weight	2	2.50
	921		Net weight	2	1.00

Production Points

Sponge temperature	**21°C (70°F)**
Tray	**2 large baking trays**
Scaling weight	**35 g (1.25 oz)**
Yield	**24**
Baking temperature	**240°C (464°F)**
Baking time	**approx 7 mins**

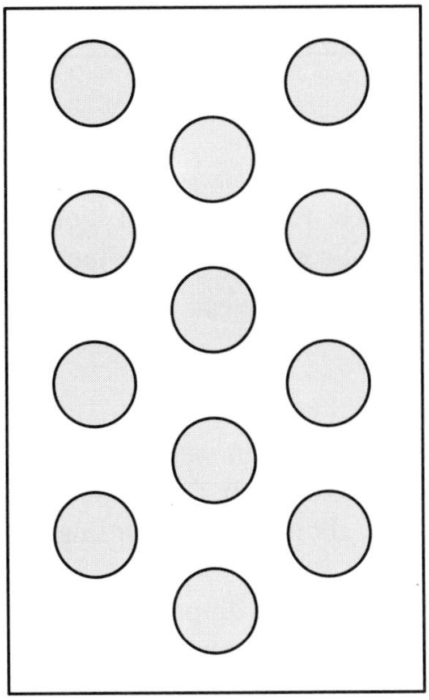

Figure 17

(See colour plate 17.)

Mixing method

1 Prior to weighing and mixing, wash and rinse all equipment and allow to drain.
2 Place the egg, egg yolk and caster sugar into a mixing bowl and using a whisk, whisk on slow speed to blend them together.
3 Whisk on top speed for 10–20 minutes until a full sponge is obtained.
4 When a full sponge has been obtained, add the glycerine and whisk through on top speed until thoroughly dispersed.
5 Sieve the flour, add to above and fold through carefully by hand or on slow speed until the sponge is clear and remains aerated.

Note:

- at this stage, do not overmix the flour through the sponge
- this sponge must be processed and baked immediately.

Processing method

1 Using a savoy bag and plain tube, pipe 24 at approximately 35 g (1.25 oz) of sponge onto a baking tray lined with silicone paper.

Note: To ensure the curls do not flow into each other, they must be piped onto the tray in a 3 × 4 formation. The middle curl in each row of three should be positioned slightly off centre – see Figure 17.

2 Bake at 240°C (464°F) for approximately 7 minutes.

Note: It is essential not to overbake the sponge curls to ensure that they can be folded successfully.

3 On withdrawal from the oven, dredge the curls with caster sugar and allow to cool.
4 When cool, fold the curl and place into a finger shaped packaging container.
5 Pipe a line of jam or curd along the base of the curl.

Note: A variety of fresh fruit or fruit fillings can be used to replace the jam or curd.

6 Fill the curl with a piped rope of fresh cream.
7 Decorate the curl with grated chocolate, roasted, flaked or nibbed nut or fruit.

Note: This is a perishable product and must be stored or displayed under refrigerated conditions.

SPONGE DROPS AND FINGERS

(See colour plate 17.)

Ingredients

Kilo	Gram	%	Ingredients	lb	oz
	480	107.00	egg at 21°C (70°F)	1	1.00
	75	16.60	egg yolk		2.50
	450	100.00	caster sugar	1	0.00
	450	100.00	cake flour	1	0.00
1	455		Gross weight	3	3.50
1	396		Net weight	3	1.50

Production Points

Sponge temperature	**21°C (70°F)**
Tray	**2 large baking trays**
Scaling weight	**approx 15 g (0.5 oz)**
Yield	**approx 90 drops or fingers**
Baking temperature	**240°C (464°F)**
Baking time	**approx 7 mins**

Mixing method

1 Prior to weighing and mixing, wash and rinse all equipment and allow to drain.
2 Place the egg, egg yolk and caster sugar into a mixing bowl and using a whisk, whisk on slow speed to blend them together.
3 Whisk on top speed for 10–20 minutes until a full sponge is obtained.
4 Sieve the flour, add to the above and fold through carefully by hand or on slow speed until the sponge is clear and remains aerated.

Note:

- at this stage, do not overmix the flour through the sponge
- this sponge must be processed and baked immediately.

Processing method

1 Using a savoy bag and plain tube, pipe approximately 90 drops or fingers at approximately 15 g (0.5 oz) of sponge onto a baking tray lined with silicone paper. Pipe into the following formations:

- drops: 5 × 9
- fingers: 4 × 11.

2 Prior to baking, dredge the drops or fingers with caster sugar.
3 Bake at 240°C (464°F) for approximately 7 minutes.
4 On withdrawal from the oven, allow the drops or fingers to cool.
5 When cool, the drops or fingers can be dipped or spun with chocolate flavoured coating and sandwiched together in pairs using jam or curd and fresh cream as follows:

- drops – large rosette
- fingers – rope.

6 Decorate the drops and fingers with fruit.

Note: These are perishable products and must be stored or displayed under refrigerated conditions.

Plain Sponge/Chocolate Sponge

RECIPE USING THE EMULSIFIED SPONGE PROCESS

PLAIN AND CHOCOLATE SPONGE CAKES

Ingredients

Kilo	Gram	%	Ingredients	lb	oz
	300	100.00	egg at 21°C (70°F)		10.75
	75	25.00	water at 21°C (70°F)		2.75
	45	15.00	emulsifier		1.50
	300	100.00	cake flour		10.75
	300	100.00	caster sugar		10.75
	pinch	0.25	salt		pinch
	18	6.00	baking powder		0.50
	15	5.00	milk powder		0.50
	90	30.00	water		3.25
1	143		Gross weight	2	8.75
1	097		Net weight	2	7.00

Production Points

Sponge temperature	**21°C (70°F)**
Shallow tin	**15 cm (6") diameter round**
Scaling weight	**180 g (6.5 oz)**
Yield	**6**
Baking temperature	**204°C (400°F)**
Baking time	**20–25 mins**

To produce chocolate emulsified sponge cakes, simply:

1 Add 60 g (2 oz) cocoa powder with the dry ingredients.
2 Increase the tempered water to 85 g (3 oz).
3 Add 5 g (0.25 oz) of chocolate compound.

Mixing method

1 Place the egg, tempered water and emulsifier into a mixing bowl and using a whisk, whisk together on slow speed for 30 seconds.
2 Sieve together the flour, caster sugar, salt, baking powder and milk powder, add to the above and blend through on slow speed until the dry ingredients are hydrated. Scrape down.
3 Whisk on top speed for 3 minutes to form a full sponge. Do not overmix the sponge at this stage.
4 Add the remaining water and blend through on slow speed for 10 seconds. Scrape down. Whisk on slow speed for 20 seconds to form a smooth, clear sponge.

Processing method

1 Scale 6 at 180 g (6.5 oz) of sponge into shallow 15 cm (6") diameter round tins which have been greased and floured.
2 Follow stages 2, 3, 4, 5 and 6 for Traditional Sponge Cake (p. 290.).

Note:

- this is a perishable product and must be stored or displayed under refrigerated conditions
- for larger sponge cake bases increase the recipe and use the following scaling weights:
  17.50 cm (7") scale at 210 g (7.50 oz)
  20 cm (8") scale at 350 g (12.5 oz)
  22.50 cm (9") scale at 430 g (15.5 oz)
  25 cm (10") scale at 500 g (1 lb 2 oz)

RECIPES USING THE DELAYED SODA PROCESS

PLAIN AND CHOCOLATE SWISS ROLL

Ingredients

Kilo	Gram	%	Ingredients	lb	oz
	320	107.00	egg at 21°C (70°F)		11.50
	60	20.00	water at 21°C (70°F)		2.00
	2.5	0.83	egg colour		0.12
	2.5	0.83	vanilla essence		0.12
	300	100.00	cake flour		10.75
	300	100.00	caster sugar		10.75
	15	5.00	cream powder		0.50
	10	3.30	milk powder		0.50
	7	2.30	bicarbonate of soda		0.25
	25	8.30	cold water		1.00
1	042		Gross weight	2	6.50
1	000		Net weight	2	3.50

Production Points

Sponge temperature	**21°C (70°F)**
Tray	**4-sided large tray**
Scaling weight	**1 kg (2 lb 3.5 oz)**
Yield	**1 sheet = 5 rolls**
Baking temperature	**240°C (464°F)**
Baking time	**approx 8 mins**

(See colour plate 23.)

Chocolate Swiss Rolls: To produce Chocolate Swiss Rolls, simply:

1 Add 60 g (2 oz) cocoa powder with the dry ingredients.
2 Increase the tempered water to 75 g (2.5 oz).
3 Replace the egg colour with 5 g (0.25 oz) of chocolate compound.

Mixing method

1 Place the egg, tempered water, egg colour and vanilla essence into a mixing bowl.
2 Sieve together the flour, caster sugar, cream powder and milk powder, add to the above using a whisk. Blend through on slow speed until the dry ingredients are hydrated. Scrape down.
3 Whisk on top speed for 20 minutes until an aerated sponge is obtained.
4 Mix together the bicarbonate of soda and cold water, add to the above and whisk on slow speed for 10 seconds. Scrape down. Whisk on medium speed for 20 seconds to form a smooth, clear sponge.

Note: The bicarbonate of soda and cold water must not be mixed together until required at stage 4 of the mixing process.

Processing method

1 Scale 1 kg (2 lb 3.5 oz) of sponge onto a large four sided baking tray which has been greased and floured.
2 Spread the sponge over the tray until even and level.
3 Bake at 240°C (464°F) for approximately 8 minutes.

Note: It is essential not to overbake the Swiss Roll, to ensure that it can be rolled up successfully without cracking.

4 On withdrawal from the oven, tip the Swiss Roll onto greaseproof paper dredged with caster sugar. While it is warm, roll it up with the greaseproof paper inside, and allow to cool.

5 When cool, unroll the Swiss Roll and spread a thin layer of appropriate filling evenly over the surface of the sponge. Suitable fillings are:
   - plain – jam, curds and cream
   - chocolate – creams.

   Roll up the Swiss Roll.
6 Mark and cut the roll into five equal portions and wrap.

MATERIALS REQUIRED FOR CAKE FINISHES

BAR GATEAUX

Bases and materials required for six bar gateaux

LEMON:

- 45 × 22.5 cm (18 × 9") piece of Lemon Genoese (see p. 280)
- 160 g (5.75 oz) lemon curd
- 1100 g (2 lb 7 oz) lemon buttercream
- 450 g (1 lb) toasted coconut
- 30 crystallised lemon slices.

RASPBERRY:

- 45 × 22.5 cm (18 × 9") piece of Raspberry Genoese
- 160 g (5.75 oz) raspberry jam
- 700 g (1 lb 9 oz) raspberry buttercream
- 500 g (1 lb 1.75 oz) roasted flaked almonds
- 220 g (8 oz) chocolate buttercream
- 440 g (15.75 oz) vanilla buttercream.

CHOCOLATE:

- 45 × 22.5 cm (18 × 9") piece of Chocolate Genoese
- 160 g (5.75 oz) raspberry jam
- 700 g (1 lb 9 oz) chocolate buttercream
- 500 g (1 lb 1.75 oz) grated chocolate
- 140 g (5 oz) melted chocolate flavoured coating
- 450 g (1 lb) vanilla buttercream
- 30 halved walnuts.

Sandwiching and coating

1 Using a sharp knife, remove skin from the Genoese and level if necessary.
2 Mark and cut the Genoese as follows:

- into three pieces measuring 45 × 7.5 cm (18 × 3")
- using a confectioner's harp, cut each piece horizontally through the middle to form six even pieces.

3 Sandwich three pieces of Genoese together using jam or curd and buttercream as illustrated below.

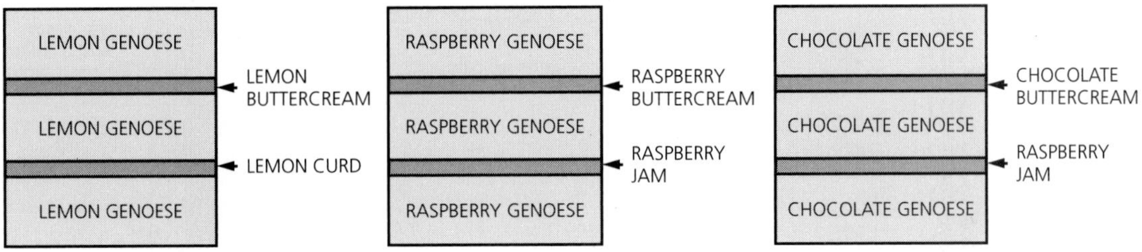

Figure 18 Sandwich three pieces of Genoese together

4 Trim the ends from the assembled base, then mark and cut the base into three equal bars.
5 Coat the top, sides and ends of each bar with the appropriate buttercream.

Final decoration

LEMON

1 Mask the sides and ends of the bar with toasted coconut.
2 Using a number 13 piping tube, pipe lemon buttercream shells along the top edges of the bar.
3 Place 5 crystallised lemon slices down the centre to complete the decoration.

RASPBERRY

1 Comb-scrape the raspberry buttercream on top of the bar.
2 Mask the side and ends of the bar with roasted flaked almonds.
3 Using a number 13 piping tube, pipe:

- three lines of chocolate buttercream down the centre of the bar
- a vanilla buttercream rope along the top edges of the bar.

CHOCOLATE

1 Spin fine lines of chocolate flavoured coating over the top surface of the bar.
2 Mask the side and ends of the bar with grated chocolate.
3 Using a number 13 piping tube, pipe a rope of vanilla buttercream along the top edges of the bar.
4 Place five half walnuts down the centre to complete the decoration.

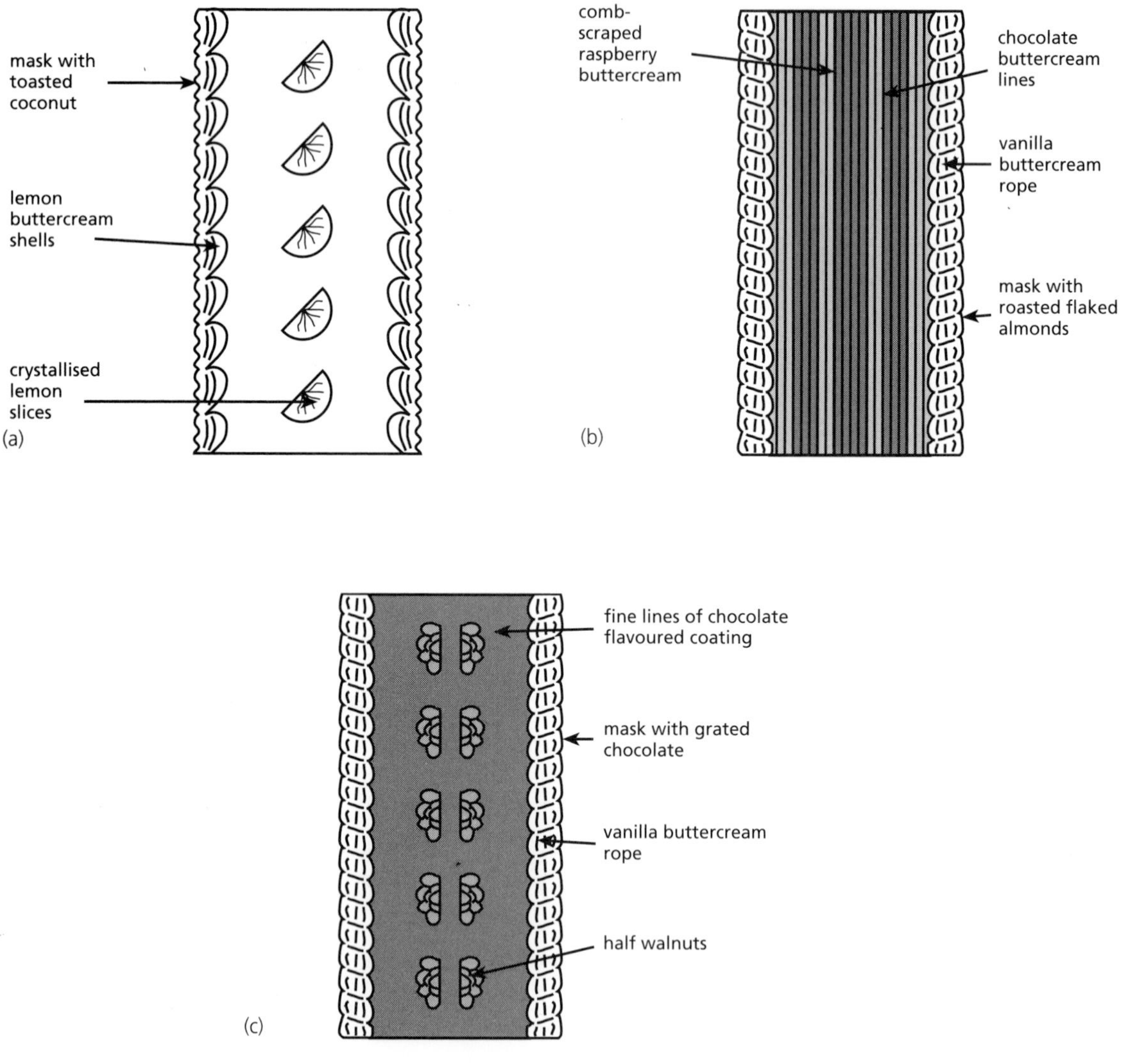

Figure 19 Final decoration for bar gateaux: (a) lemon (b) raspberry (c) chocolate

DECORATED BUTTERCREAM GATEAUX

Bases and materials required for four gateaux

LEMON:

- 4 × 15 cm (6") diameter lemon gateau bases
- 500 g (1 lb 2 oz) lemon curd
- 600 g (1 lb 5.5 oz) lemon buttercream
- 50 g (1.75 oz) chocolate flavoured coating
- 80 g (3 oz) toasted coconut.

ORANGE

- 4 × 15 cm (6") diameter orange gateau bases
- 240 g (8.5 oz) orange curd
- 400 g (14.25 oz) orange buttercream
- 100 g (3.5 oz) roasted flaked almonds
- 160 g (5.75 oz) chocolate flavoured coating
- 28 g (1 oz) icing sugar.

RASPBERRY:

- 4 × 15 cm (6") diameter raspberry gateau bases
- 240 g (8.5 oz) raspberry jam
- 450 g (1 lb) raspberry buttercream
- 100 g (3.5 oz) roasted nibbed almonds
- 100 g (3.5 oz) chocolate flavoured coating.

Sandwiching and coating

1. Using a sharp knife, remove the skin from the gateau base and level if necessary.
2. Cut the base horizontally through the middle to form two even pieces.
3. Sandwich the two pieces of gateau base together using the appropriate filling, lemon curd, orange curd or raspberry jam. Turn the gateau base over for a flat, top surface.
4. Coat the sides and top with the appropriate buttercream.

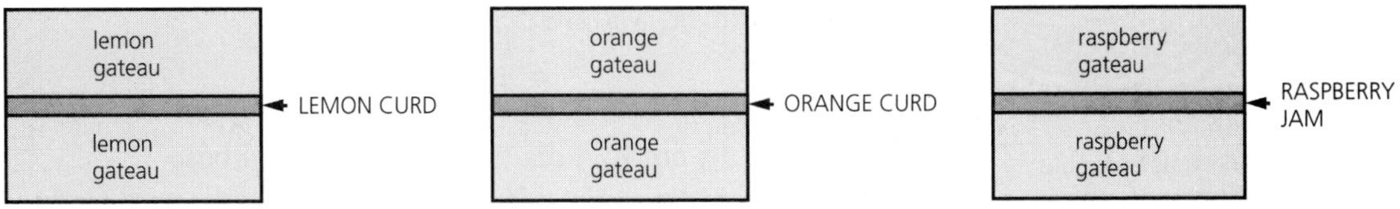

Figure 20 Sandwich two pieces of gateau together

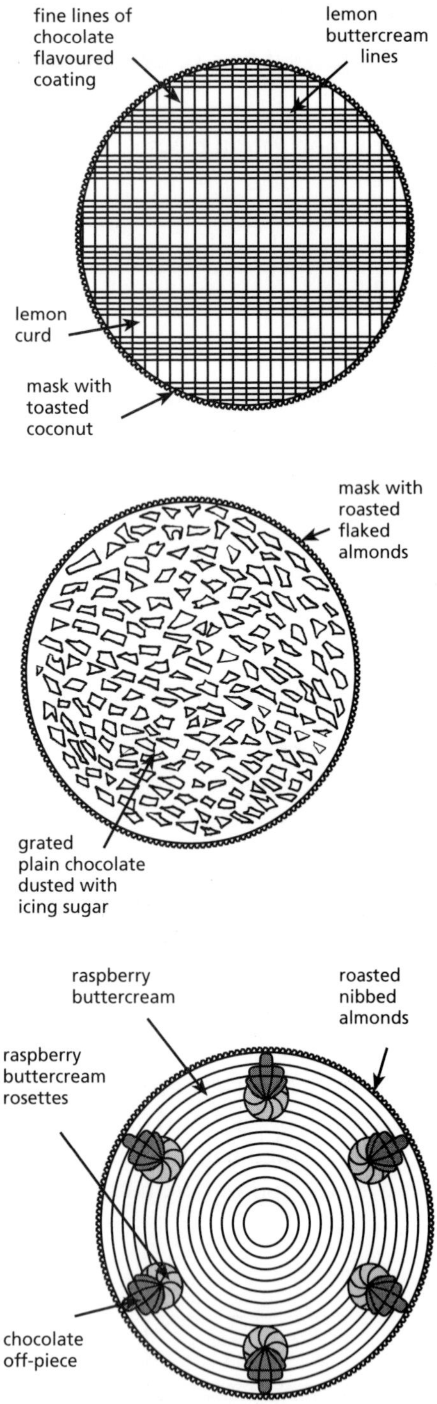

Figure 21 Final decoration for buttercream gateaux: (a) lemon (b) orange (c) raspberry

Final decoration

LEMON

1 Using a number 13 piping tube, pipe narrow lines of lemon buttercream set 5 mm (0.125") apart over the top of the gateaux.
2 Pipe lemon curd in between the lines of buttercream.
3 Spin fine lines of chocolate flavoured coating over the buttercream and curd as illustrated.
4 Mask the side of the gateaux with toasted coconut.

ORANGE

1 Mask the side of the gateaux with roasted flaked almonds.
2 Grate plain chocolate onto the top of the gateaux.
3 Dust the top of the gateaux with icing sugar.

RASPBERRY

1 Comb-scrape the raspberry buttercream on the top of the gateaux in a circular movement.
2 Mask the sides of the gateaux with roasted nibbed almonds.
3 Using a number 13 piping tube, pipe six small rosettes as illustrated.
4 Place a piped chocolate off-piece on each rosette – see illustration.

DECORATED FONDANT GATEAUX

Bases and materials required for four gateaux

WALNUT:

- 4 × 15 cm (6") diameter vanilla gateau base
- 240 g (8.5 oz) vanilla buttercream
- 60 g (2 oz) boiled apricot puree
- 400 g (14.25 oz) fondant
- 40 g (1.5 oz) stock syrup
- 160 g (5.75 oz) finely broken walnuts
- 1–3 g (0.0625 oz) chocolate compound
- 12 halved walnuts.

COFFEE:

- 4 × 15 cm (6") diameter coffee gateau base
- 240 g (8.5 oz) coffee buttercream
- 60 g (2 oz) boiled apricot puree

- 400 g (14.25 oz) fondant
- 40 g (1.5 oz) stock syrup
- 3–5 g (0.125 oz) coffee compound
- 110 g (4 oz) roasted flaked almonds.

CHOCOLATE:

- 4 × 15 cm (6") diameter chocolate gateaux base
- 240 g (8.5 oz) chocolate buttercream
- 60 g (2 oz) boiled apricot puree
- 400 g (14.25 oz) fondant
- 40 g (1.5 oz) stock syrup
- 60 g (2 oz) melted chocolate flavoured coating
- 3–5 g (0.125 oz) chocolate compound
- 100 g (3.5 oz) grated plain chocolate
- 8 g (0.25 oz) crystallised violets.

Sandwiching and coating

1. Using a sharp knife, remove the skin from the gateau base and level if necessary.
2. Cut the base horizontally through the middle to form two even pieces.
3. Sandwich the two pieces together using the appropriate buttercream filling. Turn the gateau base over for a flat, top surface.
4. Coat the sides and top with the appropriate buttercream.
5. Spread boiled apricot puree over the top of the gateau to provide a smooth, sealed surface.

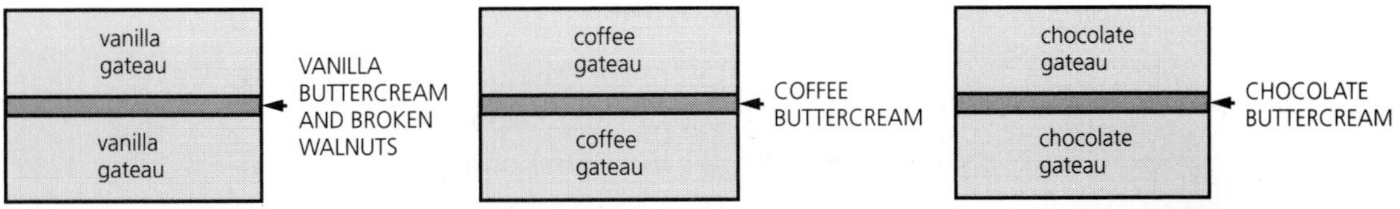

Figure 22 Sandwich two gateau pieces together

Final decoration

WALNUT

1. Spread and level prepared white fondant over the top surface of the gateau.
2. Mask the side of the gateau with finely broken walnuts.
3. Allow the fondant sufficient time to set.

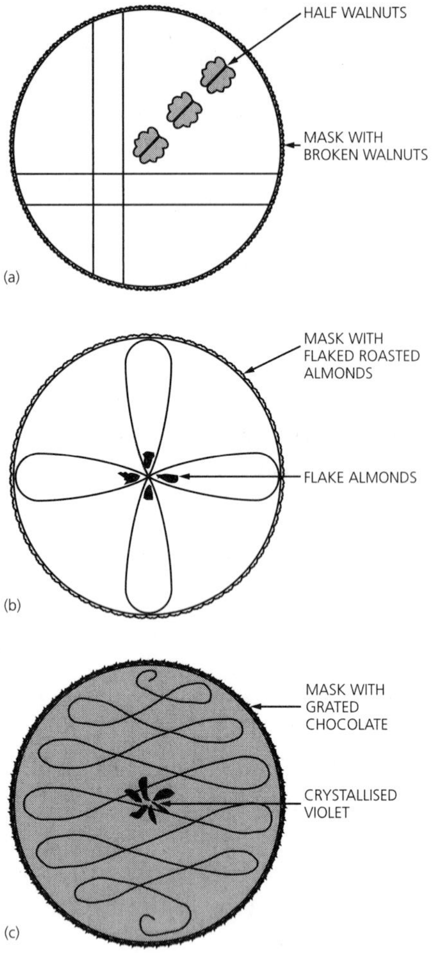

Figure 23 Final decoration for fondant gateaux: (a) walnut (b) coffee (c) chocolate

4 Using prepared chocolate fondant, pipe the fine linework as illustrated.
5 Place three half walnuts as illustrated.

COFFEE

1 Spread and level prepared coffee fondant over the top surface of the gateau.
2 Mask the side of the gateau with roasted flaked almonds.
3 Allow the fondant sufficient time to set.
4 Using slightly darker coffee fondant, pipe the fine linework as illustrated.
5 Sprinkle some roasted flaked almonds in the centre of the gateau.

CHOCOLATE

1 Add the melted chocolate flavoured coating to the prepared fondant and adjust the consistency with stock syrup.
2 Spread and level the chocolate fondant over the top surface of the gateau.
3 Mask the side of the gateau with grated plain chocolate.
4 Using slightly darker chocolate fondant, pipe the fine linework as illustrated.
5 Place some crystallised violet in the centre of the gateau.

COCONUT SPONGE

Bases and materials required for six Coconut Sponge Cakes

- 6 × 15 cm (6") diameter round Sponge Cakes
- 300 g (10.75 oz) raspberry jam
- 600 g (1 lb 5.5 oz) non-dairy cream
- 300 g (10.75 oz) desiccated coconut
- 6 whole glacé cherries.

Processing and finishing method

1 Remove any loose crumbs from the sponge base.
2 Using a sharp knife, cut the base horizontally through the middle to form two even pieces.
3 Sandwich the two pieces together using raspberry jam and non-dairy cream. Turn the sponge base over for a flat, top surface.

4 Coat the sides and top with non-dairy cream.
5 Mask the top and sides of the sponge with desiccated coconut.
6 Place a whole glacé cherry in the centre of the top of the sponge.

Note: This is a perishable product and must be stored or displayed under refrigerated conditions.

FRUIT TORTE

(See colour plate 19.)

Bases and materials required for a 16-portion torte

- 1 × 25 cm (10") diameter thin board
- 1 × 25 cm (10") diameter round Sponge Cake
- 1 kg (2 lb 4 oz) fresh cream
- 150 g (5.5 oz) chopped peach slices
- 16 peach slices
- 55 g (2 oz) brandy syrup
- 150 g (5.75 oz) roasted flaked almonds
- 100 g (3.5 oz) chocolate flavoured coating
- 75 g (2.75 oz) glazing jelly.

Filling and assembly

1 Remove any loose crumbs from the sponge base.
2 Using a long, sharp knife or confectioner's harp, cut the base twice horizontally through the middle to form three even, level pieces. Turn the sponge base over for a flat, top surface.
3 Place the bottom third of the sponge base onto the thin board.
4 Using a savoy bag and star tube pipe an even layer of fresh cream over the base. Distribute 150 g (5.5 oz) of chopped peach slices evenly over the layer of fresh cream.
5 Place the middle section of the sponge base over the peaches and cream. Press to secure a level position.
6 Sprinkle 55 g (2 oz) of brandy syrup evenly over the middle section of the sponge base.
7 Pipe an even layer of fresh cream over the middle section of the sponge base.
8 Place the top third section of sponge base over the cream and press to secure a level position.

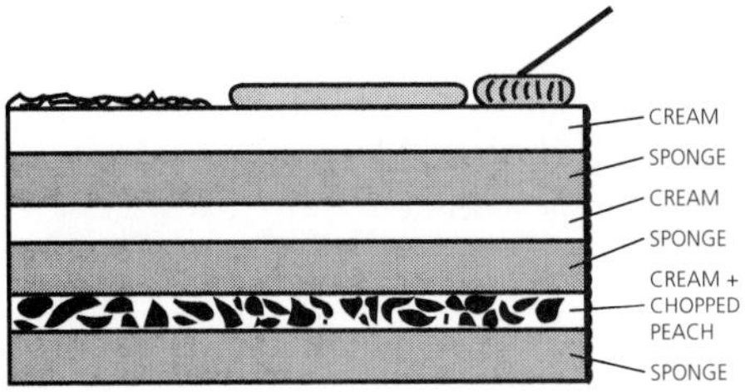

Figure 24 Fruit Torte filling and assembly

Coating and masking

1 Using a turntable and palette knife, spread and level fresh cream over the top surface of the sponge base to obtain a smooth, flat coating.
2 Spread and level fresh cream around the side of the sponge base and form a sharp corner between the top and side of the torten.
3 Mask the side of the torten with roast flaked almonds.

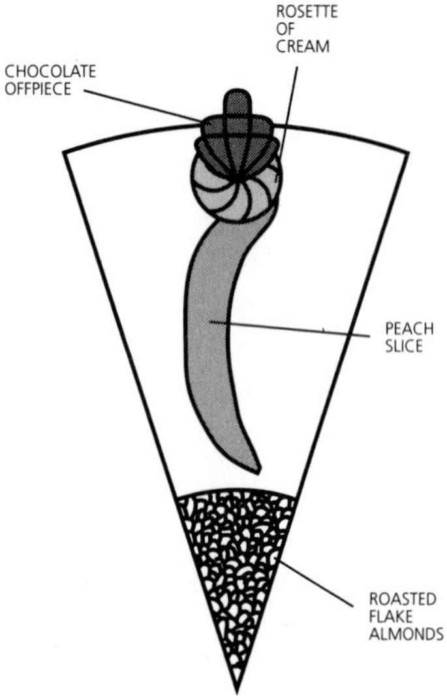

Figure 25 Fruit Torte final decoration

Final decoration

1 Using a 16 section torten divider, mark the top surface of the torten into 16 equal portions.
2 Place an 8 cm (3") plain cutter in the centre of the top of the torten and sprinkle a thin layer of roasted flaked almonds over the cream. Press the almonds to secure in position, and remove the plain cutter.
3 Drain and dry 16 peach slices. Place one peach slice on each portion as illustrated.
4 Brush each peach slice with glazing jelly.
5 Using a savoy bag and star tube, pipe a rosette of fresh cream on each portion as illustrated.
6 Place a pipe chocolate off-piece on each rosette – see Figure 25.

Note:

- This is a perishable product and must be stored or displayed under refrigerated conditions.
- A wide range of tortens can be produced from large sponge cake bases. A variety is possible because:
  - i A coloured and flavoured sponge cake base can be used.
  - ii The many fruits and fruit based fillings available can be used with an appropriate liqueur or spirit based syrup.
  - iii Countless number of designs can be used or created.

FONDANT DIPS

Bases and materials required

Yield 24

- 45 × 15 cm (18 × 6") piece of Plain Genoese
- 140 g (5 oz) apricot puree
- 240 g (8.5 oz) marzipan
- 800 g (1 lb 12.5 oz) fondant
- approx 80 g (3 oz) stock syrup
- 1–3 g (1⁄16 oz) chocolate compound.

Processing and finishing method

1 Using a sharp knife, remove the skin from the Genoese and level if necessary. Trim the ends from the Genoese.
2 Knead the marzipan until it is in the appropriate condition for rolling out. Roll out the marzipan to 2 mm (1⁄16") thick and cut to fit exactly on top of the Genoese.
3 Spread the apricot puree evenly over the surface of the marzipan.
4 Place the Genoese onto the marzipan, secure together and turn the Genoese upright.

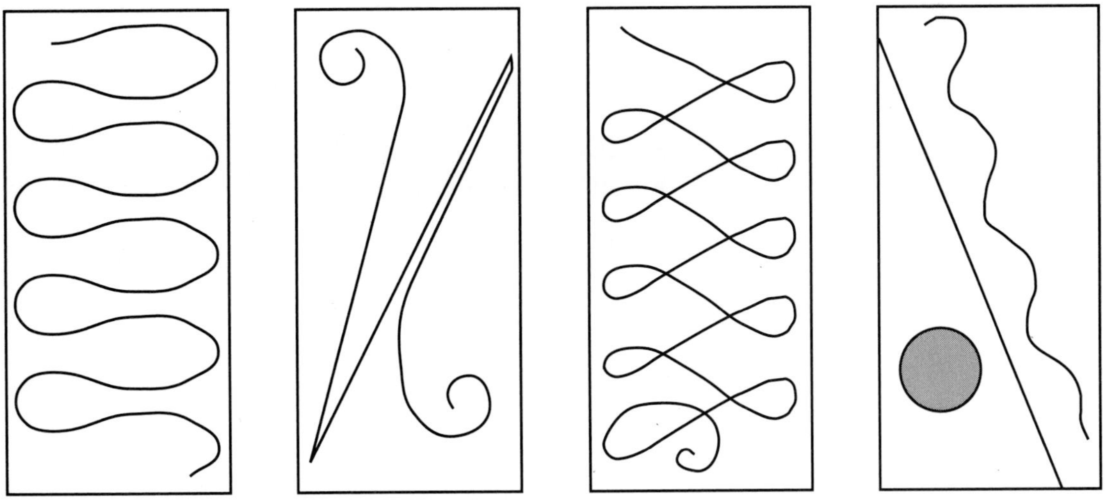

Figure 26 Fondant Dips

5 Mark and cut the Genoese as follows:

- into two pieces measuring 45 × 7.5 cm (18 × 3")
- each piece into 12 individual units measuring 7.5 × 3.5 cm (3 × 1.5").

6 Using prepared fondant of the appropriate consistency dip or enrobe the small cake bases and allow to drain on a draining wire.
7 Allow the fondant sufficient time to set.
8 Using chocolate coloured fondant, pipe one of the designs on the top; see Figure 26.
9 To remove the fondant dips from the wire, use a palette knife to slide under the dip and place into a paper case.

Note: A wide range of fondant dips can be produced from Genoese. A variety is possible because:

- the Genoese and fondant can be coloured to compliment each other
- the Genoese can be cut into many shapes, eg square, wedge, triangle and diamond
- glacé cherries, crystallised lemon slices and other small decorative media can be used to enhance the general appearance.

TRIFLES

Bases and materials required for 12 Trifles

- 12 individual trifle cases
- 48 small cubes of Sponge Cake or Genoese
- 200 g (7 oz) softened raspberry or strawberry jam
- 240 g (8.5 oz) fruit cocktail
- 360 g (13 oz) strawberry jelly
- 360 g (13 oz) custard
- 600 g (1 lb 5.5 oz) fresh cream.

Filling and assembly

1 Place 4 small cubes of sponge cake or Genoese into the trifle case and soak with approximately 15 g (0.5 oz) of softened jam.
2 Add approximately 20 g (0.75 oz) of fruit cocktail to the sponge or Genoese and jam in the trifle case.

3 Prepare the strawberry jelly and fill each trifle case with approximately 30 g (1 oz) of jelly and allow to set.
4 Prepare the custard and deposit approximately 30 g (1 oz) over the jelly. Allow to cool and set if necessary.
5 Using a savoy bag and star tube pipe fresh cream over the custard in a zig-zag pattern.

Note: This is a perishable product which must be stored or displayed under refrigerated conditions.

CHAPTER

thirteen

Popular confectionery

The baker produces a wide range of products based upon almonds, choux pastry, meringues and japonaise. We have selected some favourite products from these categories and placed them under the title of popular confectionery.

CHARACTERISTICS OF POPULAR CONFECTIONERY

Almond products

Products which contain almonds are rich in flavour and associated with high class confectionery. Almonds are available as ground, nibbed, flaked, strip, halved and whole. This enables almonds to be used in the manufacture of many types of cakes, slices, tarts and biscuits.

Choux pastry

Choux pastry bases will have some of the following characteristics:

- a high volume
- a crisp exterior
- an even crust colour
- a hollow, leaf-like interior.

These properties make choux pastry an ideal base to be combined with sweet and savoury light, moist fillings.

Meringue and japonaise

Meringue and japonaise bases will have some of the following characteristics:

- a bold volume which is light and crisp
- a sweet flavour
- a chewy interior
- japonaise products have a nutty taste.

These properties make meringues and japonaise an ideal base to be combined with cream based fillings.

THE PROCESSES

As with all processes, skill, knowledge and judgment are required to produce almond, choux pastry, meringue and japonaise products successfully. It is important to observe and perform each stage of the mixing process as stated in the detailed recipes.

The aim of mixing

- to disperse and dissolve all of the ingredients
- to incorporate air.

Basic ingredients

The basic ingredients required to make almond, choux pastry, meringue and japonaise products are:

- Almonds – this category contains a variation of products and processes, therefore please refer to the recipes.
- Choux pastry:
  Water
  Soft Fat
  Strong Flour
  Egg
- Meringues:
  Egg Whites
  Sugar
- Japonaise:
  Egg Whites
  Sugar
  Ground Almonds

MIXING METHOD

This is an outline of the mixing methods used to make almond, choux pastry, meringue and japonaise products. A more detailed description can be found in the recipes.

ALMOND

This category contains a variation of products and processes, therefore please refer to the recipes.

CHOUX PASTRY – ROUX-BASED PROCESS

1 Boil together the water and soft fat.
2 Sieve the flour, add to the above and cook until a roux is obtained. Allow to cool.
3 Add the egg in three additions and beat in thoroughly.

MERINGUES – COLD PROCESS

1 Whisk together the egg whites and half the sugar to a stiff foam.

2 Add the remaining sugar and whisk through until thoroughly dispersed.

JAPONAISE – MERINGUE-BASED PROCESS

1 Whisk together the egg whites and 60% of the sugar to a stiff foam.
2 Fold the dry ingredients through carefully.

Points to consider when processing almond, choux pastry, meringue and japonaise

The following points are common to each product group within this category.

1 Prepare all ingredients correctly before addition.
2 Adhere strictly to the mixing instructions.
3 Scrape down regularly as instructed.
4 Accurate scaling is essential to ensure that the yield is obtained and a uniform product is produced.

The following points are specific to each product group within this category:

ALMOND PRODUCTS

This category contains a variation of products and processes, therefore please refer to the recipes.

CHOUX PASTRY

1 Ensure that the roux is cooked thoroughly.
2 The consistency must allow the piped base to be just able to maintain its shape.
3 Allow sufficient space between bases to allow for expansion.

MERINGUE AND JAPONAISE

1 Ensure that all weighing and mixing equipment is free from grease.
2 Ensure that a stiff foam is obtained.
3 Once the ground nuts have been added, do not overmix japonaise.
4 It is essential to process and bake japonaise products immediately to maintain aeration.

THE BAKING PROCESS

A general guide to the baking temperature of products within this category:

- 110°C (230°F) – Meringues
- 177°C (350°F) – Macaroon Biscuits
- 180°C (356°F) – Congress Tarts, Japonaise
- 190°C (374°F) – Florentines.

During the baking process

ALMOND PRODUCTS

- Cake based – please refer to the baking section of cake and sponge products
- Biscuits – there is an increase in volume, the egg whites coagulate and the sugar caramelises to give a golden brown colour to the surface.

CHOUX PASTRY

The moisture of the choux pastry is converted into steam. The steam lifts the choux pastry product to its full volume and eventually the mixtures gelatinises and coagulates to form a hollow base. Under-baking will cause collapse, therefore ensure choux pastry products are thoroughly baked.

MERINGUES

There is an increase in volume and the egg whites eventually coagulate during an extended drying out period. Meringues must be baked at a very low temperature because of the high sugar content needed to obtain the desired characteristics.

JAPONAISE

The process is similar to that of meringues, but japonaise products are baked at higher temperatures. This is to retain the shape of the product and confer a light brown colour to the surface.

The baking temperature will depend upon the following:

- shape, size and depth
- density
- sugar content
- product characterisics.

Cooling

On withdrawal from the oven, almond, choux pastry, meringue and japonaise products should be allowed to cool until they can be handled without being damaged. All of the products within this category that are to be wrapped or finished must be cooled thoroughly before processing.

Final decoration

Popular confectionery products are decorated with suitable finishing materials to enhance their appearance, add flavour and improve the general eating qualities.

The practical application of the materials should be reproduced consistently to a good standard to maintain the quality and appeal of the product. As with cake and sponge products, this product group provides the baker and confectioner with the opportunity to be creative.

OVEN CHART

Product	Baking temperature in °C (°F)	Baking time in minutes	Additional control procedures
Congress Tarts	180 (356)	20	Open damper for final 5 mins
Frangipane Tarts	190 (374)	20	" " " "
Bakewell Tarts	190 (374)	25	" " " "
Macaroon Biscuits	177 (350)	20–25	" " " "
Florentines	190 (374)	15–20	" " " "
Choux Buns	230 (446)	40–45	Bake under a tin or lid
Eclairs	230 (446)	25–30	Open damper for final 5 mins
Meringue Bases	110 (230)	90	Dampers open and oven door ajar
Japonaise Biscuits & Fingers	180 (356)	20–25	Open damper for final 10 mins

RECIPES FOR ALMOND PRODUCTS

CONGRESS TARTS

Use recipe A, B or C for sweet pastry (see p. 172); all are suitable for this product.

Processing method

Yield approx 50

Note: The appropriate mechanical blocking machine may be used for stages 1, 2 and 3.

1 Pin out the sweetpaste to approximately 4 mm (0.25") thick.
2 Using a fluted cutter which is slightly larger than the shallow foil or tin, cut out the bases.
3 Place the sweetpaste base into the foil or tin and carefully thumb it into position.
4 Pipe a spot of jam into each sweetpaste base.
5 Prepare the macaroon filling as follows:

Ingredients for filling

Kilo	Gram	%	Ingredients	lb	oz
1	000	100.00	granulated sugar	2	3.50
	500	50.00	ground almonds	1	1.50
	70	7.00	ground rice		2.50
	400	40.00	egg whites		14.00
1	970		Gross weight	4	5.50

Mixing method

- blend the dry ingredients together
- add the egg whites in a steady stream
- scrape down
- beat on top speed for 3–4 minutes.

6 Pipe sufficient macaroon filling into each pastry case.
7 Dredge with caster sugar.
8 Bake at 180°C (356°F) for approximately 20 minutes.

FRANGIPANE TART

Use recipe A, B or C for sweet pastry (see p. 172); all are suitable for this product.

Processing method

Yield approx 60

Note: The appropriate mechanical blocking machine may be used for stages 1, 2 and 3.

1 Pin out the sweetpaste to approximately 3 mm (0.125") thick.
2 Using a fluted cutter that is slightly larger than the medium deep foil or tin, cut out the bases.
3 Place the sweetpaste base into the foil or tin and carefully thumb it into position.
4 Pipe a spot of jam into each sweetpaste base.
5 Prepare the frangipane filling as follows:

Frangipane tarts

Ingredients

Kilo	Gram	%	Ingredients	lb	oz
	270	79.40	butter or margarine		9.75
	340	100.00	caster sugar		12.25
	330	97.00	egg at 21°C (70°F)		11.75
	20	5.90	glycerine		0.75
	70	20.60	cake flour		2.50
	60	17.60	cake crumbs		2.25
	200	58.80	ground almonds		7.50
1	290		Gross weight	2	14.75
1	238		Net weight	2	12.75

Mixing method

- cream the butter or margarine with the sugar on top speed until light
- mix the glycerine through the egg and add to the above in five additions. Each addition must be beaten in thoroughly. Scrape down regularly
- sieve together the flour, cake crumb and ground almonds and add to the above
- mix on slow speed until a smooth batter is obtained.

6 Pipe sufficient frangipane filling into each pastry case.
7 Bake at 190°C (374°F) for approximately 20 minutes.
8 On withdrawal from the oven, allow the baked frangipane bases to cool.

FRANGIPANE FINISHES

Flaked Almond:

1 Brush the top of the frangipane base with boiled apricot puree.
2 Dip the frangipane into roasted flaked almonds.
3 Using a template, dredge half of the frangipane top with icing sugar.

Marzipan:

1 Pin out green coloured marzipan to approximately 4 mm (¼") thick.
2 Using a basket roller, mark the top of the coloured marzipan.
3 Using an appropriately sized fluted cutter, cut out small discs.
4 Brush the tops of the frangipane with boiled apricot puree, then place and secure a marzipan disc.
5 Place a split almond that has been half dipped in chocolate flavoured coating in the centre of the marzipan.

Buttercream and Fondant:

1 Using a No. 13 tube, pipe a ring of coffee buttercream around the edge of the frangipane.
2 Flood the centre of the ring with coffee fondant.
3 Place a half walnut over the join of the buttercream ring.

Fondant:

1 Brush the top of the frangipane with boiled apricot puree.

2 Flood the top of the frangipane with lemon or orange fondant and allow to set.
3 Spin fine lines of chocolate flavoured coating across the fondant.

BAKEWELL TARTS

Use recipe A, B or C for sweet pastry (see p. 172); all are suitable for this product.

Processing method

Yield approx 9

Note: The appropriate mechanical blocking machine may be used for stages 1, 2, 3 and 4.

1 Scale 9 at 195 g (7 oz) and mould round.
2 Pin out the bases to cover a 15 cm (6") diameter flan foil or tin. Place the base into the foil or tin and thumb into position.
3 Using a knife, trim the excess sweetpaste from the top edge.
4 The top edge of the sweetpaste can be crimped between the thumb and the forefinger or left plain.
5 Pipe a spiral of raspberry jam into each sweetpaste base.
6 Using the frangipane filling, deposit approximately 120 g (4.25 oz) into the bases and spread evenly.
7 Bake at 190°C (374°F) for approximately 25 minutes.
8 On withdrawal from the oven, allow the Bakewell Tarts to cool.
9 Brush the top with boiled apricot puree.
10 Coat the top with a thin layer of fondant or water icing.

Note: A variety of fruits can be used as part of the filling. After preparation, the fruit should be placed over the jam content within the sweetpaste base, prior to depositing the frangipane filling. The fruit content can be fresh or tinned; some of the most popular varieties are: apple, blackberry, cherry, raspberry, apricot and peaches.

MACAROON BISCUITS

Ingredients

Kilo	Gram	%	Ingredients	lb	oz
	625	100.00	granulated sugar	1	6.25
	40	6.40	ground rice		1.50
	315	50.40	ground almonds		11.25
	195	31.20	cold egg whites		7.00
1	175		Gross weight	2	10.00
1	128		Net weight	2	8.25

Production Points

Macaroon paste temperature	**Cool**
Scaling weight	**approx 30 g (1 oz)**
Yield	**approx 37**
Baking temperature	**177°C (350°F)**
Baking time	**20–25 mins**

Mixing method

1. Mix together the granulated sugar, ground rice and ground almonds and place into a mixing bowl.
2. Using a beater, add the cold egg whites to the dry ingredients in a slow, steady stream on slow speed. Scrape down.
3. Mix on top speed for 8 minutes until a smooth, lightly aerated macaroon paste is obtained.

Note: The consistency of this mixture can vary and may require some adjustments to the level of egg whites.

Processing method

1. Using a savoy bag and plain tube, pipe approximately 37 biscuits weighing approximately 30 g (1 oz) each, onto a baking tray lined with silicone paper in a 5 × 7 formation.
2. Place a split almond in the centre of the top of each biscuit.
3. Bake at 177°C (350°F) for 20–25 minutes.
4. On withdrawal from the oven, allow the macaroon biscuits to cool on the baking tray until they can be removed without being damaged.

FLORENTINES

Ingredients

Kilo	Gram	%	Ingredients	lb	oz
	150	66.60	cake margarine or butter		5.25
	75	33.30	milk		2.75
	225	100.00	caster sugar		8.00
	30	13.30	cake flour		1.00
	225	100.00	flaked almonds		8.00
	100	44.40	sultanas		3.50
	70	31.10	chopped glacé cherries		2.50
	60	26.60	mixed peel		2.00
	935		Gross weight	2	1.00
	888		Net weight	1	15.50

Production Points

Mix temperature	**Warm**
Scaling weight	**approx 35 g (1.25 oz)**
Yield	**24**
Baking temperature	**190°C (374°F)**
Baking time	**15–20 mins**

Mixing method

1 Place the cake margarine or butter, milk and caster sugar into a pan and heat gently to a temperature of 50°C (122°F). Remove from the heat.
2 Sieve the flour, mix it together with the flaked almonds, add to the above and stir through.
3 Add the sultanas, chopped glacé cherries and mixed peel. Stir through until thoroughly dispersed.

Processing method

1 Deposit approximately 35 g (1.25 oz) of florentine mixture into 7 cm (3") diameter round silicone paper cases.
2 Bake at 190°C (374°F) for 15–20 minutes.
3 On withdrawal from the oven, allow the florentines to cool on the baking tray.
4 Using a palette knife spread a thin layer of chocolate flavoured coating over the flat side of the florentine. Place the coated side onto greaseproof paper and allow to set.
5 Apply a second coat of chocolate flavoured coating and using a comb scraper, make a ripple pattern. Allow to set.

RECIPES USING CHOUX PASTRY

CREAM BUNS AND CHOCOLATE ECLAIRS

Ingredients

Kilo	Gram	%	Ingredients	lb	oz
	520	168.00	water	1	2.50
	200	64.50	cake margarine or butter		7.00
	310	100.00	bread flour		11.00
	600	193.00	egg	1	5.25
1	630		Gross weight	3	9.75
1	530		Net weight	3	6.25

Production Points

Scaling weight	**approx 50 g (1.75 oz)**
Yield:	
buns	**approx 30**
eclairs	**approx 30**
Baking temperature	**230°C (446°F)**
Baking time:	
buns	**40–45 mins**
eclairs	**25–30 mins**

(See colour plate 22.)

Mixing method

1 Place the water and cake margarine or butter into a pan and bring to the boil.
2 Sieve the flour and add to the boiling liquor. Cook for 2–3 minutes until a roux is formed.

Note: An indication that the roux is thoroughly cooked is when it leaves the side of the pan.

3 Allow the roux to cool thoroughly.
4 When the roux is cool, place it into a mixing bowl and add the egg in three additions. Each addition must be added in a slow, steady stream on slow speed, the mixture scraped down then the egg beaten through on top speed for up to 1 minute.

Processing method

COFFEE CREAM BUNS

1 Using a savoy bag and plain tube, pipe choux pastry bulbs weighing approximately 50 g (1.75 oz) in a suitable formation onto a greased baking tray.

Note:

- the formation of the bulbs must be considered to ensure that the baking tray is fully utilised, and each bulb can be covered by a lid or bread tin during the baking process
- the space between the choux pastry bulbs must be sufficient to allow full expansion during the baking process.

2 Cover the bulbs with a lid or bread tin.
3 Bake at 230°C (446°F) for 40–45 minutes.

Note:

- the lid or bread tin must not be removed or disturbed until the choux buns are at no risk of collapse
- choux buns must be thoroughly baked to prevent collapse on withdrawal from the oven.

4 On withdrawal from the oven, remove the lid or bread tin and place the choux buns onto a cooling wire.
5 When cool, split the choux bun horizontally through the middle and fill the base with fresh cream. Replace the top.
6 Pipe a topping of prepared coffee fondant over the surface of the cream bun and allow to set.

CHOCOLATE ECLAIRS

1 Using a savoy bag and plain tube, pipe choux pastry fingers approximately 10 cm (4") long and weighing approximately 50 g (1.75 oz) in a suitable formation onto a baking tray lined with greaseproof paper.

   Note: Using greaseproof paper ensures a flat base, without excessive sticking. The flat base allows the chocolate fondant to be applied neatly.

2 Bake at 230°C (446°F) for 25–30 minutes.

Choux buns and eclairs

3 On withdrawal from the oven, allow the eclair bases to cool on the baking tray until they can be removed without being damaged.
4 Remove the eclair bases and place onto a cooling wire.
5 When cool, split the eclair base horizontally through the middle, turn it over and place one half of the eclair base into a finger shaped packet.
6 Using a savoy bag and star tube, pipe a rope of fresh cream along the base. Replace the flat top.
7 Using prepared chocolate fondant which must include plain chocolate, pipe the fondant over the flat surface of the eclair using a flat piping tube or a greaseproof bag with a V shaped end, and allow to set.

Note: Coffee Cream Buns and Chocolate Eclairs are perishable products and must be stored or displayed under refrigerated conditions.

RECIPES USING THE COLD PROCESS

MERINGUES – SHELLS, FINGERS AND NESTS

(See colour plate 20.)

Ingredients

Kilo	Gram	%	Ingredients	lb	oz
	300	100.00	egg whites		10.75
	360	120.00	caster sugar A		13.00
	360	120.00	caster sugar B		13.00
1	020		Gross weight	2	4.75
	990		Net weight	2	3.75

Mixing method

1 Prior to weighing and mixing, wash and rinse all equipment and allow to drain.
2 Place the egg whites and caster sugar A into a mixing bowl. Using a whisk, whisk on slow speed to blend them together.
3 Whisk on top speed for 5–10 minutes until a stiff foam is obtained.
4 Add caster sugar B and blend through on slow speed for 15 seconds. Mix on top speed for up to 2 minutes to ensure thoroughly dispersed.

Processing method

1 Using a savoy bag and plain or star tube, pipe one of the following shapes onto a baking tray lined with silicone paper.

- Shell – 7.5 cm (3") long: 4 × 8 formation

Production Points

Mix temperature	**Cool**
Scaling weight	**approx 15 g (0.5 oz)**
Yield	**approx 66**
Baking temperature	**110°C (230°F)**
Baking time	**1 hour 30 mins**

- Fingers – 10 cm (4") long: 3 × 11 formation
- Nests – 7.5 cm (3") diameter round: 4 × 8 formation.

2 Bake at 110°C (230°F) for approximately 1 hour 30 minutes with the dampers open and the oven door ajar, to ensure that the baking process takes place in a dry atmosphere.
3 On withdrawal from the oven, allow the meringue bases to cool on the baking tray until they can be removed without being damaged.

Finishing method

SHELLS AND FINGERS

1 Dip the flat surface of the shells or fingers into chocolate flavoured coating to obtain a thin coat. Place the coated side onto greaseproof paper and allow to set.
2 Place two shells or fingers into a suitably shaped packet.
3 Using a savoy bag and star tube, sandwich the two shells or fingers together with a rope of fresh cream.
4 Decorate the top of the meringue with a piece of fruit.

NESTS

1 Dip the flat bottom surface of the base into chocolate flavoured coating to obtain a thin coat. Place the coated side onto greaseproof paper and allow to set.
2 Using a savoy bag and star tube, fill the hollow with a large rosette of fresh cream.
3 Decorate the top of the nest with roasted nibbed or flaked almonds and fruit.

Note: These are perishable products which must be stored or displayed under refrigerated conditions.

RECIPE USING THE MERINGUE-BASED PROCESS

JAPONAISE BISCUITS AND FINGERS

Ingredients

Kilo	Gram	%	Ingredients	lb	oz
	250	100.00	egg whites		9.00
	250	100.00	caster sugar A		9.00
	1	0.40	cream of tartar		pinch
	185	74.00	caster sugar B		6.50
	40	16.00	bread flour		1.50
	40	16.00	ground rice		1.50
	200	80.00	ground almonds		7.00
	966		Gross weight	2	2.50
	930		Net weight	2	1.00

Production Points

Mix temperature	**Cool**
Scaling weight	**approx 12 g (0.5 oz)**
Yield	**approx 76**
Baking temperature	**180°C (356°F)**
Baking time	**20–25 mins**

Mixing method

1 Prior to weighing and mixing, wash and rinse all equipment and allow to drain.
2 Place the egg whites, caster sugar A and cream of tartar into a mixing bowl, and whisk on slow speed to blend them together.
3 Whisk on top speed for 5–10 minutes until a stiff foam is obtained.
4 Sieve together caster sugar B, bread flour, ground rice and ground almonds, add to the above and fold through carefully by hand or on slow speed until the dry ingredients are dispersed. To ensure that the mixture remains aerated, do not overmix at this stage.

Note: The japonaise mixture must be processed and baked immediately.

Processing method

1 Using a savoy bag and plain tube, pipe the japonaise mixture into biscuits or fingers onto a baking tray lined with silicone paper. Pipe in the following formation:

- biscuits: 5 × 9
- fingers: 4 × 11.

2 Bake at 180°C (356°F) for 20–25 minutes.
3 On withdrawal from the oven, allow the japonaise bases to cool on the baking tray until they can be removed without being damaged.

Finishing method

1 Dip the biscuits and fingers into chocolate flavoured coating as follows:

- biscuits – half dipped
- fingers – ends dipped.

Remove the excess chocolate and place onto greaseproof paper. Allow to set.

2 In pairs, place the biscuits or fingers into a suitably shaped packet.
3 Using a savoy bag and star tube, sandwich the biscuits or fingers together with fresh cream as follows:

- biscuits – large rosette
- fingers – rope.

4 Decorate the biscuits or fingers with fruit.

Note: These are perishable products which must be stored or displayed under refrigerated conditions.

C H A P T E R

fourteen

Sandwiches

The popularity of sandwiches within the take-away food sector has increased, and sandwiches have become an important part of production for today's baker. The success of the sandwich can be attributed to these factors:

- the wide range of bread and fermented products which can be used to form the foundation of a sandwich
- the freshness and tastes offered by the range of bread and fermented products
- the combination of products are endless, and so it is possible to cater for all tastes. The wide variety of fillings available range from traditional to exciting and refreshing flavours from countries all around the world.
- sandwiches are an excellent source of nutrition; they are filling, satisfying and represent good value for money
- the use of packaging garnishes and thoughtful presentation, linked to all the above factors, have enhanced the image and profile of the sandwich.

With good planning and organisation, the production of sandwiches can provide the opportunity to develop an exciting range of take-away food.

TYPES OF BREAD

Each of the following types of bread are suitable for the production of sandwiches (The recipes and processing methods are provided within Chapters 4, 5, 6 and 7.):

- Sliced Tin Breads – white, brown, wholemeal, granary and country cereal
- Stotties
- Rye Bread
- Huffkins
- Vienna Bread and Rolls
- Soft Fancy Rolls
- Brown Rolls
- Muffins
- French Breads
- Bridge Rolls
- Bread Rolls and Scotch Baps
- Brown Fancy Rolls
- Milk Bread Rolls
- Croissants
- Finger Rolls
- Burger Buns
- Barm Cakes
- Ciabatta.

(See colour plate 25.)

CATEGORIES OF SANDWICHES

Closed sandwiches

Closed sandwiches are the most popular type of sandwich. The types of bread most suitable for making closed sandwiches are:

- all Sliced White and Brown Tin Breads
- Stotties
- Huffkins
- All rolls, baps and buns
- Muffins
- French Bread
- Croissants
- Barm Cakes
- Ciabatta.

Buffet sandwiches

Buffet sandwiches are made from sliced white or brown breads which have had the crusts removed and are then cut into four small triangles. Small Bridge Rolls are also a suitable base for a buffet sandwich.

Toasted sandwiches

Toasted sandwiches are made from sliced white or brown bread which contain a moist filling. The whole sandwich is toasted under a grill and is served hot.

Open sandwich

The open sandwich can be made from any type of bread which can form a suitable base on which to place the sandwich ingredients in an appetising and decorative style.

MAIN PRODUCTION POINTS

To ensure that sandwiches are produced satisfactorily, efficiently and hygienically, the following points must be observed.

Equipment

1 Use sharp knives for all cutting processes.
2 Use a flexible palette knife to apply spreads and fillings.
3 Always use a suitable chopping board during production.
4 Always use plastic containers with lids to hold fillings during production and storage.
5 Storage and display units must be refrigerated areas.
6 The work surface must be a comfortable height and well lit.

Spreads

1 Firm spreads such as butter must be beaten to ensure quick and easy application.
2 Always ensure the spread reaches the edge of the bread, in order to:
   - prevent drying
   - create a barrier between the bread and moist filling, which will prevent the bread from becoming soggy.

Fillings

1 Include a suitable quantity of filling.
2 Ensure that fillings are of a consistency which allows quick and easy spreading.
3 Remove excessive fat, gristle and skin from meats.
4 Fillings such as lettuce, tomatoes and cucumbers must be cleaned and dried in advance.
5 All fillings must be within easy reach during production.

SANDWICH FILLINGS

The following recipes have been calculated to give one of these yields:

- 4 rounds using sliced bread
- 4 × 60 g (2 oz) rolls or baps

When using smaller or larger units of bread and fermented products, the filling recipes will require adjustment.

Buttering: Allow approximately 35 g (1.25 oz) of softened butter or margarine per four rounds of sliced bread or four baps.

SANDWICH RECIPES USING SALAD

FRESH SALAD

Ingredients

Gram	Ingredients	oz
4 leaves	lettuce	4 leaves
60	cucumber	2
85	tomatoes	3
60	hard boiled egg	2
	salt to taste	

Method of preparation

1 Wash, inspect and dry the lettuce, cucumber and tomato.
2 Slice thinly the cucumber, tomatoes and hard boiled egg.
3 Apply salt after assembly of filling.

Salad varieties

To produce a wide range of salad sandwiches, use the recipe given above and combine it with any one of the following:

1 *Cheese:*
- sliced or grated firm cheese, eg Cheddar
- cream cheese
- cottage cheese.

2 *Cold meats:*
- sliced chicken, ham, corned beef, pork, beef, turkey and smoked bacon
- continental meats, eg salami and smoked sausage
- spiced and curried meats, eg chicken Tikka and Mexican chicken.

3 *Seafood:*
- tuna, prawn, crab and salmon.

DICED HAM SALAD

Ingredients

Gram	Ingredients	oz
4 leaves	lettuce	4 leaves
40	cucumber	1.50
60	tomatoes	2.00
25	carrot	1.00
40	onion	1.50
60	hard boiled egg	2.00
80	tinned ham	3.00
	salad cream or mayonnaise to bind	
	salt to taste	

Method of preparation

1. Wash, inspect and dry the lettuce, cucumber and tomatoes.
2. Peel, rinse and dry the carrots and onions.
3. Dice finely all of the ingredients.
4. Add sufficient salad cream or mayonnaise and mix all of the ingredients together.
5. Add salt to taste.

SANDWICH RECIPES USING EGG

EGG MAYONNAISE

Ingredients

Gram	Ingredients	oz
180	hard boiled eggs	6.50
15	cress	0.50
pinch	cayenne pepper	pinch
	mayonnaise to bind	

Method of preparation

1. Grate the hard boiled eggs.
2. Add the cress to the eggs.
3. Mix the cayenne pepper through the mayonnaise, add to the eggs and cress and mix together thoroughly.

EGG AND TOMATOES

Ingredients

Gram	Ingredients	oz
110	hard boiled eggs	4.00
70	tomatoes	2.50
	mayonnaise to bind	
	salt and pepper to taste	

Method of preparation

1. Grate the hard boiled eggs.
2. Wash, rinse, dry and chop the tomatoes.
3. Add the mayonnaise, salt and pepper to the egg and tomato and mix together thoroughly.

EGG AND SMOKED BACON

Ingredients

Gram	Ingredients	oz
100	hard boiled eggs	3.50
80	smoked lean bacon	3.00
	mayonnaise to bind	
	pepper to taste	

Method of preparation

1. Grate the hard boiled eggs.
2. Dice the smoked bacon and cook until crisp. Allow to cool and add to the above.
3. Add the mayonnaise and pepper and mix together thoroughly.

SANDWICH RECIPES USING CHEESE

CHEESE AND ONION

Ingredients

Gram	Ingredients	oz
160	Cheddar cheese	5.75
40	onion	1.50

Method of preparation

1 Slice or grate the Cheddar cheese.
2 Peel, rinse and dry the onion.
3 Slice or chop the onions.

CHEESE AND TOMATO

Use the recipe above, but replace the onion with 100 g (3.5 oz) of clean, thinly sliced tomato.

CHEESE AND CHUTNEY

Use the recipe above, but replace the onion with 60 g (2 oz) of chutney.

CHEESE SAVOURY

Ingredients

Gram	Ingredients	oz
120	Cheddar cheese	4.25
40	onion	1.50
40	carrot	1.50
	salad cream or mayonnaise to bind	

Method of preparation

1 Grate the Cheddar cheese.
2 Peel, rinse and dry the onion and carrot.
3 Dice finely the onion and grate the carrot.
4 Add sufficient salad cream or mayonnaise and mix all of the ingredients together.

CREAM CHEESE AND CELERY

Ingredients

Gram	Ingredients	oz
55	butter or margarine	2.00
130	Cheddar cheese	4.50
40	celery	1.50
	celery salt to taste	

Method of preparation

1 Beat the butter until light.
2 Grate the cheese and mix through the butter.
3 Wash, inspect and dry the celery.
4 Chop the celery finely and mix through the butter and cheese with the celery salt.

CREAM CHEESE AND PINEAPPLE

Use the recipe above, but replace the celery with 40 g (1.5 oz) chopped pineapple and omit the celery salt.

COTTAGE CHEESE, HAM AND PINEAPPLE

Ingredients

Gram	Ingredients	oz
110	cottage cheese	4.00
50	tinned ham	2.00
50	pineapple	2.00

Method of preparation

1 Dice the tinned ham and pineapple, and mix through the cottage cheese.

SANDWICH RECIPES USING MEAT

CHICKEN WITH SAGE AND ONION

Ingredients

Gram	Ingredients	oz
180	cooked white chicken	6.50
100	sage and onion filling	3.50

Method of preparation

1 Dice the cooked chicken.
2 Prepare the sage and onion filling and allow to cool.

HAM AND PEASE PUDDING

Ingredients

Gram	Ingredients	oz
180	sliced cooked ham	6.50
100	pease pudding	3.50

Method of preparation

1 Freshly made pease pudding must be cooled before use. No other preparation required.

CORNED BEEF AND ONION

Ingredients

Gram	Ingredients	oz
180	sliced corned beef	6.50
40	onion	1.50

Method of preparation

1 Peel, rinse and dry the onion, then slice thinly. No other preparation required.

CORNED BEEF AND TOMATO

Use the recipe above, but replace the onions with 100 g (3.5 oz) of clean, thinly sliced tomatoes.

PORK WITH SAGE AND ONION

Ingredients

Gram	Ingredients	oz
180	sliced cooked pork	6.50
100	sage and onion filling	3.50

Method of preparation

1 Prepare the sage and onion filling and allow to cool. No other preparation required.

PORK, APPLE AND SAGE AND ONION

Use the recipe above, but reduce the sage and onion filling to 85 g (3 oz) and include 85 g (3 oz) cooked diced apple.

TURKEY WITH SAGE AND ONION

Ingredients

Gram	Ingredients	oz
180	sliced cooked turkey	6.50
100	sage and onion filling	3.50

Method of preparation

1 Prepare the sage and onion filling and allow to cool. No other preparation required.

SALAMI AND COLESLAW

Ingredients

Gram	Ingredients	oz
180	sliced salami	6.50
100	coleslaw	3.50

Method of preparation

1 Remove the skin from the salami. No other preparation required.

CHICKEN, BACON AND SWEETCORN

Ingredients

Gram	Ingredients	oz
100	lean bacon	3.50
100	cooked white chicken	3.50
40	sweetcorn	1.50
	black pepper to taste	
	mayonnaise to bind	

Method of preparation

1 Dice the lean bacon and cook until crisp. Allow to cool.
2 Dice the cooked chicken and add to the above.
3 Add the sweetcorn, pepper and mayonnaise and mix all ingredients together.

MEXICAN CHICKEN

Ingredients

Gram	Ingredients	oz
180	cooked white chicken	6.50
45	tomato ketchup	1.75
10	sweet chilli sauce	0.50
20	soy sauce	0.75
	salt and pepper to taste	

Method of preparation

1 Dice the cooked chicken.
2 Add the sauces, salt and pepper to the chicken and mix together thoroughly.

CORONATION CHICKEN

Ingredients

Gram	Ingredients	oz
180	cooked white chicken	6.50
35	curry paste	1.25
20	mango chutney	0.75
25	mayonnaise	1.00
20	roasted flaked almonds	0.75

Method of preparation

1 Dice the cooked chicken.
2 Blend together the curry paste, mango chutney and mayonnaise, add to the chicken with the roasted flaked almonds. Mix all of the ingredients together thoroughly.

CHICKEN TIKKA

Ingredients

Gram	Ingredients	oz
180	cooked white chicken	6.50
30	Tikka paste	1.00
	mayonnaise to bind	
30	sultanas	1.00

Method of preparation

1 Dice the cooked chicken.
2 Blend together the Tikka paste and mayonnaise, add to the chicken with the sultanas.
3 Mix all ingredients together thoroughly.

SANDWICH RECIPES USING SEAFOOD

TUNA AND SWEETCORN

Ingredients

Gram	Ingredients	oz
160	tuna flakes	5.75
55	sweetcorn	2.00
	mayonnaise to bind	
	salt and pepper to taste	

Method of preparation

1 Drain the tuna flakes.
2 Add the sweetcorn, mayonnaise, salt and pepper to the tuna. Mix together thoroughly.

PRAWN COCKTAIL

Ingredients

Gram	Ingredients	oz
120	peeled, cooked prawns	4.25
40	celery	1.50
40	white cabbage	1.50
	mayonnaise and tomato ketchup in equal quantities to bind	
10	lemon juice	0.50

Method of preparation

1 Wash, rinse and dry the celery and white cabbage.
2 Finely chop the celery and shred the cabbage.
3 Add the mayonnaise, tomato ketchup and lemon juice to the prawns, celery and cabbage. Mix together thoroughly.

CRAB AND CUCUMBER

Ingredients

Gram	Ingredients	oz
150	flaked crabmeat	5.50
50	cucumber	1.75
	mayonnaise to bind	
10	lemon juice	0.50

Method of preparation

1 Wash, rinse and dry the cucumber.
2 Finely dice the cucumber and add to the crab meat.
3 Add the mayonnaise and lemon juice to the crab and cucumber. Mix together thoroughly.

SALMON

Ingredients

Gram	Ingredients	oz
200	flaked salmon	7.00
5	chives	0.25
	mayonnaise to bind	
10	lemon juice	0.50

Method of preparation

1 Finely chop the chives.
2 Mix all of the ingredients together thoroughly.

bakery terms

Aerate To increase in volume by a mechanical or chemical process.
ADD Activated Dough Development.

Bain Marie A vessel used for warming that is protected from direct heat.
Bake-Off The baking of a product.
Basket Roller Patterned rolling pin.
Batter A soft smooth mixture.
BFT Bulk Fermentation Time.
Bloom The colour and glaze on the surface of the product.
Bookfold A method of rolling and folding puff pastry.
Bun Frame A metal frame used to hold small paper cases.
Butterfat The fat content of cow's milk present in cream.

Caramelise The partial decomposition of sugar.
Coagulate The setting of protein.
Clear The formation of a smooth mixture.
Coat To cover a product with a smooth mixture.
Comb Scrape A method of decorating a soft mixture.
Compound A blend of colour and flavour.
Confectioner's Harp A device used to cut cakes evenly.
Constituent A single part of a raw material.
Contaminate To spoil food with harmful substances.
Cream To incorporate air by beating or whisking.
Crown The top of the oven baking chamber.
Crumb The cut interior surface of a product.
Crumble A fine mixture of fat and flour.
Crimp A form of decoration for pastes.
Crust The exterior outer surface of a product.
Crystallised The addition of sugar.
Curdling The separation of fat from water.

Damper A mechanism to release humidity from the oven chamber.
Defrosting The conversion from a frozen state to the natural condition.
Depositor A device for placing fillings into bases.
Develop The formation of gluten forming proteins during mixing process.
Disperse The distribution of an ingredient within a mixture.
Divide The cutting of dough into small units.
Dock The puncturing of paste and dough.
Dredge To cover the surface of a product with a fine material.
Dressing Decorative materials such as cracked wheat, sesame seeds, etc.
Dust The distribution of flour to prevent sticking.

Eggwash A mixture of egg and milk used to glaze the surface of a product.
Emulsifier A material that allows oil and water to mix together into a smooth solution.
Emulsion A smooth mixture containing oil and water.
Enrich To add sugar, fat, egg, milk, etc.
Enzyme A substance that can start a chemical or biological change.
Enrober Apparatus used to coat confectionery.
Ester A substance used in the manufacture of artificial flavours.
Extensibility The ability of a dough to stretch without breaking.

Fermentation The action of yeast within a dough.
Final Proof The expansion of dough pieces before baking.
Final Prover A controlled environment in which dough pieces expand prior to baking.
Finishing The decoration of a product.
Flash To colour the surface of a product quickly with heat.
Foam A stable aerated mixture of egg whites and sugar.

Full Sponge A mixture of egg and sugar aerated to the maximum volume.

Garnish The use of extra materials to enhance the presentation of a product.

Gelatinise The bursting open of starch cells when heated in water to form a gel.

Germination The early stages of growth.

Glaze To preserve and/or enhance the appearance of a material or product.

Gluten The insoluble gluten forming proteins present in wheat flour.

Greased The application of a thin film of oil or fat to a baking tray or tin.

Greaseproof A paper used during the baking of cakes to aid release and retain moisture.

Gross Weight Total weight of ingredients in a recipe.

Half Clear The midway point in the formation of a smooth mixture.

Half Turn A method of rolling and folding puff pastry.

High Ratio Refers to a high level of sugar and liquids to flour in a cake batter.

Hoop A round band of metal used for baking products.

Hopper A holding and feeding container used in large scale production.

Hydrate To add water to dry ingredients.

Hygroscopic The ability to absorb moisture present in the atmosphere.

Incorporate To combine and blend ingredients together.

Infestation The unwanted presence of eggs, insects, rodents, etc.

Intermediate Proof The rest period given to dough pieces prior to the final mould.

Knead The manipulation of dough and other suitable mixtures.

Knock Back The manipulation of dough during bulk fermentation time.

Lamination The process of rolling and folding puff pastry to create layers of dough and fat.

Mask The application of decorative ingredients to the side of a product.

Mature A period of time allowing the product to reach prime condition.

MDD Mechanical Dough Development.

Mechanical Blocking Machine Apparatus used to shape and cut out pastries.

Mould a. The manipulation and shaping of dough, etc.
b. Microscopic organism belonging to the fungi family of plants.

Net Weight The actual weight of ingredients in a recipe after production losses.

Notch A decorative cutting procedure.

Organic Acid Acid obtained from edible sources.

Oven Bottom Breads that are baked on the sole of the oven.

Oven Spring The increase in the volume of bread during the initial stages of baking.

Oxidising Agent A substance that stabilises the gas cells within a dough.

Pasteurised Heat treated to destroy bacteria.

Pastry Wheels A tool used for measuring, marking and cutting.

Peel An oar shaped tool used to load and unload the oven.

Pectin A natural setting agent found in fruit.

Perforated Tray A baking tray consisting of small holes to assist the frying process and the baking of crusty bread.

Pin To roll out a paste or dough thinly using a rolling pin.

Pipe The extrusion of a soft mixture from a piping bag.

Pre-gelatinised Starch A thickening agent for cold fillings.

Production Points A summary of the main details involved in the production of a product.

Pup Tins Very small bread tins.

Rancidity The spoilage of fat as a result of chemical changes.

Reconstitute The addition of water to dry raw materials.

Recover A period of time allowed for gluten to become relaxed.
Relative Humidity The amount of moisture present in a given volume of air.
Retard The slowing down of yeast activity.
Ripe The point at which gluten is in ideal condition for processing.
Roux A cooked mixture of flour and fat.

Savoy Bag A large piping bag used to extrude soft mixture.
Scotch Scraper Flat tool made from a wooden or plastic handle and metal blade.
Scrape Down The removal of mixture from the side and base of a mixing bowl.
Scraper A curved plastic tool used to remove mixture from the side and base of a mixing bowl.
Scaling The weighing of a mixture into a smaller unit.
Setting Placing unbaked units in the oven.
Shelf Life The period of time that a product will remain in good condition for consumption.
Shorten To give a firm but tender eating quality.
Silicone Non-stick baking paper.
Simmer To maintain a liquid at boiling point.
Skinning The drying of the surface of a dough.
Sole The bottom of the oven baking chamber.
Stabiliser An agent that prevents the separation of fat and water.
Stock Rotation A system of using existing stock before new.
Sterilising Process of destroying bacteria.
Stock Syrup A near saturated solution of sugar and water.
Sweating The inability of moisture to escape from a product during the cooling process.

Tempered Liquids that have been warmed to a specific temperature.
Texture The appearance and feel of the crumb structure.
Torten Large flat cake divided into portions.
Toughen The over development of gluten.
Toxic Harmful or poisonous.
Trimmings Excess paste and dough from final shaping.
Tube A shaped decorating tool for soft mixtures.
Turntable A rotating apparatus that aids the decorating process.

Uniform Consistency in the characteristics of a product.

VAT Value Added Tax.
Volume The depth of a baked product.

Watt Hours The measurement of energy input for high speed mixing.

Yield The number of units obtained from a recipe.

INDEX